TAKEDOWN

Other Books by JON LAND

The Alpha Deception
*Betrayal (nonfiction)
*Black Scorpion: The Tyrant Reborn
*Blood Diamonds
The Blue Widows
The Council of Ten
Day of the Delphi
*Dead Simple
*Dolphin Key
The Doomsday Spiral
The Eighth Trumpet
*The Fires of Midnight
The Gamma Option
*Hope Mountain
*Keepers of the Gate
*Kingdom of the Seven
Labyrinth
The Last Prophecy
The Lucifer Directive
The Ninth Dominion
The Omega Command
The Omicron Legion
Pandora's Temple
*The Pillars of Solomon
*The Seven Sins: The Tyrant Ascending
*Strong at the Break
*Strong Darkness
*Strong Enough to Die
*Strong Justice
*Strong Light of Day
*Strong Rain Falling
*Strong Vengeance
The Tenth Circle
The Valhalla Testament
The Vengeance of the Tau
Vortex
*A Walk in the Darkness
*The Walls of Jericho

*Published by Forge Books

TAKEDOWN

A Small-Town Cop's Battle
Against the Hells Angels and
the Nation's Biggest Drug Gang

JEFF BUCK

with Jon Land
and Lindsay Preston

A Tom Doherty Associates Book

New York

TAKEDOWN: A SMALL-TOWN COP'S BATTLE AGAINST THE HELLS ANGELS AND THE NATION'S BIGGEST DRUG GANG

Copyright © 2016 by Jeff Buck, Jon Land, and Lindsay Preston

Map by Rhys Davies

A Forge Book
Published by Tom Doherty Associates, LLC
175 Fifth Avenue
New York, NY 10010

www.tor-forge.com

Forge® is a registered trademark of Tom Doherty Associates, LLC.

The Library of Congress Cataloging-in-Publication Data is available upon request.

ISBN 978-0-7653-3809-9 (hardcover)
ISBN 978-1-4668-3789-8 (e-book)

Our books may be purchased in bulk for promotional, educational, or business use. Please contact your local bookseller or the Macmillan Corporate and Premium Sales Department at 1-800-221-7945, extension 5442, or by e-mail at MacmillanSpecial Markets@macmillan.com.

First Edition: March 2016

Printed in the United States of America

0   9   8   7   6   5   4   3   2   1

For my mother, father, and sister, who were always there

Acknowledgments

All drug cases and books are true team efforts. For help along the way of both this case and this book, I'd like to thank and acknowledge: Sheriff Drew Alexander, Mayor Sam Alonso, Phyllis Azar, assistant editor Elayne Becker, Sergeant Rick Beverly, Sergeant Jeff Breznak, Kathi Buck, law director Paul Carpenter, the Honorable Derek Champagne, dispatchers of the City of Twinsburg, publisher Tom Doherty, Detective Jim Gilchrist, editor Bob Gleason, attorney Gary Himmel, Congressman David Joyce, Captain John Korinek, Jon Land, Special Agent Bill Leppla, publicist Emily Mullen, attorney Ken Myers, Narcotics Border Task Force, Franklin County, New York, officers of the City of Beachwood, officers of the Village of Reminderville, Lindsay Preston, associate publisher Linda Quinton, Detective Rod Smith, Lieutenant Kirk Snodgrass, Detective Larry Weppler, and Chief Keith Winebrenner.

Yulia Abramovich: The Russian woman I arrested on a domestic assault beef in October 2008 who provided the first clue to drug dealing in my Ohio backyard by elements of the Russian mob.

Ralph "Sonny" Barger: Founder of the Hells Angels and kingpin who turned the biker gang into a criminal force coast to coast and, ultimately, north of the border.

Robert "Robbie" Barnes and Frank Courtland Teek: The two sources that provided product to Richard Heckman.

Al Beauchamp: Fairlawn, Ohio, police detective who helped me score a "reverse" drug deal after we arrested Kevin Sorin.

Maurice "Mom" Boucher: Joined the Montreal chapter of the Hells Angels in 1987 after completing a forty-month sentence for sexually assaulting a teenager. He led the Hells Angels in their war against the Rock Machine.

Rudolph Brancel: Subject of another of my biggest drug investigations, resulting in him being imprisoned.

Kathi Buck: My wife, mother of my daughter, and the woman who's been by my side through almost all of my career.

Salvatore Cazzetta: Successor to Sonny Barger as head of the Hells Angels, a position he held when the Angels solidified their hold on the Quebec drug trade and their "arrangement" with the Akwesasne Nation.

Derek Champagne: Ambitious, driven Franklin County, New York, district attorney cross-designated as an Assistant U.S. Attorney who wanted to put an end to the drug trade originating with the Hells Angels and members of the Akwesasne Mohawks as much as I did. He's currently a family court judge.

Matt Cody: Low-level target of the Geauga, Ohio, drug task force investigation that could have destroyed my case.

Kim Cook: Danny Simonds's fiancée, who introduced Danny to Alan Jacobs and then helped pick up the slack after Danny was murdered.

Derek Cooke: Alan Jacobs's boyhood friend who helped him sell drugs and one of the thugs who attacked Danny Simonds. No relationship to Kim.

Daniel Desrochers: An eleven-year-old boy killed in a Hells Angels bomb blast in Montreal, the incident attributed with igniting the Quebec biker wars.

Chad Edwards: One of the thugs that attacked Danny Simonds.

Sam Fields: The Native who introduced Alan Jacobs to the world of drug running on the reservation when Alan was just a boy.

Harold and Sabrina Fraser: Franklin County farmers who replaced Danny Simonds as Kevin Sorin's suppliers.

"Frenchie": Undercover drug officer from the Ontario Provincial Police who was working Operation SharQc north of the border while my task force was working our investigation south of the border.

Leo Fritz: A lower-level drug dealer who became a confidential informant and helped me break one of my biggest drug cases ever involving a kingpin named Brancel.

Phil Garillo: DEA agent who assisted me on the Heckman case.

Richard Heckman: Kingpin of a national, and international, drug network another of my investigations brought down.

Bryan "Wildcat" Herne: Alan Jacobs's chief enforcer and leader of the thugs who attacked Danny Simonds.

Benjamin Hudon-Barbeau and Frédéric Landry-Hétu: Full-patch members of the Hells Angels of Quebec involved in the drug trade north of the border.

Mike Hughes: A Reminderville, Ohio, uniformed policeman I enlisted as part of the multi-jurisdictional task force that extended from Ohio to Franklin County, New York.

Ivan Ivashov: Computer salesman friend of Kevin Sorin's and boyfriend of Yulia Abramovich whose tip was the beginning of my entrance to the case and Kevin's ultimate undoing.

Alan Jacobs: A drug runner from boyhood who rose to become de facto head of the drug trade on the Akwesasne Mohawk Nation reservation and spearhead of moving drugs through the reservation supplied by the Hells Angels out of Montreal.

Rosalie Jacobs: Alan's mom and currently CEO of Jacobs Tobacco Company.

Curtis Jones: A high-level drug dealer who tried to evade my arresting officers by jumping out a fifth-story window in my last case undercover.

Dave Joyce: Chief prosecutor from the Geauga County Prosecutor's Office and now an Ohio congressman.

Terry Kincade: A drug dealer targeted by me in 1995 in one of my last cases as an undercover drug officer, using my alias of "Jimmy Morgan."

Noah King: Alan Jacobs's right-hand man who replaced him as head of the drug trade on the Akwesasne reservation after Alan was arrested and jailed.

John Korinek: Beachwood, Ohio, detective who was already looking at Kevin Sorin when I got involved. Korinek remained involved the whole way.

Brad Kottler: Low-level dealer of Kevin Sorin's I nailed in a rare "reverse" that added more funds to my forfeiture coffers.

Brian LaTulipe: One of the thugs that attacked Danny Simonds.

Robert McDivitt and Joe Thatcher: Major players in the Heckman case.

Randy McGuire: New York state trooper who introduced me to Derek Champagne and the Franklin County wire room that was instrumental in the ultimate success of my task force in bringing down the network.

Brandon Meyers: Korinek's detective partner with the Beachwood, Ohio, police department I pegged right away as someone I didn't want sticking on the case.

Detective Joe Miles: One of my top detectives with the Reminderville, Ohio, police who was with me from the very beginning of the case depicted in *Takedown*.

Mitchell: A drug runner for Terry Kincade I turned into a confidential informant.

Jimmy Morgan: My undercover alias as the Dope Ghost.

Ashley Schmid: Kevin Sorin's young, feisty, and drug-addicted girl-friend.

Danny Simonds: Ex-marine and doomed drug runner who lost his life after trying to cut Alan Jacobs out of the process.

Rick Sinnigan: DEA agent assigned to St. Lawrence County, New York, who I felt never grasped the enormity of the problem he was facing.

Boris and Loudmilla Sorin: Parents of Kevin Sorin.

Kevin Sorin: The young Beachwood, Ohio, drug dealer who was getting his product from Danny Simonds, prime courier of Alan Jacobs, titular head of the drug trade on the Akwesasne Indian reservation.

Stevenson and Walters: Members of the Geauga, Ohio, drug task force whose tangential investigation involving Kevin Sorin could have blown my whole case.

Frank Tawlberg: The main warehouser in the Heckman case. It took three years to find him.

Mark Ververka: Longtime friend and associate of Kevin Sorin.

"Whiskers": The bartender in the dumpy watering hole where Alan Jacobs has his first encounter with the Hells Angels on the Canadian side of the border.

The enemy is within the gates; it is with our own luxury, our own folly, our own criminality that we have to contend.

—Marcus Tullius Cicero

This is a true story, though some names and details have been changed.

PROLOGUE

On the last day of his life, eleven-year-old Daniel Desrochers rode his bike to a local schoolyard playground where he was supposed to meet some friends. The friends were late, so Daniel waited on the sidewalk directly across the street from an innocuous white slab of a building that was actually the headquarters of the Rock Machine biker gang there in the Hochelaga-Maissoneuve area of Montreal.

Daniel sat on his bike with his hands tucked in his pockets. He'd brought his baseball glove along, but somewhere along the path of his ride the ball had slipped out. He was pretty sure his friends would be bringing one with them, though that ball had been his favorite, well-worn and broken in just right. It was hot, so he took off his T-shirt and tucked it into the back of his shorts. His short dark hair was damp with sweat, and if he was lucky, a local ice-cream truck would soon edge near, its annoying jingle announcing its approach ahead of the jangling of its bell at each stop.

If he was lucky.

A year before, two members of the Hells Angels had strolled into a downtown motorcycle-repair shop and gunned down Pierre Faucher, brother of the Rock Machine's leader, igniting a turf war over control of Quebec's lucrative drug trade. On this day, Frank "Bull" Quellette, another member of the Angels, had managed to pack a Jeep parked overnight in front of the Rock Machine headquarters with explosives. The Jeep belonged to Marc Dubé, one of the gang's top drug runners and allegedly one of its de facto leaders.

Quellette, a stocky, muscular man with slicked-back hair, was American by birth whose family relocated to Canada when he was eight.

Industrious as well as brutal, Quellette was reputed to operate three stripper agencies and an escort service. The Hells Angels battle with the Rock Machine gave him the opportunity to rise through the ranks by proving his mettle with another specialty:

Explosives.

Quellette, who fancied himself a porn star and would later make X-rated films at a sprawling Lavigueur estate, went on to become a full-patch member of the Montreal Angels' chapter the following year in large part because of the role he played in the so-called biker wars.

The Rock Machine began as a loose amalgamation of bar owners who distributed drugs in what became known as the Dark Circle. When the Hells Angels, reborn and reinvented, looked to muscle in on the local drug trade, the Dark Circle recruited members of various other outlaw biker gangs to counter those efforts by forming an organization every bit the Angels' equal in violence and ruthlessness.

Their purpose was to provide Montreal with an alternative to the Angels as a source of drugs, especially cocaine. So to better make their mark, the Rock Machine undercut the Angels' prices, flooding the streets with drugs, sometimes at a loss, just to cut into their rival's market share and hopefully lead the Angels to pull up stakes and move elsewhere.

In the summer of 1994 the Hells Angels decided to go to war instead, muscling in on the Rock Machine's territory by taking a monopolistic approach to the drug trade and punishing any vendor who dared defy them. With good reason, since this was about much more than just supplying a single city or even province. Billions of dollars in drugs were crossing into the United States annually through a single fifteen-mile, essentially unguarded stretch of the US-Canada border.

As he waited for the explosives packed into the Jeep to detonate, Frank Quellette reached into his pocket and pulled out a pack of Nations Best cigarettes. An eagle was stamped on the front of the Indian brand, specifically a symbol of strength of the Akwesasne Mohawks who manufactured them a few hundred miles away in a factory on tribal land. That stretch of land, sitting on the St. Lawrence River that separates the Canadian and US tribes, represented a world entirely unto itself with its own government, its own laws, and its own ways that happen to include one of the most lucrative smuggling routes in the entire country.

Quellette himself didn't know a lot about Indians or profit margins and didn't care much about the internecine struggles that would ultimately determine the winner in Quebec's biker wars. But he did know plenty about the hundreds of hydroponic greenhouses across Quebec that produced the most potent marijuana in the world. Their intricate design was something any green-thumbed botanist would envy. The interiors had been hollowed out and gutted. No walls, no furniture. Just a perfect electrical setup, water pipes, a nutrient-rich mix of soil, and millions of dollars' worth of pot plants that thrived in such ideal conditions. But these homes could take only so much of the moisture and humidity before mold ate away at the structure's very integrity. At that point, after one final harvest, men like Frank Quellette were called to burn them to the ground so no trace whatsoever would remain.

The real stakes in the war between the Rock Machine and the Hells Angels was control of the export of this "bud" into the United States across the St. Lawrence River and onto the very Indian reservation that produced Quellette's favorite cigarettes. This part of the river cut through Akwesasne tribal land, traversing Quebec and Ontario en route to forming part of the international boundary between Canada and the United States. Frozen for up to four months a year, it was essentially a vast, unmanned road—an "ice bridge," as the locals called it—and as busy as any other road in town.

So just after three o'clock that afternoon in August of 1995, with the Rock Machine headquarters packed with the very soldiers who were battling the Angels for control of that ice bridge as well, Marc Dubé climbed into his Jeep and started the engine. The explosives set by Frank Quellette ignited instantly and the Jeep exploded in a single blast, sending steel, rubber, and plastic bursting from orange flames that briefly swallowed all of the vehicle's frame, killing Dubé instantly. The blast's percussion and shrapnel blew out all the windows of the Rock Machine headquarters, wounding several and laying waste to, among other things, a pool table, a faux-leather couch, and a beer-packed refrigerator that sent bottles flying in all directions.

Across the street, Daniel Desrochers was still seated atop his bike on the sidewalk when a wave of steaming steel shards from the Jeep's carcass slammed into him. The force knocked him from his bike and into a nearby waist-high rock wall, bracing him there half on and half off it with shrapnel having turned his young body into a pincushion, including an ultimately fatal fragment that lodged in his brain.

The boy was rushed to a hospital and lay in a coma for four days before dying, not the first and far from the last victim of a war that was about to spill over the border into the United States. But Daniel Desrochers's death ignited a firestorm that led the Canadian government to declare its own war against the outlaw biker gangs. That war raged for years, through 2002. And along the way the Hells Angels vanquished their rivals and consolidated their power, in large part owing to a smuggling operation in which St. Regis Mohawk tribal leaders moved drugs supplied by the bikers off the reservation and across a large swath of the country.

The fact that the reservation straddles the St. Lawrence River has allowed the trafficking in all manner of contraband transported back and forth through the most lawless stretch of land in North America today. And when the river freezes it becomes, quite literally, an ice highway to hell. In addition to Nations Best cigarettes, foreign sex slaves and illegal aliens are trafficked across the St. Lawrence through Mohawk land. One of the 9/11 hijackers entered the United States this way, and the Department of Homeland Security still considers it to be a potential hotbed of terrorist incursion.

But what this relatively small stretch of border, measuring only six to eight miles, is known best for by far is drug smuggling. The entire two-thousand-mile-long border between the United States and Mexico is estimated to produce somewhere around $40 billion a year in drug revenue. In 2008, the year I got involved with the flow of drugs coming over the St. Lawrence, this six-to-eight-mile stretch alone accounted for an estimated $2 billion, a staggering figure when you compare eight miles against two thousand. And, thanks in large part to that fact, some estimates now put drugs smuggled over our northern border to be greater than that $40 billion coming in through the south.

As I would later learn, the reservation is a neglected, forgotten wasteland where federal agents and police play cat-and-mouse with those Natives involved in criminal activities along a mostly unmarked and unfortified frontier with Canada. These same Natives are beholden to the Hells Angels out of Quebec in an unholy marriage of convenience and mutual gain, the money involved is so staggering that it more than outweighs the risk mitigated by the geopolitical realities. Unlike the southern border with Mexico, where drug-related violence has exploded in recent years, the northern border rarely makes headlines. But this particular stretch, which widens to thirty miles on the Canadian side, just might be the most vicious, corrupt, and dangerous strip of border anywhere in the country and possibly the world.

Federal officials in both Canada and the United States have become increasingly aware of the problem, thanks in some part to the Quebec biker wars. It wouldn't be those officials, though, who years later would ultimately bring down what was one of the biggest and most powerful drug gangs on either side of the border. It would be the police chief in the small town of Reminderville, Ohio, hundreds of miles away.

Me.

1

THE FOOD CHAIN

A shocking crime was committed on the
unscrupulous initiative of few individuals,
with the blessing of more, and amid the
passive acquiescence of all.

—Tacitus

CHAPTER ONE

Youngstown, Ohio; 1995

Right around the time that Hells Angels bomb killed Daniel Desrochers, a single incident made me wonder if my time as an undercover drug officer was coming to an end. Incidents like this were what led me to give up the life I loved to spend the rest of it free of the kind of criminals who had left an eleven-year-old boy to die in a hospital bed four days after his brain was pierced by shrapnel.

I'd been working undercover for more than a decade already in 1995, an eternity in a world of deception, betrayal, loneliness, and constant danger. This particular case started with a guy named Mitchell. Mitchell was a runner that the Geauga County, Ohio, drug task force (DTF) had been watching for a year. They knew he was an underling for Terry Kincade, one of the most powerful drug guys in the entire Midwest. They knew that Kincade was impossible to find, let alone touch. Mitchell was his mope and a bad one at that, picked up by a simple beat cop for doing sixty-five in a forty-miles-per-hour zone. What idiot speeds when he's carrying ten ounces of marijuana? It didn't take long for me to get wind that Mitchell had been picked up. This was the task force's chance to finally get to Terry Kincade, one of our primary targets. But things had to happen fast. I had to convince Mitchell to become an informant before Kincade got word that Mitchell was late for wherever he'd been headed.

Mitchell, pathetic mope that he was, was shaking and near tears when I arrived. He was so relieved I put freedom on the table as an option that he'd have turned in his own mother to avoid a stretch behind bars. He agreed to become an informant and get me into Kincade's inner circle and, as a result, was back on the street an hour later to continue his run. We tagged the drugs he'd been carrying into evidence, then provided him with the money he needed to continue his run and maintain his credibility with Kincade. Six months later, with Mitchell's help, I'd immersed myself in Kincade's criminal organization under the undercover alias I went by, Jimmy Morgan.

That's where the patience kicked in. Most ordinary narcs would've had Mitchell lead them to Kincade, set up some sort of deal, and pop him immediately. Not me. I wanted to build a case first. I was more a strategist than a cowboy and played a case the way a skilled gambler played poker. It was about not grabbing a guy like Kincade until you had everything you could possibly get on him. If you want to take down a drug dealer and make it hurt, you take his drugs, his money, his house, and his toys. If you don't get everything, the dealer will get out of jail and open up shop again. Business as usual. My philosophy when it came to a drug bust was simple: If it floats, flies, or drives we seize it. Pulling this off, though, required time and research, as well as detailed search-and-seizure warrants. I was willing to do whatever it took to make the strongest possible case, the best way to ensure my climb up this particular drug-dealing food chain, toppling links as I went. Patience.

When I was finally ready to take down Kincade, I had agents at all of Kincade's banks, and tow trucks ready to take his speedboat, Porsche, Lexus, Mercedes, two Jet Skis, three snowmobiles, turboprop plane, and bulldozer. I could never figure out why he had a bulldozer, but what the hell, I'd take that too. Hit the bastard everywhere to make it hurt as much as possible.

Everyone was in place for the final takedown. Detective Joe Miles from Reminderville was taking charge of the group of officers waiting for my command. I'd spent my undercover years as Jimmy Morgan and became Jimmy again that day, picking up three kilos of cocaine. Those three kilos would cost $75,000, and in a well-organized sting I, in the guise of Jimmy, would present Kincade with a suitcase packed with that amount in hundred-dollar bills. Unfortunately, the task force couldn't pull together all the cash, so my suitcase was $30,000 short. Thirty thousand dollars! That left no room for error. The officers sitting outside couldn't afford to waste any time moving on my position when I yelled out the signal phrase, "You ready to count?"

Mitchell and I pulled up to Terry Kincade's house, where Kincade and his three drug soldiers were waiting for us inside the barn out back. I got out of the car and pulled out the suitcase short thirty grand in cash, helping to make Mitchell even more of a wreck.

Guys like Kincade could smell a setup plain as skunk odor. I needed Mitchell to pull it together and fast.

"You're going to get us both killed!" I told him. "Stay cool. We'll be out of there before you can blink an eye."

Mitchell just looked at me.

"I've kept you safe and out of jail so far, haven't I? Do you trust me? . . . Come on."

Mitchell finally nodded. He was sweating badly and I was glad he'd at least chosen a dark shirt to better disguise it.

"We're going in," I whispered into the hidden microphone that was wired to the police van out front. "Stand by. Shouldn't be more than five minutes."

I walked into the barn just behind Mitchell. Kincade was rubbing the head of his thoroughbred racehorse. The kindness he was showing to his horse made him seem human, almost. Kincade had been running drugs for a good twenty years. His trips to Miami to find the goods had wrinkled and cratered his face thanks to too much sun. The dark hairs that hadn't fallen out of his head were lacquered to his scalp. A chewed cigar hung from his dry thin lips. His three soldiers, clearly armed, stood back in the shadows like statues, not radiating any particular menace for now.

"How ya doing, Jimmy?" Kincade asked.

"I'm good. You?" I replied.

"Just fine. You wanna see the product?"

"Sure do," I said, walking toward a fold-out card table set up in the middle of the barn under the watchful eye of Kincade's soldiers.

Kincade had already begun pulling out the tightly packed bricks of white powder and laying them out for my inspection. I picked up a few, pretending to check the weight.

"Looks good," I said, following up with the takedown signal. "You ready to count?"

My prosecutor, who'd accompanied us on the bust, was driving the takedown van and I waited for the welcome sound of the tires of the van and the other squad vehicles crunching gravel en route to the barn. The expected sixty seconds passed, but it didn't come.

What the fuck was going on?

I felt my stomach drop. Drug dealers don't like to chat and hang out. I'd stall as best I could, but before too much longer I was going to have to open that suitcase, at which point Kincade would know something was amiss as soon as he realized I was short.

"That my money?" Kincade asked, pointing to the suitcase.

But I moved his gaze away from the case to the thoroughbred instead. "Hey, that's a nice-looking horse you have over there."

"He's a good moneymaker. Hand me the suitcase."

There was no way I could stall any further. The officers outside were going to have to figure out something.

"You ready to count?" I asked him, uttering the takedown signal again.

"I am."

I still couldn't hear cars approaching. Shit! And not far away from me, Mitchell began sucking in big gulps of air. The man looked like he was about to cry.

"What's the horse's name?" I asked, still in distraction mode. "So I can bet on him sometime."

"Miami Glory," Kincade said.

"I like that."

"Could you please just hand me the suitcase?"

"Oh, you're ready to count," I said, giving the takedown signal a third time, as I handed him the case.

"Didn't I just say that?"

I felt my heart thudding in my chest, loud enough, I thought, for Kincade to maybe hear. I was going to have to think of something and fast. I started slowly backing up toward the barn door. My only option was to run. I was unarmed; I always went in unarmed on an undercover buy. Believe it or not, guns make big drug dealers nervous. So now here I was unarmed and trapped in a barn with a drug dealer and his three bodyguards.

As Kincade unzipped the suitcase, my mind raced and I calculated my chances of making it out the door before the bodyguards drew their guns.

"What the fuck is this?" Kincade said, looking up from the bag.

Before I could offer some lame explanation, the door burst open and tossed me across the length of the dirt floor, where I found myself lying at Kincade's feet.

"*Police!*" a voice shouted. "*Police! Police!*"

And my officers surged in wielding the most-welcome guns I'd ever seen in my life. They arrested everyone, including me in my guise of Jimmy Morgan, my heart still pounding as the cuffs were slapped on.

Turned out my prosecutor was slowed by a school bus when he approached the scene, accounting for the delay. Meanwhile, anyone listening to the police band for a five-hundred-mile radius heard the angered plea of the driver of my squad's lead vehicle behind the van:

"*Get around the fucking school bus and get up there!*"

CHAPTER TWO

A week later, while Terry Kincade was out on bail awaiting trial, the number I kept for "Jimmy Morgan" rang. It was Kincade.

"Jimmy, I got a shipment of good shit if you want it," he said.

"Huh? After what happened?"

"It's good shit. Forget that you were short last time. We're cool."

"Cool with me. Where should we meet?" I laughed.

The asshole was out on bail and already back in business. But I greeted this as his opportunity to turn Kincade from a guy who would just do hard time to a guy who could work for me as an informant. Sure enough, a week later when the deal went down, Kincade rolled over to reduce his sentence, helping me take down the kingpin in his organization, which proved enough to keep me in the game for yet another decade.

That's the thing about being undercover. It becomes an addiction. But nothing lasts forever, and my forever moment came in Cleveland in 2004. The Trumbull County drug task force and I had been after a known dealer, an inner-city man who'd climbed the food chain at a surprisingly rapid pace. At only twenty-two, Curtis Jones was moving mass volumes of anything you could shoot, snort, or smoke. He was the go-to guy for true street junkies, for whom drugs were no less vital than breathing.

This particular task force had worked a sting on Jones for six months before they were finally ready to nail him. I was already worn out, tired of "the Life" by this time. I'd just wrapped up a case where I had been undercover for seven years. Seven long years mostly away from my family, surrounded by drugs in a world utterly devoid of honor and dominated by paranoia and double crosses. I'd decided that the Curtis Jones case was going to be my last, my swan song.

Interestingly enough, and probably contrary to what most would think, my wife never minded me working narcotics; in fact, she preferred it. She was never afraid of me getting hurt on the job because, in her words, I did the undercover life "as easy as I breathed." She worried plenty more about me in my job as chief of police later on than working undercover. I'm a team player and a big part of being a team player is keeping everyone happy, from the officers under me to the town councilmen, the prosecutors, the judges, the mayor—everyone. And Kathi worries that the stress of trying to manage that will kill me a long time before a bullet will.

While the Trumbull County DTF was setting up the sting, I told them I'd hang back and handle the wire, that I had no intentions of chasing or shooting anyone that night. They agreed, content with having me there and grateful for my help in getting them as far as I had.

So I parked my car behind the building where the bust was going to go down, no door or exit anywhere in sight, meaning no way anyone was escaping from the five-story apartment complex.

I sat in my car with the tape running. Everything was going as planned. The informant was in place, Curtis Jones was there, and the drug task force was ready to move in. I listened as the DTF agents entered the apartment, everything going just as planned until a piercing scream came over the wire.

"Shit! The guy jumped!" I heard one of my guys yell next.

My eyes crawled up the bricks to the fifth-floor apartment's window just as Curtis Jones took a flying leap into the night. It was a sight to behold, one I would never forget, since this guy floated toward the ground like goddamn Batman. He'd grabbed hold of the floor-length curtains and now appeared to be soaring through the sky wearing a cape, albeit plaid instead of black.

"I'm going to have to fucking chase this guy?" I muttered to myself, annoyed by the bizarre turnabout my insistence on running the wire had brought on.

Curtis Jones ran out of curtains three stories above the pavement and plummeted the rest of the way, his body crashing to the ground.

"Maybe not," I said, relieved as I reported in to my men over the radio. "Guy's gotta be toast. Just come and hook him up."

But as I was getting ready to pull my car around to the front of the building, Curtis somehow climbed to his feet.

"You gotta be fucking kidding," I muttered to myself, before returning to the radio. "This jackass is standing up, you hear me? Five-story fall and he's on his feet!"

The other officers would be there in no time and I figured this guy wasn't in any shape to get anywhere fast. I was wrong again. Jones had somehow shaken off his five-story fall and had begun running. So maybe he was Batman; either way, I had to run after him now, exactly what I'd been trying to avoid. I lit out in pursuit, following Curtis over one fence and two hedges and down three blocks, my lungs burning the whole way, before I finally tackled him to the ground.

"You're under arrest, asshole! You're finished!"

And so was I.

CHAPTER THREE

My involvement with both the Hells Angels and arguably the biggest drug gang in the country began as a domestic-assault case nearly three years later in my new capacity as chief of police for the Reminderville, Ohio, police department, the same department I'd served in as both detective and undercover narcotics officer.

"This is too fucking funny," I said, laughing as I stepped over a broken desk lamp, a trampled gardenia plant, a shattered picture, and fragmented pieces of computer hardware.

These were just some of the items that had fallen victim to the temper tantrum of one Yulia Abramovich, a Russian immigrant who was already no stranger to my police department. Reminderville, a small town forged in the heart of middle America, hard in the center of the American dream, boasted a population of only 3,800. I'd been with the Reminderville PD for going on seventeen years, most of them spent in drug enforcement, before being appointed as chief following the Curtis Jones case. I figured I was lucky to be alive without the repercussions that had broken up the families of many undercover drug officers, and I'd promised my wife of thirteen years, Kathi, that I was done for sure.

This was the third time Reminderville police had been called out to Yulia and her boyfriend, Ivan Ivashov's apartment on domestic-assault charges. I continued stepping over the debris, including glass and pasty hunks of plaster from jagged holes in the apartment's walls. As was the case with the other two calls, it wasn't hard to figure out that it was Yulia who'd done the bulk of the damage, since Ivan was once again found cowering in a corner of the twelve-hundred-square-foot apartment.

"Chief, the guy is right here," my lead detective, Joe Miles, said, gesturing toward the corner.

Ivan Ivashov popped up from his protective cover behind the murky green couch. His long skinny fingers were still clenched around the phone that he'd used to call 911 yet again.

Ivan was a gangly thing, like a puppy that wasn't quite sure how to handle its lanky frame. He was in his midtwenties but had a teenager's severe case of acne and the physical awkwardness of a boy who'd not yet grown into his body. At first glance, he looked like the computer geek he very much was. At second, you could see that his left eye was beginning to swell and a claw mark from Yulia's red fingernails streaked down his cheek. His hair was spiky to the point of looking like the quills of a porcupine glued atop his scalp.

"She beat me up. She chased me and was throwing things. She even tried to stab me! *Stab me*, can you believe that!"

"I wouldn't admit that to anyone if I were you, my friend," I warned, trying not to smile.

The remark could have sounded condescending but it didn't, because all of my years undercover had taught me how to talk to people in whatever guise fit the moment. But the guise that fit me best was the air of power and righteousness that made me appear much taller than my five-foot-ten-inch frame before the eyes of guys like Ivan. I didn't beat around the bush and always carried myself with a sense of humor bred of a life lived in the dark netherworld of the undercover cop, where if you didn't learn to laugh and smile at the right time you were much more likely to end up on the wrong side of a gun.

Ivan was right. Yulia did try to stab him. Several times, in fact, with several different weapons. As I continued to patrol the apartment, I took note of each and every attempt that had punched holes in the walls and left powdery plaster residue coating the floor, occasionally kicking up a thin mist into the air. A kitchen knife protruding from the living-room wall, a letter opener jutting out of the tan wall of the hallway, and a pair of scissors wedged deep in the bathroom door.

Creative girl, I thought. Good thing for both her and Ivan she had lousy aim.

Detective Miles had managed to restrain Yulia before I had arrived. She was sitting quietly, her thin arms crossed over a white button-down.

Surprisingly pretty and petite, with soft features that belied the fury it had taken to do so much damage and come only inches from lodging a weapon in flesh instead of plaster. Blond strands of hair had escaped from her ponytail, but other than that she was unscathed by the battle with her boyfriend.

"You did all this?" I asked with a nod.

"I was defending myself."

"Sure you were, tornado," I said, continuing to note the damage.

An open umbrella, turned inside out, was caught in the sink. The kitchen chairs had been turned over and one was missing a leg. I wondered if it too had ended up in a wall somewhere.

"I was defending myself," Yulia repeated. She had a Russian accent that thickened when she was under stress, or maybe she played it up when she felt it was needed.

"With an umbrella?"

"You don't understand," Yulia said, trying to sob.

I watched her bottom lip quiver as she did her utmost to muster a fake tear.

"Nice try," I said with a smirk, not bothering to add that I'd seen my young daughter try the same façade with no better results.

"Should I cuff her, boss?" Miles asked.

"You don't have to, if she'll behave. So you going to behave, Yulia, or do you want to try Miles here?"

Miles was a big guy with a baby face dominated by plump cheeks and a mischievous grin. If not for his expanding gut, he could've passed for twenty-five instead of the forty-three listed on his Ohio driver's license. I considered him a good cop. Miles liked rules; he needed rules, so much so that he still lived with his mother, who woke him up every morning for work. A fascination with guns had drawn him into law enforcement, and he remained an excellent marksman to this day. That and his size made him intimidating and maybe a bit unpredictable at the same time. I knew that I couldn't give Miles much freedom, rules and orders forming a leash that kept him from going astray.

In my twenty-eight years as a cop, serving every day since I was twenty-one, I'd known a lot of cops like Miles, but cops like Miles seldom encountered someone like me. My long tenure undercover, chasing the drugs, had earned me the nickname "Dope Ghost." I was like a drug dog sniffing his way to the top of the food chain. It was never good enough for me to catch the average dealer; I wanted the kingpin or snowman, as they were called. Take down the guy who made a difference. I was wise enough to know that there was an ass for every seat and someone to move in when the big guy went down, but there was something intrinsically rewarding and fulfilling in the awareness that taking down that right guy could dramatically affect the supply of drugs on the street and their respective price. It had always been about making a difference, and I had made a big one with service on the drug task force that left even the higher-ups at the Drug Enforcement Administration in Washington, DC, scratching their heads in amazement over what I'd managed to accomplish with limited resources. It was all about running the investigation, not letting the investigation run you.

But that all seemed like a lifetime ago. I was now chief of police for Reminderville, happy to deal with table legs splitting plaster as opposed to the dangerous, deceit-riddled world of men like Terry Kincade and Curtis Jones. Sure, working a desk job had padded my middle a bit. Sure, I missed the charge, the adrenaline rush of bringing down real bad guys who, in turn, could lead me to bigger bad guys.

But I was happy standing watch over a middle-class town where Ivan and Yulia's regular battles royal passed for exciting. And yet Reminderville, despite its size, boasted a considerable drug fund, one of the largest in the state. A fund that had ballooned because I was good at busting the pushers and distributors all the way up the food chain to the kingpin. I'd long proven myself and now Reminderville was reaping the rewards of that. So much so that the current home of Reminderville's police department had been paid for entirely by a single drug-bust seizure I'd led a few years before.

Busts like that helped to explain why my wife, Kathi, loved Jimmy Morgan just as she loved Jeff Buck. I'd operated undercover for most of our marriage and she'd never begrudged that, welcomed it, in fact, because the Dope Ghost was the man she'd married. Like I said before, she preferred me in that life rather than a normal cop's life, that of patrol officer or even police chief. I'm not saying the undercover world was intrinsically less dangerous than the duties of a regular cop, but it tended to be more predictable and she trusted the fact that I was placing myself in positions and conditions where I was in control. Being in the room with the bad guys instead of kicking the door down without being sure what was waiting on the other side. But she understood I'd had my run. No more chasing the dope, no more Dope Ghost. It was time to relegate myself to going after folks like this crazy Russian chick and her spineless boyfriend. Spend more time with my daughter and the horses we raise on our farm. As close to a normal life as I'd ever known.

"We're going to charge your girlfriend," I told Ivan. "We'll call you when she can make bond. That is, if you want to get her out."

Ivan's bony arms and elbows swayed in and out, as he replied. "Officer—"

It was "Chief," but I never corrected anyone. Even after four years, I hadn't gotten used to the sound of it.

"I run a successful computer company," Ivan continued. "I take care of her and this is what I get. Hell, no way am I bailing her ass out!"

Hearing this from the kitchen, Yulia broke free of Miles's grasp and flew screaming into the living room.

"You son of a bitch!"

Yulia surged past me, slamming into Ivan and knocking him into the couch.

I could only shake my head, covering my face to keep from laughing again as Miles finally pulled Yulia off of Ivan.

"You are a special one, Yulia," I said, chuckling. "Read the girl her rights, Miles."

Miles did just that, as he dragged Yulia in handcuffs to the door.

"Take that, you bitch," Ivan spat, throwing a pillow at her.

"Now you have balls?" I smirked at him and shook my head again.

Yulia kicked and screamed the entire way down the four flights of steps of the apartment building to the police car. Her tantrum escalated when Miles tried to stuff her thin frame into the rear of the police car. That's when she latched her hands onto the roof in a last-ditch effort to fight her confinement; the sound like fingernails on a chalkboard made me think of Freddy Krueger from the *Nightmare on Elm Street* movies. I'd seen nightmares for real, I'd lived them, and this was no nightmare by comparison. Not even close.

It was still warm outside and the leaves were just beginning to change. Little kids were swinging on swings, neighbors walking their dogs,

Yulia giving them a show until Miles finally got the car door closed behind her.

"Hey, Chief," greeted one of the neighbors, tossing me a friendly wave.

I waved back. Funny how I'd become so recognizable in direct counterpoint to my years spent in the anonymity of an undercover cop.

"Is that Yulia?" the neighbor continued.

"Guess you'll just have to read tomorrow's police blotter to find out," I said, and winked.

CHAPTER FOUR

With me in the passenger seat and Yulia securely behind the bulletproof divider in the back, Miles headed toward the police station.

"I didn't do anything wrong!" she protested, back in sobbing mode. "It's all him! I don't know why you men don't get it! The way you do things in your country is *crazy*! Back in Russia, I'd be a hero!"

Yulia continued to ramble and I continued to ignore her, ultimately turning on the radio to drown her out. Yulia responded by raising her voice another few octaves. I turned back to her and put my finger over my mouth.

"Shhhhh!" I shook my head yet again. "You are a real pain in the ass, aren't you?"

Yulia slouched back in her seat and began to pout. Glad for the silence, I turned the radio down the rest of the way to the station house.

And house is exactly what it is. The Reminderville Police Department looks like something out of Mayberry, or Pleasantville, or an old-time Norman Rockwell cover on *The Saturday Evening Post*. The building is a quaint white house with a picket fence, a two-car garage, and a manicured lawn. A simple post-mounted sign perched in the front yard and a row of police cars parked off to the side are the only way to tell that this isn't just another house in the neighborhood which, in fact, it used to be. All that's missing is a basketball hoop.

It seemed as if Yulia had run out of gas. Her thrashing and tantrum had subsided by the time Miles escorted her into the station.

"Throw her into the cell," I ordered. "I'll be down in a minute."

The inside of the station had barely been renovated from its previous incarnation. My office consisted of one of the smaller bedrooms, and the receptionist held court in what used to be the dining room. The chandelier was gone, replaced by a simple light fixture, while upstairs closets that once held dresses and suit jackets now contained a collection of papers, reports, and files.

My predecessor as chief, by the way, had used the sprawling master bedroom as his office. My first order of business upon succeeding him was to change that by giving the biggest room to my detectives and sergeants. I always believe in giving my men the most I possibly can to let them know they've got my support, that I've got their back. I try to lead by example and that meant using the biggest room for my office would've been a dick move. All Reminderville's officers, for instance, are allotted $850 per year for uniforms, equipment, and clothing. But after ten years or so they've accumulated everything they need, so I encourage them to let the younger officers use that money for bulletproof vests and duty leather that would otherwise have to come out of their own pockets. It all starts at the top.

Yulia, meanwhile, was taken to the basement, where a makeshift cell had been erected. Just one, since the likelihood that Reminderville would ever need more than that was virtually unthinkable; the petty criminals who occasionally turned up for lodging were pretty much par for the course. Upstairs, I stopped in the house's original kitchen and grabbed myself a glass of water before walking down to the basement to question Yulia.

I could hear her from the top of the stairs, clearly recharged and rejuvenated based on the clanging, banging, and fresh squealing shrieks coming from the basement.

A waft of spearmint tingled my nostrils, alerting me to the presence of Patrolman Mike Hughes, who'd returned from cruising the ten primary streets that bisected the town. Mike was the youngest guy on the force and he always smelled like mint, thanks to the gum he smacked in his mouth until he replaced it with the more discreet Life Savers.

"Chief, is that pretty girl making all that noise?"

"The pretty ones always make the most noise, Mike."

Not yet twenty-three, with dark skin and even darker eyes, Hughes was viewed by girls as a handsome kid. His hair always seemed to fall perfectly in place, which I couldn't understand; even on my best days my hair never did that, especially now that there was so much less of it.

When I reached the basement, Yulia was pacing back and forth, stammering in Russian. The holding cell was small but surprisingly clean, smelling of Lysol and air freshener. The dim lighting of a typical basement remained, much of it focused in a narrow beam shining on a metal folding chair set directly in front of the single cell. I took a seat on that chair, in front of Yulia as if she were some sort of zoo animal.

"Let me go! You can't keep me here!"

"Actually, I can. But if you answer my questions we can see about getting you out."

"I have nothing to say to you!"

"I'm sure you'll have something to say when you have to go pee," I said, and motioned toward the toilet in the cell, exposed for all to see.

The thought of using that toilet made Yulia's shoulders slump, quieting her back into vulnerable mode. And finally she sat down on the bench inside the cell. I waited for some story of woe, some misplaced and perfunctory explanation I'd nod my way through. In my experience, bullshit was pretty much all that came out of people's mouths when they were behind bars; the trick was being able to decipher it.

"It was all Ivan's fault," Yulia began.

"Sure. And why was it Ivan's fault?"

Yulia paused. Her eyes narrowed and she scratched her head. I could see the wheels turning.

"It is his fault because he deals drugs and I told him not to and he wouldn't listen to me."

I perked up slightly, leaned forward a bit in the metal chair. "Really? Drugs, huh?"

I'd heard every tale under the sun from suspects. But this was something different, especially stemming from nothing more complicated than a domestic-assault beef. Usually at this point the suspect, unless trained and schooled in such things, would get caught up and fumble over what came next.

"Yes," Yulia continued. "Ivan buys drugs from this Russian guy named Kevin and his American piece of ass girlfriend. He then sells the drugs he has to other people."

I leaned farther forward, enough to make the metal chair shift slightly on the linoleum floor beneath my feet. It was common knowledge that the Russian population stuck closely together in the suburban Cleveland area, forming a finely tuned and well-organized criminal network. It wasn't the mafia per se, more like an amalgamation of Russians networking only with each other. They tended to fly under the radar, sticking mainly to mortgage fraud, minor drug dealings, and money laundering. They weren't violent in the northern Ohio area that's my backyard, and it was almost always violence that led even the most successful, and normally restrained, criminal to get caught.

"Kevin . . . You say this guy's name is Kevin?" I prompted Yulia.

"Yes. He lives in Beachwood. His name is Kevin. From Beachwood," she repeated, naming a neighboring town of ours in Ohio. "I don't know his last name."

I wasn't sure whether Yulia was telling the truth or not. The Russians tended not to turn on each other. Secrecy was power. But it didn't seem that this girl would know anything about such inner dealings and, in my experience, suspects normally stayed within the story to better explain themselves, not expand the tale to include something like drug-dealing comrades.

"I'll be right back," I said, rising from the folding chair.

"Wait a minute! I thought you would let me go if I told you something!"

"We'll see," I told her, and headed off.

Mike Hughes was waiting for me at the top of the stairs.

"Book her and set her bail," I told Mike when I got up the stairs.

I walked up to my second-floor office. The mere thought of the potential of a Russian organized-crime drug ring's involvement in this minor domestic-assault beef raised the stakes considerably. The old flutter of excitement from my undercover days found my stomach and held there. I looked at the picture of my wife and daughter on my desk. Kathi would remind me that it was Beachwood's problem, because that's where this Russian named Kevin was from, and I should let it stay Beachwood's problem.

Maybe, sure. *But what was the big deal about making one phone call to the Beachwood police department?* I thought, as I reached for the phone.

Plenty, as things turned out.

CHAPTER FIVE

Ten months earlier, Kevin Sorin, the man Yulia Abramovich identified to me as a drug dealer, waited impatiently at his home. Sorin lived with his girlfriend, Ashley Schmid, and his friend Mark Ververka in a traditional brick-and-cedar-sided home nestled amid other similar ones in an upscale suburban neighborhood in tony Beachwood, where he plainly didn't belong. The trees were bare this time of year, forcing Kevin to keep his blinds drawn at all times to prevent anyone from seeing inside, starving their six-thousand-square-foot house of light. That's right, six thousand square feet. The drug business definitely paid dividends.

Kevin gently rolled a bud between his fingers, watching as the pieces flaked onto the clean white sheet of paper he had laid on the table. The bright green leaves and sticky red crystals made the paper look like a Christmas decoration. Kevin took pride in the quality of pot he was distributing throughout northeast Ohio. It was still strange for him to think that most of the pot being smoked in the area was courtesy of him. Kevin was the top of the food chain as far as the northeast Ohio drug trade was concerned. Ivan Ivashov was just a peon in the game, a small-time buyer of Kevin's weed and OxyContin.

Kevin swept the pot into a piece of rolling paper and rolled a perfect joint. He began passing it around the room to pass the time. Mark looked up from unscrewing the back of a computer tower to grab the joint from Kevin. The heavenly smoke was a good distraction while they waited.

—————

And they'd be waiting a while longer, because their prime supplier of product, Danny Simonds, had gotten a late start and was still three hundred miles up Interstate 90, somewhere outside of Syracuse, New York. Danny's 1999 blue Dodge Ram pickup truck had seen a lot of miles since he started making the five-hundred-mile trip from St. Lawrence County, New York, to Beachwood, Ohio, every other weekend. The truck cab that he purchased especially for this job was chipping, and the plastic windows were cracked. The doorjambs were rusted, the tires worn, the windshield chipped, and the paint peeling. And there wasn't much point in fixing the cosmetic issues, since the harsh St. Lawrence elements and moist frigid air ate away at new cars as well as old. St. Lawrence, as far as Danny Simonds was concerned, had a tendency to destroy everything, spirits as well as paint.

In the process of adding yet another thousand to his mileage count, Danny found himself running late for the first time. A former marine, he prided himself on being systematic and punctual, especially for Kevin. Kevin wasn't known for his patience, but then neither was any drug pusher. As the runner who supplied Kevin's product, Danny didn't want to be the source of angst in a business where reliability was the next best thing to cash. He lived by the clock, maintaining the discipline that had been ingrained in him since boot camp.

That made him a reliable runner, but control of his own situation extended only so far. And in this case the man from whom he picked up the load wasn't one to be rushed or pressured for any reason, at any time. Alan Jacobs, perhaps the wealthiest and most powerful member of the Akwesasne tribe residing on an Indian reservation that straddled the US-Canada border, represented the absolute top of the food chain as far as Danny was concerned. In a business generally devoid of rules, there was one that stuck: Pushers like Kevin were beholden to their distributors and had to work on their timetable. Kevin would have to understand; he didn't have much of a choice, since Danny wasn't going to risk doing anything that might run him afoul of Alan Jacobs.

He'd heard about the kind of violence the man was capable of and well practiced in. And there were plenty of rumors about his coziness with the Hells Angels, just a phone call away if he needed something from them other than drugs. Word was Jacobs had first met up with the gang when he was a twelve-year-old kid running backpacks full of marijuana on the back of a snowmobile. And he was the one, brass balls and all, who'd initiated the contact. At least, that was the legend.

Danny had heard plenty of stories of doing business with the Angels, both inside the res and out. But the one that stuck out the most was how the gang was known to take pictures of any "associate's" family members. Mothers, fathers, wives, children—no one was spared. And similarly no one would be spared the Angels' wrath if someone in league with them failed to deliver or pay up. There were no extensions, no grace periods. When the time came to pay up, the Angels came to collect. Short of that, they had the addresses of those of whom they'd already taken pictures, hardly shy about paying a visit to them next.

That's what I quickly learned separated the northern drug trade out of Canada from the southern trade run out of Mexico. The latter was dominated by career criminals, all about rival cartels fighting it out for market share and territory. Recruiting the toughest hombres they could find based on rap sheets and general ruthlessness. But the drug trade born of the unholy alliance between bikers and Indians had reached out into towns like Beachwood and Reminderville, involving, quite literally, the folks next door. The willing recruits in the northern world didn't lop off heads, machine-gun their enemies, or dig tunnels to sneak their product into the country; they didn't have to, with the Akwesasne Indian reservation serving as an open bridge over the border.

Loading the car was a breakneck activity for Danny, undertaken with the same regimented thinking that ruled his life. He loaded a hockey bag stuffed with two hundred pounds of top-of-the-line hydroponic marijuana, grown in Quebec, and delivered onto the res for distribution by the same Hells Angels who'd emerged victorious in their battle with the Rock Machine, into the back of his truck. Danny was smart enough to know the value of what he was toting, his end of the deal ridiculously small by comparison on the level of a hundred bucks per pound he transported. The risk of transporting all that pot across state lines for any curious highway patrolman who could manufacture probable cause to see was all his to bear, while the profits fell to someone else.

Danny's sculpted, lithe frame held sinewy muscles layered in ridges across his forearms, neck, and shoulders. He didn't look strong or intimidating at first glance any more than he looked like a special-ops ex-marine who'd been stationed in Afghanistan. Danny had enlisted hoping to get out of Massena, one of the tiny towns in St. Lawrence County. He figured the sand, bullets, and grenades of the Middle East would be a welcome respite from the snow, ice, and dark abyss of St. Lawrence County, where the sun seemed to retreat altogether for a good five months of the year. The Marine Corps had treated him well, changing his outlook on life, but hadn't offered much of an alternative for him after his tour was up and he returned to the very place he'd fled.

Running drugs for Alan Jacobs wasn't what Danny had planned to do after getting home. He had protected his country proudly and had witnessed firsthand the damage the drug trade had done to another nation. He had gone to Afghanistan to be part of the solution, only to come home and find himself part of the problem. The only remnants of his service were the military crew cut and toned body. Everything else was left behind.

The best job he could find after completing his four-year tour was at Jacobs Tobacco Company, proud producers of Nations Best cigarettes, on the sprawling grounds of the St. Regis Mohawk Reservation. The money wasn't great and opportunities for advancement were even worse, except for the ones unique to this land. The reservation straddled Canada and the United States. It was considered sovereign land, a considerable advantage when it came to smuggling goods into the United States. He knew about the truckloads of cigarettes that made their way into Canada and learned quickly that all the rumors of wholesale drug running were true as well. In fact, the drug business was expanding at a pace that challenged the ability of the suppliers at the top of the supply chain, like the Hells Angels, to keep up. There was especially a need for runners who could load, drive, keep cool, and handle themselves if push came to shove. A marine like Daniel Simonds fit all those criteria and more, a fact quickly taken notice of by Alan Jacobs.

Jacobs didn't particularly care that Danny wasn't Native; he was used to employing the local white people as his runners. But it still took several years of working for Alan as an electrician at his cigarette factory for Danny to truly earn his trust. Danny had embraced not only his job, but also the Akwesasne Nation as a whole, seeing in it a sense of belonging he'd been lacking since leaving the corps. He was engaged to an Akwesasne Indian woman named Kim Cook, Alan's cousin, to the consternation of both their families, who lent them little help in raising their son. The couple had made many pleas to the tribal council to allow them to move onto the St. Regis Mohawk Reservation to reap the benefits the Natives enjoyed and help make their lives a little easier. Their pleas fell on deaf ears, and the tribal council stuck to their strict rules that non-Natives were not allowed to reside on the res. So Danny and his family were forced to live in a slab of a house in the rural town of Stockholm, right off of the reservation, suspending them in a kind of limbo between the white and Indian worlds.

Danny needed more money than his job provided to help raise his son Danny Jr. and his future baby girl with his Native American fiancée. Danny also had full custody of his three children from a previous marriage, Jake, Rachel, and Shawn, something Kim grudgingly accepted and put on a brave face about. If acceptance wasn't coming, then at least a better life could be, once he began supplementing his income as a runner mostly for marijuana, raised in Canadian grow houses, that Alan Jacobs moved with virtual impunity off reservation land.

And run Danny did. Every two weeks he ran down to Beachwood, Ohio, to deliver Kevin and Ashley pot, oxy, ecstasy, and anything else that had been ordered. Danny knew the rules of not getting caught. Drive the speed limit, don't let anyone see the hockey bag or bags, never look guilty, and always use a chase car. The chase car was a vehicle that drove seven to ten minutes in front of the runner. Its job was simple: Inform the runner of roadblocks and law enforcement. Danny had also found that traveling on Sundays was safer—less law enforcement and the roads were pretty clear, most people staying at home or going to church, though he knew no one would be saying a prayer for him.

Danny had boyish good looks, with bright blue eyes that danced when he smiled and made him appear charming. Even if he did get pulled over, no one could possibly suspect him; he'd learned what a guilty man looked like from his years in the military, so he became remarkably adept at looking anything but that.

It always took Danny the full eight hours and twenty minutes to get to Beachwood. During the heavy winter Kevin Sorin was lucky if Danny could get out of upstate New York at all. The unpredictable weather patterns that plagued the upper tip of New York, whipping up the famed "lake effect" snows, came with the frenzied steadiness of Taliban ambushes in Afghanistan. Danny learned to live with those and, back home, he learned to live with disruptions caused by the weather. He never pushed it, even if he was running late. It wasn't worth getting caught, since he certainly didn't want to lose Alan's drugs or deal with the law.

Such rational reasoning, though, made Kevin no less irritable, not interested in excuses no matter how legitimate and prudent they might be. Then again, Kevin was irritable most of the time, though he seemed to have little reason to be. At twenty-one years old he was living in a $600,000 house with the girl of his dreams. He had plenty of cash and drugs to go around. He could travel and do what he wanted when he wanted. And to top it off, he was tall and handsome, with a thick head of dark hair and enchanting green eyes. And not just hazel, real green, green like the money he'd come to love above all else, since it had netted him all the other things he loved, including Ashley. He was living the American dream.

Kevin and his parents had immigrated to the United States from Russia when Kevin was just a boy. Kevin did everything he could to blend into the American culture, including changing his name from Konstantin. He had practiced for years to cover up his Russian accent when around Americans. But as a true-blue Russian, the way his parents, Boris and Loudmilla, had raised him, he spoke Russian and lived by the Russian ways when outside the company of his new countrymen.

Ashley was the lone exception, a kind of bridge between his two worlds. From the minute she came into his life, he was hooked. Like one of the drugs that he ingested so often, she intoxicated him in ways he couldn't understand. Even looking at her now, sitting on the couch, he found himself infatuated. It wasn't that she was the most beautiful girl he'd ever seen or the smartest by any stretch of the imagination. Maybe it was her naïveté or the way her bright eyes regarded him with such admiration. Ashley fed his need for power and the adulation that came with it. And with each successive done deal and money earned, Ashley fell more in love with the lifestyle of a drug dealer. Her thin frame, soft features, and long brown hair made her appear even younger than her twenty years, a portrait in virtue more suited to a family magazine cover than a life partnered with a drug dealer.

Until she opened her mouth.

"Fuck," she said, gazing out at a day already turning dark. "How the fuck long are we supposed to wait? I'm getting hungry!"

Kevin glanced at the roman numerals on the decorative wood wall clock that Ashley had bought at Pottery Barn last week. It was 6:30 P.M. and Danny was already two hours late.

"Yeah, where the fuck is that kid?" Kevin said, not really expecting an answer, just making known his frustrations.

"Be patient, Kevin. It's always worth the wait, isn't it?" Mark reminded him, as he took a deep inhale off the joint. He handed the joint over to Ashley before leaning back into the leather couch, exhaling the smoke.

Kevin had loaned fellow Russian Ivan Ivashov money to start a computer company. Ivashov had taken Kevin's start-up capital and built a somewhat successful computer company, which proved very fortuitous for Kevin indeed. Not only was it a way to launder his money, but it also provided him with the ability to purchase all of the shells of the computer towers that he needed without raising an eyebrow. Computer towers, essentially large monolithic steel boxes with vast amounts of storage capacity once hollowed out, made for perfect vehicles for smuggling. Their presence was innocuous and easily explicable, and a single computer tower could carry a whole bunch of the cash they'd be exchanging for the drugs. Kevin always found it curious how buying too much of one thing without obvious purpose raised suspicions and, sometimes, flags. The people should just shut up and be thankful for a sale, which didn't change the fact that Ivan had a business that made for the perfect cover and abettor for what Kevin needed.

"I like to get the deal done early in the day so I have the evening to relax," Kevin explained to Mark. "I like to keep to my routine."

"Some routine," Ashley said playfully.

Kevin didn't smile back at her. This was business, his operation, and he didn't have to justify himself to anyone. In a town like Beachwood you didn't get any higher up the food chain than Kevin Sorin.

Kevin wanted to call Danny, just to get an idea on time. But he knew better. If a runner was late, you never called. Because if getting nabbed was the reason, you didn't want your number on his caller ID.

"The sides are off the towers. Do you want me to load them up?" Mark asked, reaching for one of the neatly wrapped stacks of hundred-dollar bills on the table.

Kevin smacked his hand away. "Only I touch the money."

Trust ran only so deep in this business where anyone could turn at anytime. That was why Kevin had very few friends and dealt only to select people, mainly Russians, who worked in large volumes of dope. His dad, Boris, was the only other person that he'd allow to have the money or dope in his possession without Kevin present. And it was Boris who was helping Kevin stash and launder through legitimate business dealings the vast amounts of cash he was bringing in.

Mark backed off quickly. He knew this was Kevin's show. He was just glad that Kevin even let him be part of it at all. He would have been just another pothead kid with no money working at a gas station if it weren't for Kevin. It was because of Kevin that he was able to afford to do anything that he wanted, more than he could ever dream.

"Yeah, back the fuck off, Mark!" Ashley rang in like a parrot.

Kevin rolled his eyes. Sometimes the girl was ridiculous.

"Shut up, bitch," Mark snapped back.

"Who you calling a bitch?"

"You!"

"Well, you're a dumb-ass."

"Really, that was the best you could come up with?" Mark replied, laughing at her, igniting her hot temper.

Kevin was ignoring the two of them, concentrating on counting the money. His head lifted from the crisp hundred-dollar bills.

"Will the two of you shut the fuck up?" Kevin ordered.

The two quieted quickly. Ashley stuck her tongue out at Mark and slouched back into her chair.

Kevin was standing over their new Dalton slate pool table counting the bundles of hundred-dollar bills. The pool table was a great accessory to the freshly furnished house, which Ashley had decorated. She might have been young, and ditzy more often than not, but she had great taste. She'd turned the house into a traditional, elegantly furnished home, knick-knacks and all. The elaborate security system that tracked every move in the house was Kevin's only requirement. You could never be too careful. A fellow Russian immigrant had hooked him up with the top-of-the-line computer and camera system, so that nothing that happened in or out of the house would go unrecorded. In Cleveland, Russian immigrants stuck together. They did business only among themselves and had a tendency for illegal activities and laundering money. Most of the individuals Kevin dealt with were members of the Russian mafia.

After counting out the $235,000 in increments of a thousand, Kevin began to place the money inside the hollowed-out computer towers. This was a safe way to travel. Kevin would never risk packing the cash into something like duffel bags or suitcases; computer towers were the way to go. If he got pulled over, he'd just whip out Ivan Ivashov's legitimate-computer-company business card and, voilà!, no questions asked.

The cash had to get where it needed to be whether Danny got here with the drugs or not. Kevin didn't want any hiccups or complications with his supplier. The keys to a profitable and successful drug business were to keep your supplier happy, remain low-key, and never use your own stash—which was the one rule Kevin broke.

Constantly.

"Danny's here!" Ashley said, springing to her feet at the sound of a car pulling into the driveway.

Danny had been delivering to Kevin for over a year now, and he could never get over how Kevin lived compared to how he did in the slab house off the res. It wasn't that Danny wasn't well taken care of; the hundred dollars per pound Alan Jacobs paid him for each run was top of the line for runners, but still nothing like what the dealers like Kevin made after paying $2,300 a pound wholesale to ultimately double his investment on each pound thanks to buying and moving such bulk. Danny knew it took money to make money, and all he could hope was that after a while he would accumulate enough to make a move up the food chain. He just had to force himself to be patient, just like Kevin awaiting his delayed arrival in Beachwood.

Because things were going to change. He was going to make them change.

And soon.

CHAPTER SIX

Ashley always liked to open the door for Danny. Kevin liked to think it was because she was so excited to get the drugs, but it really had to do more with the striking good looks of the thirty-one-year-old ex-marine, on whom she had a schoolgirl crush.

Ashley always had a little skip in her step, like a child hopping up and down pleading for a cookie, but when Danny came that tendency turned downright weird. As she twinkle-toed her way through the living room to the foyer she tripped, tripped over the same muted and tastefully appointed tan rug that had been there since they moved in, the same rug she tripped over every time Danny arrived with a delivery.

"Hiiiii," she squealed, sounding like a giddy fourteen-year-old, and waved.

The warm tingly feeling that Danny sent through her in waves numbed Ashley's nerve endings to the point where she didn't even feel the icy thirty-five-degree air blowing through the now-open door. Even the light dusting of snow didn't trigger a shiver, only Danny.

"Hey," Danny said, and waved back, showing no interest in her whatsoever.

Ashley leaned on the white doorframe of the brick front porch, twiddling her long dark brown hair between tiny delicate fingers, as he unloaded the hockey bag from his truck.

"Er, need a hand?"

"I got it. Don't you worry your pretty little self." Danny winked.

She was still gushing when Danny carried the black hockey bag into the living room.

"Hey, sorry I'm late," he said, addressing Kevin as he wiped his brow. "I got a late start."

"No worries," Kevin replied.

"It's totally cool," Ashley chimed in.

Kevin shot her a disapproving glance, silencing her at least for the time being.

Kevin knew that while he might have been the biggest dealer in the area, that didn't give him license to upset Danny. Danny was the key to Alan Jacobs, and Alan didn't like to deal with many people in the first place. Piss off Danny, Alan's runner, and Kevin could end up dry, likely to be gobbled up by the food chain's current bottom-feeders.

Kevin unzipped the hockey bag and pulled out one of the many one-pound bags of pot, vacuum-sealed for freshness and odor control. He continued digging for something that he was having trouble finding.

"Did you bring the oxy?"

"I did," Danny told him. "It's in there. There are also five hundred pills of ex."

Kevin finally came out with one bag of white tablets and another of blue ones.

"They're blue this time?"

"Al got them from someone new."

"How are they?"

"He said you'd be very pleased."

Kevin opened the bag of little blue pills and popped one in his mouth, using only his saliva to swallow it down.

"Anyone want one?" Kevin offered the others in the room.

Ashley and Mark each reached into the bag and took a blue pill as well.

"Danny?" Kevin prompted.

"Nah, I'm good, man. Going to get back in the car and drive home."

"You sure you don't want to stay and play?" Ashley said, sounding more disappointed than seductive.

Her clear flirtation with him clearly embarrassed Danny, especially with Kevin not five feet away. "Thanks, but I'd rather drive on Sunday, less risky since I'm carrying the towers and all."

The pill was already starting to make Ashley's eyes glaze. Something about the way she continued to look at him made Danny want to get out of there even more.

"Speaking of which, are those for me?" Danny asked, motioning toward the computer towers.

Kevin nodded. "Sure are. It's all there."

"As always."

Danny knew that Kevin would never try to rip him off, tantamount to ripping Alan Jacobs himself off, and that wouldn't be in anyone's best interest. Especially Kevin's.

Danny loaded the computer towers into his truck. Mark was starting to look at him as well, his eyes even more glazed than Ashley's but somehow intense and virtually unblinking.

"Well, I'm off," Danny said with a wave, forcing a smile.

"Drive safe," Kevin told him.

"Enjoy your trip, too," he tried to muse, but didn't care whether the line drew any smiles or not.

"We will." Ashley giggled.

"See you in two weeks, man," Kevin said, as more of a reminder than a farewell. True to form, the two men did not shake hands.

Danny started his Dodge Ram and backed out into the wide suburban street, breathing a hefty sigh of relief that he'd made a clean getaway from what seemed to him to be little more than an upscale crack den. With an eight-hour-and-twenty-minute drive ahead of him, he could still make it back by three A.M. to see his kids before they went to school Monday morning.

Another run done, he thought as he headed back down Bryden Road. He was always more at ease hauling money than dope. Smooth cruising from here, so he eased the window down a crack to let the winter air in, refreshing compared to the deep chill back home. Ashley and Kevin didn't know how good they had it nestled here in a world dotted by shopping malls, great schools, and roads where the pavement was actually visible this time of year.

Danny found himself envying this suburban life. This was where he wanted his kids to grow up. In a neighborhood where swing sets and barbecues occupied backyards and front lawns weren't cluttered with rusted-out lawn furniture, broken-down cars, and trash. Here his kids could make friends and his fiancée, Kim, could borrow a cup of sugar from one of the wives next door.

He drove slowly to take it all in, lit a cigarette, and turned on the radio, losing himself in the pleasant daydream of living on a street like this sometime in the not-so-distant future, once Alan Jacobs arranged a higher place in the organization for him. It was all coming together.

At least in the dream. In reality, the drug world offered little chance of advancement, since runners like him were often nabbed before their checkered careers could evolve at all. Sure, the money was good, damn good given how few opportunities were available in St. Lawrence County. Danny wasn't unskilled; he was an electrician, just short of his license. He could get into private security, something like that; hell, he'd be a great candidate for law enforcement, and he quipped to himself how experience as a drug runner would look on his résumé.

But true opportunities back home were limited and shrinking fast. So every time he drove through Beachwood, he left the town limits with a lump the size of a baseball in his throat. If a couple of pissant punks like Ashley and Kevin could stake their claim to a share of the American dream, why couldn't he? But it wasn't like he could go somewhere to file a complaint, and the drug business offered no human-resources department. Forget the food chain; this was a man-eat-man proposition, and Danny wondered how long he could continue running before his luck ran out. All he wanted was to make enough money to take care of his family and stay safe until they had enough to go legit.

Danny spun the tuner, finally locking in on 98.5, Cleveland's classic-rock station. He hadn't noticed the black Honda CRV, being driven by a local undercover cop, emerge from its hiding spot across the street from Kevin's house when he pulled away, nor did he notice it now. The CRV discreetly stayed on his tail until Danny turned onto the US 271 North on-ramp, just as the Stones' "Sympathy for the Devil" blared over the Ram's speakers.

CHAPTER SEVEN

As Danny was heading home, a Ford extended-cab pickup truck was making its own run through southern Quebec on the outskirts of Montreal. Behind the wheel was Frédéric Landry-Hétu, with Benjamin Hudon-Barbeau riding shotgun. Both were full-patch members of the Hells Angels, the equivalent of being made guys in the Mafia. And they were carrying product in the covered bed of the truck that might well become part of Danny's next run or the one after, certain to make its way somewhere into the United States, if not my own backyard.

The pungent aroma of that much weed trimmed, bagged, and bundled behind them soaked the air of the truck's cab, forcing the two men to crack the windows to let in the frigid air of the night. They always made these runs at night, since the swing took them through residential suburbia and several of the dozens of grow houses the Angels operated. Often purchased at foreclosure sales, the once-stately homes were converted into interior jungles where hydroponic weed was grown and harvested. The workers were often Chinese immigrants lured to Canada and employed based on a promise that the HAs would ultimately get them across the border into the United States, but I couldn't find a single case where this promise was ever made good on.

Instead, the Chinese workers were either discarded or transferred to another grow house once their current house was deemed so mold-and-mildew-infested as to no longer be a viable growing environment. They could probably escape, but where would they go? Having been lured into Canada didn't exactly make them credible witnesses, and that was before the language barrier was even considered; few, if any, spoke

English. They were virtual slaves, going about their daily chores like drones in suburban homes, the normalcy of which created the ideal cover.

But how exactly did this happen?

"In 1967 Canada invented a way to remove discrimination and prejudice from the process of choosing which immigrants to let in," explained *The Economist* in its January 10, 2015, issue. "The points system ignored an applicant's race and country of origin (until then it helped to be white). Instead, it rewarded education, fluency in English or French and work experience. With the change, Asians supplanted white Europeans as the dominant immigrant group."

But all with the system, as it turned out, was not well.

"When William Lin moved to Canada in 1999 from Gutian County, in the southeastern Chinese province of Fujian, he was full of hope," *The Huffington Post* reported on December 19, 2012. "He had almost 10 years of experience as a mechanical engineer and a bachelor's degree from one of the most prestigious schools in China. He had a master's degree from a university in Japan and had worked in the country, a place more racist toward other Asians than he thought Canada could ever be. Lin estimated it would take him a few months to find professional work. Instead, after sending out 150 résumés over the course of six months, he didn't receive one call."

That same *Huffington Post* article reports that 14 percent of all immigrants to Canada were Chinese. Unable to find the jobs they'd expected, many ended up turning to the pornography industry for jobs. Others had no choice but to work in the kind of grow houses maintained by the Hells Angels.

Frédéric Landry-Hétu and Benjamin Hudon-Barbeau were armed with pistols, and a customized compartment under the rear bench seat held both a twelve-gauge shotgun and an assault rifle. Neither man ever figured to need those or any weapon during the normal course of their job, but betrayal was rife in the drug world in general and in the world of outlaw biker gangs in particular. You just never knew who you could trust or when another war, internecine or otherwise, was going to break out. And Landry-Hétu and Hudon-Barbeau certainly didn't want to be its first victims.

Picking up the harvested and cut products from the grow houses on tonight's route could have just as easily been a one-man job. But each was there to police the other as much as anything. Eliminate the temptation of going rogue, siphoning off part of the product, or delivering the "evidence" to the authorities as part of some plea deal. Call the notion of pairs the ideal insurance against CIs, or confidential informants.

The pickups they had already made tonight were especially large loads, to the point where there wasn't room in the truck for the product from the last two houses on the route. One of the few freedoms they enjoyed was discretion, being able to pass a signal through their throwaway cell phones that additional pickup was required. So they were carrying the latest harvest from just three of the houses on tonight's route, probably around fifteen-hundred pounds of weed, which had been loaded onto the truck in each house's garage, once they'd pulled in and the door had slid down after them.

Landry-Hétu had actually blown the horn outside the first grow house to signal their arrival.

"What the fuck you doing?" Hudon-Barbeau snapped at him in French.

"Letting them know we're here, asshole."

"Them and the fucking neighborhood," Hudon-Barbeau shot back. "Maybe there's a fucking cop living next door. Maybe you should walk up and knock on his door, introduce yourself."

"Knock-knock," Landry-Hétu tried to joke through a smirk.

Landry-Hétu and Hudon-Barbeau were just one of several HA teams assigned to such runs. I don't know how much they actually knew about the ultimate destination of the product they were carrying; not much, for sure, or even nothing more than what they heard being passed down from higher up the food chain. They'd truck their pickup to one of several warehouse-type buildings that, even more than the grow houses, were quickly phased out to always stay one step ahead of the authorities that might have caught on to some aspect of the operation.

And that operation was compartmentalized and almost militaristic in that respect. The growers grew, drivers like Landry-Hétu and Hudon-Barbeau picked up, and at scheduled times HA runners brought the weed from the various warehouses to the shores of the St. Lawrence, where it would be exchanged for cash coming in from the Akwesasne reservation. Then it would be portioned out for runners like Danny Simonds to deliver on the routes they ran through much of the country on a regular basis. If HA drivers got pinched, the most they could provide the authorities was the location of a few of the grow houses and warehouse fronts, which in all likelihood would already have been shut down. In other words, the system was designed to be self-protecting, and so regular that it ran like clockwork. The HAs at the top of the food chain north of the border were no different in this respect from their counterparts to the south of it.

That's what makes building a successful drug case so challenging and detailed. The low-hanging fruit isn't all that hard to pick, but the closer you get to the top the more insulated the targets become. It's a painstaking process made all the more complicated by the fact that many of these guys can't give up the kingpins even if they want to. All they can give you is those immediately above them.

So you keep climbing.

Landry-Hétu and Hudon-Barbeau kept driving through the frigid night, trying not to suck in more of the stench that seemed to thicken in the truck's cab with each mile. BC Bud, the strain the Hells Angels specialized in growing across Quebec and beyond, was immensely popular for a reason, and its potency was evident not just in the crystals that glistened on the weed, but also in its skunklike odor. By the time they neared tonight's drop point, both men had literally held their noses for stretches at a time.

But they weren't holding them now, as Landry-Hétu turned down a lonely road leading to the warehouse. If an ambush or pinch was coming, it would be now, and both men needed their hands free to go for their pistols if it came to that. Although none of these truck runs had ever been knocked off, dissension and infighting were part and parcel of any biker gang. Leaders were known to switch allegiances, although in the case of the HAs it would be far more likely for a few to form a splinter group that would need resources to build itself out. The Rock Machine, for example, had actually been established by former Hells Angels. The last thing Landry-Hétu and Hudon-Barbeau wanted was to become collateral damage in such a struggle, and if a takedown by law enforcement was coming, it would likely be here too; they normally clung to back roads wherever possible to avoid roadblocks or at least be able to spot them as far ahead as possible.

Strange to think of the drug world as normally nonviolent in this case, even for the Hells Angels, but violence was bad for business. In this case, it really was all about the money.

I didn't know all this when I first got involved, the night I arrested Yulia Abramovich on a domestic-violence beef. In fact, I knew very little about how this particular operation was run. Sure, it mirrored those of the other drug organizations I'd brought down in enough respects to create a sense of familiarity. There also, though, was an equal sense of foreboding over the additional jurisdictional issues cast by running an investigation that needed to cross international borders as well as tribal ones. I just needed to learn the territory on which I was operating, starting in Beachwood and branching out from there.

All drug organizations are indeed different.

But the food chain is the food chain.

CHAPTER EIGHT

A few weeks after my interview with Yulia in that basement holding cell, I made my way through the busy town of Beachwood on the very same road that Danny Simonds took to get to Kevin Sorin's house every other Sunday. I felt a welcome rush of excitement knowing that I might be on to another high-profile case. I hadn't really missed the undercover life, playing my part in the war against major criminals. But that didn't stop me from continuing to adamantly believe that drugs were the scourge of American society. The source of endless crime, heartache, and tax dollars spent prosecuting offenders. I'd left that world in body, though not mind. And Yulia Abramovich's naming this "Kevin" as a major player in the Beachwood drug trade stoked old fires I thought were extinguished that turned out to only be smoldering.

Less than fifteen miles away from Reminderville, Beachwood might as well have been a million, at least as far as I was concerned. The city officials had followed the perfect playbook in building their town of twelve thousand. Comprehensive municipal planning allowed for shopping, restaurants, parks, and more. Beachwood Place and Legacy Village alone, two high-end shopping centers, brought in more tax dollars by themselves than all of Reminderville collected in a year. And the easy access provided by three convenient exits off of I-271, like the one used by Danny Simonds, made Beachwood a great location for residents, visitors, and drug dealers alike. The combination of thriving businesses and wealthy residents generated well over ten times the tax revenue that Reminderville did, leaving Beachwood flush with the kind of cash it had taken to build a spanking new municipal complex that was a source of envy to its neighboring communities.

I hadn't told Kathi what I was up to; there was no point yet, not until I had some idea whether Yulia's story checked out. To find out, I'd be meeting in Beachwood with Detective John Korinek. That left me on edge, the discomfort adding to the anxiety I was feeling. Narcotics guys are always uneasy about meeting new people, and I didn't want Korinek to feel like I was stepping on toes or trying to steal his case. Drug guys always felt that the arrival of a new face was a threat, someone swooping in to rob them of their hard work and glory.

It wasn't about the glory of a case for me, though. There were two types of cops that worked narcotics, "show horses" and "workhorses," with me squarely falling into the latter category. Sure, I had to tread cautiously with Korinek and earn the cop's trust. But to do that I first had to figure out where Korinek fell. Because in my world, a show horse would be infinitely harder to deal with, more territorial and less willing to share information. "Mutually beneficial" was a phrase not in a show horse's vocabulary; they were in the game for themselves.

"Nice building," I muttered to myself, as I passed the Beachwood Police Department.

Beachwood's recently built community center boasted two swimming pools, a lavish park, and a new ultramodern structure that housed city hall, the fire department, and the police department. The building had large open windows, streamlined siding, and an art-deco stainless-steel sculpture jutting out of the front that was a little too much for me.

My disdain for the architecture, though, was not why I drove past the complex and made my way to a Ruby Tuesday restaurant down the street. That was because I made it a point never to meet inside a police station. I was always cautious of wandering eyes. Having worked narc and undercover for so long, I'd learned to be cautious above all else. Bad guys are smart. You never want to let someone see you going in and out of a police station. It's the quickest way to blow your cover and let them know you're up to something.

I pulled in to a back parking spot at the restaurant, a spot hidden from street view. Old habits die hard. I'd made a lot of enemies over the years; most of them were still in prison, but with a wife and a young daughter I'd learned to play it safe. I shut the door of my black Ford Expedition and scanned the parking lot for anything suspicious before walking into the restaurant.

"May I help you?" the hostess asked.

"I'm meeting some people," I responded, eyes crawling across the restaurant. "There they are," I continued, and walked toward Detective John Korinek and his partner, Detective Brandon Meyers, who were seated side by side in a booth waiting for me.

Though I'd never met either man, I could spot a narcotics guy from a mile away. I was never sure if it was the tightly cropped hair, their alert posture, or just a look in their eyes. Either way, I could tell for sure that Korinek was a narc but Meyers was not, at least hadn't been for very long.

Korinek was younger than I was expecting, thirty-one or thirty-two tops. His hair was cropped neatly against his scalp. He stood up stiff and straight, not smiling, and making sure I could see the harshness of his eyes directed at no one in particular. Like me, Korinek had been working narcotics since he graduated from the academy. He had worked a few "good cases," as I called them, cases that were more than some dumb kid and a bag of weed or mope dealing. Meyers, on the other hand, was a beat cop, with a rough complexion and a cop mustache. A veteran of more than fifteen years on the force, Meyers had spent most of his time writing tickets. He fit the typical cop profile to an almost comical level, right down to the distended belly of someone who's eaten too many doughnuts. His cheeks were flushed with red and had a nest of spider veins sprouting. He was a heart attack waiting to happen.

"Chief Buck?" Korinek asked as I approached him.

"Indeed. Call me Jeff. You're John Korinek?"

Korinek nodded. "And this is my partner, Detective Brandon Meyers."

"Good to know you," I said, rotating my eyes between them, but focusing mostly on Korinek. "Thanks for meeting me."

I slid into one side of the booth across from Korinek and Meyers, positioning myself to better face Korinek. Body language was everything in meetings like this, and I wanted to make sure Korinek understood I knew the score.

But then Korinek surprised me.

"It's really great to meet you," the detective said, showing deference. "You worked the Heckman case, right?"

"I did."

"And the Brancel case?"

"Did that one, too," I said, not bothering to add that cases like that had earned me the nickname "Dope Ghost."

"'The Dope Ghost,'" Korinek said, clearly impressed. "That's what they call you, right?"

"Well, not anymore."

I nodded in appreciation, still on edge and on guard, but seeing Korinek a bit differently. I was proud of my cases, proud of the amount of times that I was able to change the price of street drugs to help make them less accessible and available. Supply and demand; capitalism spills over into the criminal world, too. Although I was proud of my accomplishments, I was never cavalier. I knew that what I did was not rocket science by any means. It was all a matter of knowing what to do, having the patience to get it done and, most important of all, putting in the time.

That's the thing very few outside this world understand about what it takes to build a successful drug case. It isn't flashy and requires long hours poring over recorded tapes, turning suspects into informants, and climbing the food chain until you've got those at the top in your sights. Car chases and shoot-outs, for the most part, are the stuff of movies. They happen, but those of us who've survived this long in the game know how to avoid them and use our wits instead of bullets to win out. I believed that any detective willing to work the case, *really* work the case, could catch a dealer. But it was the special ones, the workhorses, who could follow that lead all the way up the food chain to the kingpin.

I'm not saying that guys I call show horses aren't good men or good cops in other ways. But they just aren't my kind of cop nor did I believe they're cut out for the laborious, meticulous work required in order to put together a coordinated drug sting operation. Instead, they're satisfied with the small fry rather than the big fish. It comes down to ambition, coupled with vision.

The three of us ordered lunch and continued to chat idly for a time. Korinek bragged about his three little boys, how they loved baseball and fireflies and math. Kids and families didn't make for a good narcotics officer. The hours were long and the commitment overbearing. But I was cognizant of the fact that through it all Korinek never once produced a picture. I doubted he even carried one in his wallet, an ingrained habit of old-school narcs who want to insulate their loved ones from the danger of their work. The more Korinek spoke, the more I could tell that he fell squarely into the workhorse category. He had the drive and passion to get the job done. Detective Meyers was another matter. He sat silent and smug for a time before revealing his showmanship.

"You're interested in Kevin Sorin? In *our* case?" Meyers asked me, his mouth full of french fries, after I explained what I had.

I'd been prepared for this, glad it had come from the clearly junior man. "I had a recent domestic dispute in my town," I responded cautiously. "The suspect was a young woman."

Korinek raised an eyebrow at that.

"Yeah, a young *woman*," I repeated. "We'd been called out to the couple's home several times. On our last visit, the young lady made a statement that the boyfriend she'd just beaten up was a drug dealer who associated with *your* Kevin Sorin. She said she could put them in the same room with a major supplier out of New York."

"We did have a case on Kevin Sorin, but it went cold this past June," Korinek told me, drawing a disparaging look from Meyers.

"Can you tell me more?" I asked, keeping direct eye contact with Korinek while avoiding the disapproving gaze of the show horse Meyers. My decision to position myself directly before the senior man was paying dividends. Body language.

Korinek seemed to be ignoring Meyers as much as I. The Beachwood PD's interest in Kevin Sorin, he explained, had begun about three years earlier, with a routine traffic stop.

Korinek was running radar right down the street from their current lunch spot when a spanking new blue Tahoe came whisking by doing fifty-five in a thirty-five. Korinek threw on his siren and chased after the SUV, which pulled over without incident. When Korinek arrived at the open window, a clearly stoned seventeen-year-old looked up at him from the passenger seat, shaking.

"Driver's license and registration, please."

The boy's face went from pale to paler as he slowly reached over to the glove compartment. He'd barely cracked it open when the car filled with the smell of skunk. And when the boy reached inside for his registration, an ounce of pot tucked in a ziplock bag fell to the floor. Korinek called for backup and the boy was hauled in for questioning. It didn't take long before the kid's dad had one of Beachwood's most well-known and leading defense attorneys at the station. The attorney made the sensible decision, common with first-time drug offenses, to pursue a deal right from the start. Korinek explained that if his young client turned on the dealer from whom he'd received the ounce, he could cop a plea, a good deal for anyone in the situation the boy was in. The boy's dad and attorney did everything they could to convince him to give up his dealer, but the kid wouldn't. And the more they persisted, the more stubborn the young man became.

"The kid would rather ruin his future than turn on his dealer?" I asked Korinek three years after the fact, eyebrows raised in curiosity.

"The only thing that we were able to get from him was that his dealer was part of the Russian mafia and that he lived in Beachwood with his American girlfriend. He was genuinely terrified. We explained how we could do a setup. All he would need to do is buy a bag from his pusher and we would nab him, and the kid could get off scot-free for the effort."

"Kid still didn't take the deal?"

"He said that he couldn't do it, even if he wanted to. That he'd never met the guy. That no one could get near him. That the dealer had some 'mope,' another Russian kid, running the stuff for him so he could keep his hands from getting dirty."

I nodded, feeling that familiar sense of excitement again.

Uh-oh . . .

Beachwood had a real drug dealer, all right. A smart one who'd make a worthy adversary, someone fun to go after. Any dealer that was intelligent enough to not meet his buyers and use a mope, someone to run the drugs and to take the fall, knew the rules of operating a successful criminal enterprise. This wasn't your average small-time dealer standing on a street corner or dispensing his wares from a coffee-shop parking lot. This was the real deal.

I pressed on. "If the kid gave you nothing, then how . . ."

"Not three days later we got an anonymous phone call about some local drug dealers. All the caller told us was that the dealer was a Russian guy named Kevin and he lived with his girlfriend, Ashley."

"And from there we put two and two together and started doing surveillance on their home on Bryden Road," Meyers interjected, the show horse stealing the punch line like he'd probably try to steal credit for the bust later. Leopards weren't the only things that couldn't change their spots.

"I see," I said, bobbing my head. "Can I take a look at your files?"

Korinek pushed the stack of papers toward me. "Sure."

I flipped through the pages quickly, reading only fragments at a time. Experience had taught me what was important and what wasn't in endless reams of papers, a blessing when it came to narcotics work. This was indeed a world of paper and those who didn't learn to negotiate it agilely risked losing their way and becoming buried in ink.

Korinek proceeded to explain that Beachwood PD had been following Kevin and Ashley from the time of the anonymous phone call to no real avail. Their house on Bryden Road was always neat and clean. They were quiet and rarely did a car come and go from the house. After months of surveillance, John and Brandon realized that it was only on Sundays that they had visitors. It was usually a blue pickup truck with New York plates, and sometimes there would be a second car.

A quick scan of the surveillance notes showed that neither Ashley nor Kevin left the house much either, triggering another familiar bell in my head. Rather odd indeed, for two twentysomethings to live so lavishly without having any visible means of income. I knew real drug dealers, had busted enough of them to be acquainted with how they operated—their habits and proclivities. It was no different than a strong smell, and I didn't have to know this Kevin and Ashley personally to catch the scent.

In that moment I wasn't thinking of my wife or daughter, or of the fact that I'd be stepping on a bunch of toes in taking over Beachwood's case. I wasn't thinking of missed soccer games and parent conferences and dance lessons, or not being there to kiss Kathi good night or see my daughter off to school in the morning. I was thinking of what my years undercover taught me about the likes of Kevin and Ashley and those running drug organizations. The lives that were being ruined, the lives that would be lost. I'd seen it all before. Too many funerals re-sulted from the likes of Kevin and Ashley being allowed to continue practicing their deadly trade. In that moment, I stopped being Jeff Buck, chief of police in Reminderville, and returned to being Jeff Buck, under-cover drug operative. Back in my old world. The Dope Ghost.

I raised my head from the papers and this time made sure to include Meyers in my gaze. "I can help you get this guy."

CHAPTER NINE

From the look on Korinek's face, I knew I had him. But the scrunched, bushy eyebrows of Detective Meyers said otherwise.

"That is, if you want me to," I added in a show of deference, already contemplating how best to negotiate the politics of crossing jurisdictions to take control of this particular drug case.

Because it was time to go after the real bad guys again.

"Of course, we'd love to catch this guy," Korinek responded, "but I gotta tell you, he's good."

I started to smile and stopped. "We can get him," I said confidently. "It's all how you go about doing it."

"I just don't want you to get your hopes up," Korinek said, not swayed by my experience or swagger. "I just don't think this kid ever touches the drugs or the money."

I found it amusing that Korinek didn't want me to get my hopes up. Then again, he didn't know me. It wasn't about anything as random as hope; it was about the handling of a case, knowing what to do and when to do it and when to give up if necessary.

"Why did the case go cold?" I asked, sifting through the papers to find the answer on my own if I could.

"Blue pickup truck stopped showing up. We had no other leads and didn't know where to take things."

Didn't know where, I thought. Yeah, this was now my case all right. For sure.

"Let's get these guys!" I said, emphasis on *let's* in a show of more deference, leaning forward over the collection of pages strewn before me.

I saw that John Korinek's attention was focused solely on me,

Meyers forgotten in his mind now as much as in mine. *Body language was everything indeed*, I thought, the wheels in my head really starting to spin. There were so many ways to go about attacking a drug organization. I never knew what path a case would take until I was knee-deep into the investigation, the very definition of fluidity. But the first step was always the same: Gather information. Information was a better weapon than any gun or even army. And I wanted to make Korinek and Meyers realize that I had no intention of pushing them out; quite the contrary, I wanted to work the case with them as a team.

"What should we do first?" Korinek asked eagerly, the way a student might ask a teacher.

I didn't bother trying to hide my pleasure at the senior detective's reaction. "First thing we do is run the New York plates on that blue pickup again. Then we go from there."

Back at his desk inside the Beachwood Police Department—set in a private office on the lower level away from peering eyes, as a narcotics officer's desk should be—Detective John Korinek punched the license-plate number of the blue pickup truck into the Law Enforcement Automated Data System (LEADS). Korinek had run the plates a year back, and the registrant had come up clean. The system processed the request and turned up the same name the truck was registered to last year: Daniel Simonds of St. Lawrence County, New York. No prior arrests and no criminal history. In other words, nothing to go on. Korinek decided to wait until tomorrow to call me with his somewhat disappointing findings. Who knows, something else might turn up in the meantime.

As it turned out, something did. Just not what Korinek was expecting.

He arrived at the station early the following morning to find a note on his desk from the receptionist:

RICK SINNIGAN OF THE ST. LAWRENCE DRUG EN-
FORCEMENT AGENCY CALLED. PLEASE CALL BACK
ASAP!

Korinek felt a fire inside of him beginning to spark. And, not metaphorically, he felt hot and was beginning to sweat.

Goddammit!

It was well known in the world of law enforcement that the Drug Enforcement Administration and the Federal Bureau of Investigation were always at odds, grasping for the best cases, swiping them away from local municipalities and even, at times, from each other. The two organizations were like schoolkids who didn't always play nice. The only thing they could seem to agree on was that local law enforcement wasn't capable of handling cases approaching anything that resembled substantial. Speaking from experience, I can honestly say I never experienced any of these reputed issues in the working relationships I'd developed with the FBI or DEA on cases, like Brancel and Heckman, that Korinek had asked me about.

That may sound simple, when it's actually anything but, just as the perception of how law enforcement works in this arena has little to do with reality. Perception says the FBI handles big criminal cases that nobody else can and the DEA handles big drug cases. Perception also says that dealers like Kevin Sorin, with lifestyles vastly exceeding their apparent means, would raise flags at the IRS. Except dealers like Kevin either don't file taxes at all or have trusted accountants working out detailed, foolproof returns certain to raise no eyebrows. If somebody like me doesn't bring them to the IRS's attention, the IRS becomes like Sergeant Schultz from the old television show *Hogan's Heroes*: They know nothing, especially since the reduced level of staffing in recent years has left the agency woefully ill-equipped to conduct that kind of detailed audit or investigation.

That leaves local police departments like mine in Reminderville with everything else falling under the mundane. Domestic violence, street crime, traffic accidents, random violence of other kinds—that's local PD's lot. See, 98 percent of all police departments have thirty or fewer men and women serving as officers. So they just don't have the resources to handle big cases outside of their limited comfort zone. A major drug case, for example, would be handed off to the DEA. The DEA cares about the big import-export stuff, vast quantities of drugs coming in and out of the country. Big cases mean big numbers, and big numbers drive office staffing. It keeps agents employed and the agency itself growing and vital.

In the world of law enforcement, I've learned that drug cases come down to three things: asset seizure, drug seizure, and the number of arrests. But that kind of mentality creates this nebulous middle ground, a kind of doughnut hole, an empty gap, between the small stuff local police departments can handle and the big stuff that's really all that interests the DEA.

But here's the quandary. The DEA specializes in forming multi-jurisdictional task forces that incorporate local PDs into the mix. A majority of informants are turned by local cops like me in situations no more complicated than traffic stops. So in the Cleveland-Akron region, for example, you've got between a hundred and fifty to two hundred police departments and the vast majority of them don't have drug task force officers. That means when a traffic stop turns into a drug bust, they need to hand the case off. But to whom exactly? Very few of these cases are big enough to draw the DEA's interest, and the result of that is good leads falling through and the vast majority of the drugs the bad guys are peddling remaining on the streets.

Call it Catch-22.

The DEA isn't interested in doing any street-level stuff; their threshold level basically prohibits them from bothering. The only time it's worth them getting involved is when huge money enters the mix. That leaves a large amount of drug cases to slip through the cracks, into that gap.

That's where I come in. In the late 1980s, I started filling that gap by targeting my drug cases based on the quality of the drugs or the way a particular gang did business, meaning if I saw large amounts of weed being fronted. Here's the way it works: A big wholesaler, a pro, has five hundred pounds of marijuana he divvies up equally among ten dealers. He *fronts* the weed, as opposed to charging them for it—that's the mark of a big operation. My approach was to find the guys who are fronting the product and then follow the chain of dealers and suppliers up the food chain. Except you need what's called "walking" money, lots of it, to pull it off.

Call that Catch-23.

And my way around it was to "walk" marijuana money. "Walk" money refers to large amounts of actual cash I keep to use to purchase drugs from dealers in order to better make my case not only against them, but also to them to ultimately give me the guys the next level up. The money buys me the credibility I need to get inside and climb the ladder one rung at a time. And I'm not sacrificing the money I walk because in most cases I get it all back once the eventual bust is made. Here's something else: I photocopy a portion of every bill I walk, enough to capture the serial number. That way when a target's cash is tagged into evidence and made a record for the case, I can prove any bills I've photocopied are indeed the product of crime, making it that much easier to get a conviction. The suspect might say all the money came from legitimate sources, to which my rejoinder might be how about these bills I copied and then used to buy two kilos of cocaine from you?

Instead of arresting a suspect, I follow him. I see who he's talking to, meeting with. And more important, what are his assets? Large-scale drug dealers, the kind I'm after, can spend their money only so fast. You start seeing a pattern that allows you to identify the players and their place within an organizational tree. From that I identify my targets, establish the organization and who's a part of it, and then, most important of all, I find the weak link I can exploit to topple the whole tree. Where is the target vulnerable? Does he have a family, a record that means a bust could put him away for a long time if he's a three-time loser? What kind of guy is he? Did he play ball in high school, own his own business at some point? That kind of stuff.

The weak link gets all my attention. I target him twenty-four hours a day, seven days a week. I get him as dirty as I can and use him to give me the rest of the organization, or as much of it as he can. But it takes walk money, lots of it—sometimes as much as $50,000. Very, very few other, if any, local police departments are walking that much money on marijuana. It's worth the risk for me because once I have the guy I want to go after I look at it as an investment that's going to roll the rest of the organization. And once I get the evidence I need I hit all the players with search warrants, take them down all at once, and seize all their assets to fuel future walks.

The process, in other words, perpetuates itself. The more walk money I accumulate, the bigger buys I can position myself to make, bringing me further and further up the food chain. I hadn't found my weak link in the Beachwood case yet, but I would.

Because I always did.

CHAPTER TEN

Remember how impressed John Korinek was that I'd worked the Rudolph Brancel case? He was head of a huge marijuana distribution ring I busted in early 2000. In that case, I chose as my target within the overall organization a plumbing-supply-company owner we'll call Leo Fritz, who was moving lots of product. But he had a family, a business, and a country-club membership and liked to think of himself as legit. The kind of guy who could never do serious time; in it for the cash he was able to easily launder through his plumbing-supply company. Years before I actually busted Brancel himself, my partner and I were tailing Fritz when he stopped at a red light and, *boom!*, we snatched him out of his car, cuffed him, and put him in our car. And we're gone in thirty-five seconds. We drive him out of the county for what I like to call the Bad News Talk, while a uniform follows us driving his car.

Thing is, the clock's running at this point, which is to say that Leo's due in a particular place at a particular time. And as soon as he's late, or doesn't call in when he's supposed to, the source goes dark. Phone numbers get changed, burner phones get thrown away—the whole procedure gets shit-canned so nothing Leo can tell me leads anywhere. At that point the food chain ends for all intents and purposes with him, so I've got to make the Bad News Talk not just work, but work fast.

"Listen, Leo," I tell him, "we didn't pick your name out of a hat or a phone book, so you need to make a life-changing decision, the most important decision you'll ever make. You know I'm a narcotics agent. You know I'm here for the guy above you. I want you to think about what

you've been doing for the last ten years and I want to give you a hypothetical situation."

I look him in the eye and wait for him to nod or gesture for me to go
on. And once Leo Fritz does that, I proceed to recite for him what I
know he's been doing: all the deliveries he'd made and the dates and
times on which he made them, which we know from the surveillance
we've had up since we targeted him.

"That's how you're getting your dope, Leo, and that's how you're
moving it. Now hypothetically you can tell me I'm full of shit. But here's
a key component, something you should consider. You know all about
your Miranda warnings and you know I haven't given them yet. The
reason is I don't need to give them to you right now, because I've got
enough information and evidence without you saying a single word to
me to put you in prison for twenty-five years. That's twenty-five years
away from your family and friends. You'll lose your business. If you
don't make parole you'll probably die in jail. Now, because I haven't
Mirandized you yet, everything you tell me is strictly hypothetical, like
you never said it. Look, you have a very small window of opportunity
to help yourself out here and here's why. You're sitting in this parking
lot with me and pretty soon somebody's going to know you weren't
where you were supposed to be doing what you were supposed to be
doing. So we've got a very small window here.

"But if you work with me, Leo, I'm gonna let you help yourself out.
Work with me and that twenty-five-year sentence goes down to somewhere between fifteen and zero. The more you give me, the more years
get shaved off. There's a great chance, maybe seventy-five percent, that
I can keep your name out of this and nobody I nail will ever know it
was you who gave them up."

I then go on to talk about his kids, his grandkids, the places he likes
to travel to with the family, his interests, the college funds that are going to be confiscated along with everything else he's got if he doesn't
play ball with me. I say to Leo that all he has to do is tell the guys above
him that he's found a new dealer willing to take fifty pounds of product a week. Once he's hooked, my plan is to walk that fifty pounds (because cops can't put drugs back on the streets) and follow the money
up the food chain to its ultimate source.

Leo was nodding by the time I finished. His breathing had gone shallow, his skin pale. A man who knew he'd run out of good choices and just had to make the best one, which was me. Leo was smart enough to do exactly what I told him, and then he helped me with two more cases. Worked his sentence all the way to zero, no time served at all and not a single charge filed. He got to take care of his kids and watch his grandkids grow up, all because he cooperated. To this day, Leo calls me every year on Christmas Eve to wish me Merry Christmas.

And thanks in large part to Leo, the Brancel case became a truly major bust. Over the course of the two-year investigation, we climbed the food chain to the very top, culminating in a seventy-pound buy of pot from Rudolph Brancel himself in late January of 1999. Those seventy pounds were part of a near-fifty-ton shipment that came in from Mexico with a street value of $212.5 million. It was brought to port by a Louisiana shrimp boat and transferred to barges awaiting the shipment in Baton Rouge. This case, you see, was like so many others I've been involved in over the years. Our part of the investigation had taken me to Arizona, Pennsylvania, and California, with at least five other states involved in addition to Ohio.

But we didn't stop there. As the *Tribune Chronicle* newspaper reported in early 1999, "Prosecutors say in exchange for Brancel's cooperation, he was charged only with trafficking in marijuana, a third degree felony." That cooperation was directly responsible for us arresting Brancel's direct supplier, Edward Books, and three other men involved in the ring, which had grown into an enterprise doing more than a billion dollars in business annually. If drug organizations qualified for the Fortune 500, this one would be on it for sure, which is what I tell people who like to believe that marijuana dealing is a harmless and victimless crime. The profits don't end up going back into the economy. They go to buy more drugs or get laundered and end up in the pockets of the kingpins or stashed in offshore accounts to further hide their profits from the government and, especially, the IRS. These guys think they walk on water until they get caught by guys like me. Then they sink in a hurry.

I worked Brooks and three of his cronies right alongside Rudy Brancel; they trusted me because they trusted him, enough for us to walk money to make a series of buys that provided the evidence we needed to snatch them up. Just how big was Brancel's operation? On December 10, 1999, *The Cleveland Plain Dealer* reported that his "barges traveled up the Mississippi River to distribution ports where the drugs would be taken off the barges and reloaded onto rental trucks which, the operational outline states, would deliver the marijuana to dealers in Colorado, Michigan, Indiana, Pennsylvania, New Jersey, Maryland, Florida, Texas and Ohio."

Drugs are big business and the kingpins who stay open the longest treat them that way, maintaining several layers of precautions to keep from getting caught. A Geauga County Sheriff's Office report from December of 1999 about this particular operation read, "By using couriers, the primary suspects never touched the drugs. Couriers, who were often not the dealers, would drive the drugs to motels near Geauga County, then follow detailed instructions regarding the use of pager numbers to notify Brancel the drugs were here. The courier would then leave town. Brancel would distribute the drugs and in a totally unrelated (in time and location) transaction, pay for the drugs."

You can't follow a trail until you find one, no matter how long it takes. There's a lot of waiting; it takes a lot of patience. But in this case all that waiting and patience paid off when we put this particular drug operation out of business for good from the ground up. That same Geauga County Sheriff's Office report notes that the operation "proved to be the largest distributor of marijuana and other narcotics in Geauga County and perhaps even the entire state of Ohio." It took seven years and man-hours I can't even begin to count to do it, but that's what I do. That's what I'm about. Some of those newspapers that covered the busts printed pictures of bags and bags of marijuana piled high atop an evidence table while officials looked on. You won't find me in that picture or any other. That's the life of an undercover and I'm fine with that, more than fine. And when those photos were taken I probably was still working that case, had moved on to another one, or was continuing a parallel case that was ongoing as well. That's also part and parcel of the life of an undercover, or "UCA," for "undercover agent."

The Brancel case is illustrative of another facet of the process, which is when to bring in the DEA, because there are things for which local police departments need them even after the case is made and pretty much broken. The thing is, in cases tried in state court, the state has to prove that all the money coming into the organization is profits of the crime. But in federal court, the burden of proof is reversed—the bad guys have to prove the money *didn't* come from their crimes. They've got to prove where it came from alternatively, and that's almost impossible to do when a suspected drug dealer with no viable means of income or employment is living a lavish lifestyle.

For me, getting the DEA on board was as simple as convincing them there's good money involved, plenty of forfeiture assets to go around for everyone. In my mind, more forfeiture funds meant more walking money I could put on the street to nab more bad guys. For the DEA, it meant more positive stats that ultimately drive all their local offices and allow for more multi-jurisdictional cases with locals like me. Besides, what did they have to lose? I was serving the score up for them on a silver platter. But I had all the skin in the game and that meant I was in control. Everything in the case came back to my local property room, so they'd have to come to me for the forfeiture proceeds instead of the other way around.

Sometimes you never know where a case is going to lead. In 1993, the Grateful Dead Trucking Tour rolled into a sprawling, forty-acre campground in the town of Aurora, Ohio, outside of Kent. So we set up shop inside a ratty-looking trailer a few hundred yards away from a mobile home where our takedown team was based, close enough for them to hear everything over a wire we set up. We blended into the scenery so well, nobody suspected a thing. We started doing deals, buying dope, and making cases inside the trailer. Then the takedown team would swing in and place the targets under arrest out of sight and earshot. A van typical for a Grateful Dead show came by and we'd stuff them inside before anyone was the wiser.

This started Wednesday night and went on for four days. We arrested so many people, who seemed to flat out disappear, that the local towns were deluged with missing persons reports from their friends who had no idea what had happened to them. And the local departments couldn't be of much help because we'd booked all the targets under John Does.

But here's the thing. As a result of that operation, we recovered a whole bunch of LSD, strips of blotter paper with the individual tabs, or stamps, looking like sunshine. That was the mark of one of the biggest LSD dealers in the country whose acid was showing up coast to coast, known only as "Sunshine" for the stamps that bore his mark. Kind of like Walter White's, or Heisenberg's, blue meth on *Breaking Bad*. One of the targets we arrested gave up Sunshine's contact info, so after the Dead left town we set up a buy with him for thirty-five hundred unit doses. Sufficient bait to lure him out of his native Colorado up to my backyard in Ohio, where we nailed him in a parking lot and put him away where just one of the charges carried a penalty of fifteen to life. Something else: The parking lot where we had him meet us belonged to a school which makes any crime involving the sale of drugs that much more serious, even though the school wasn't open at the time of the bust.

Every case is different, as this latest one was sure to be once I figured out where Kevin Sorin, and whoever was driving that blue pickup truck, was taking me.

CHAPTER ELEVEN

Back in Beachwood, though, John Korinek figured the DEA wanted to steal our case right out from under us instead of waiting for us to call them once the case was made. He reached for the phone to call me before ringing Sinnigan.

"There's this DEA guy from New York trying to steal our case!" he ranted.

"No one is stealing the case," I assured him calmly. "Give the guy a call back and see what he wants. Don't tell him any more than you need to."

While I understood Korinek's concern, I wasn't at all worried about the New York branch of the Drug Enforcement Administration. If a New York connection was found, we'd go to New York, find local law enforcement that had jurisdiction, and work with them. Bring the DEA in officially when the federal thresholds were met, and the proper paperwork for the case was ready to be presented to the local US attorney's office.

Korinek felt infinitely better after his talk with me. He remained uneasy about calling Rick Sinnigan but comforted himself with my counsel and decided to follow my advice.

"Sinnigan here," the DEA agent said.

"Yeah, this is Detective John Korinek from Beachwood, Ohio, returning your call."

"Why did you run the plate of Daniel Simonds yesterday?" Sinnigan asked him, getting right to the point.

Korinek knew it! This guy *was* planning to steal our case, for sure.

Best way to prevent that from happening was to answer the question and stake his claim right from the get-go.

"We have him visiting the home of a local target numerous times over the past couple years."

"Has Simonds been there lately?" Sinnigan asked, his voice raised in a way that left Korinek distinctly unsettled.

"We haven't been surveilling the house the past several months," Korinek answered, not wanting to give Sinnigan any more information than was absolutely necessary.

A pause followed before Sinnigan's voice returned, lower and strangely flat.

"Well, Detective, I'm afraid I've got some news about Daniel Simonds. . . ."

CHAPTER TWELVE

Almost one year earlier, Danny Simonds found himself on the verge of exhaustion in the midst of his return from the drop at Ashley and Kevin's house in Beachwood. He'd had four cups of coffee and a pack of cigarettes, and kept the radio volume turned as high as it would go, but he couldn't shake the fatigue. Even the biting winter cold slipping in through the cracked driver's window wasn't helping to keep his heavy eyelids raised. His chase car was seven minutes ahead of him, so he knew the coast was clear, and with cash-filled computer towers instead of dope he figured it was okay to pick up the pace just a little.

It was three thirty in the morning when his blue Dodge Ram finally arrived at his home in the hamlet of Hogansburg, a mile from the St. Regis Mohawk Reservation, which was also known by its Mohawk name, Akwesasne. That's confusing and bears some explanation. The St. Regis Mohawks are also known by their native name, Akwesasne. Technically, the St. Regis tribe occupies the US side of the reservation while the Canadian side is referred to as the Akwesasne reserve. But over the years the terms "St. Regis" and "Akwesasne" have become virtually interchangeable in common nomenclature to the point where the confusion mirrors the border between the two tribes itself. In fact, thanks to the Jay Treaty, dating all the way back to 1795, members of the two tribes are able to move freely and lawfully between the two countries.

Unlike reservations provided with territory by the US government in its resettlement efforts, both sides of this reservation represent Akwesasne ancestral land dating back to the mid-eighteenth century. In 1755 it was established initially by Jesuit priests as the St. Regis Mission at Akwesasne. It was, actually, British land dating all the way to the end of the Revolutionary War when the fledgling United States claimed as much of it as it could, forcing the Mohawk peoples to pretty much become refugees. They gravitated toward the safe haven provided by the Akwesasne land, effectively immigrants in a country to which they were the true natives. And, according to the St. Regis Mohawk Tribe Web site today, "After this immigration, the culture at Saint Regis stayed predominately Mohawk. In 1796 the Seven Nations of Canada, which included Christian Mohawks living in St. Regis, asserted rights to their lands and were eventually confined to a small parcel of land through a treaty signed by representatives of the Seven Nations of Canada and the State of New York.

Currently the St. Regis Mohawk Tribe Web site is strung with the banner, "Helping Build a Better Tomorrow." That may well be true, but it belies a recent past riddled by the kind of drug smuggling in which Danny Simonds had become involved. He drove slowly up the gravel driveway. The frost and the chipped stones made an awful lot of noise if he wasn't careful, and he didn't want to wake up his family squeezed inside.

Danny's house was small. It looked like a cardboard box with white wood siding stapled in place. The snowpack climbed halfway up the house's sides, and thick pointy icicles hung from the gutters. The double-hung windows were completely frosted over. Danny did his best to scrape the sheets of ice that caked the glass, but it was hard to keep up with that and the residue of the relentless winter winds here in St. Lawrence County in general.

In the cold dark of that early Monday morning, Danny sat in his truck with the engine turned off, as if to punish himself for his failure to rise above his station in life. He was a war hero, for Christ's sake, he'd served his country, and this ramshackle box of a house was his reward? This, compared to a half-million-dollar-plus home owned by a drug-dealing punk?

Danny compensated for the lack of a big bright yard and spanking brick home like Kevin Sorin's by refusing to live like the rest of his neighbors. You didn't have to look far to see what Danny was trying to escape. To the left of his house was a run-down trailer home. Brown plastic garbage bags had replaced the windows. Rotted-out lawn furniture sat in the front lawn, buried in the snow. To his right sat a tiny house with chipped paint, the yard full of beaten-down junked cars. Danny felt that poverty was no excuse to live like a slob, and that's why he kept his yard as clean as he could and made sure to touch up any spots on the house where the paint had been eroded by the harsh, endless winter. And, yes, he scraped the ice from the windows relentlessly, although all that did was make it easier to see the decrepit, disheveled world from which he so badly wanted to flee. Or maybe that was the point.

Although he was tired and his body felt weak and stiff from the ride, he carried the computer towers into the house and placed them gently next to his bed. Danny was not going to take a chance with Alan's money. If someone wanted the money they were going to have to go through him, no easy task given the Marine Corps training that had been put to the test in Afghanistan often enough. Violence was most feared from a man used to practicing it; that's why he'd never do anything to risk Alan's wrath. That could lead to a confrontation with the Hells Angels, for whom violence was practically an occupation.

Danny washed up and climbed into bed next to his fiancée, Kim Cook. As his body hit the mattress and his head lowered to the pillow he sighed, a vast sense of relief pouring from him with another run completed. He looked over at Kim. To him, she was the most beautiful woman in the world. She reminded him of Pocahontas, the cartoon version. She had long, thick, flowing black hair that haloed her strong-featured face as she slept. Her dark olive-colored skin was flawless, and even when she slept her full lips seemed to form a mischievous grin. Danny was doing this for her and his kids, he told himself as he lay there. He was going to be able to give her everything she ever wanted and more.

Nighttime faded away quickly and the gray of the day arrived before Danny was ready to embrace it. But the sizzle of bacon and the giggles of innocence reenergized him. He ran down the steps and kissed all his loves, the people for whom he was doing all this. On his first few runs, Danny had placed a family picture on the dashboard to remind him of that fact, ending the practice when he realized how it could involve his family should he be caught. Stupid.

"Successful trip?" Kim asked casually, as if his Sunday run were traditional business travel.

"It was fine. Just got to get those towers to Al before eight."

"He's at the factory by eight?" Kim asked, clearly surprised. She'd known Alan Jacobs since they'd been kids, having grown up on the res; everyone on the res knew each other, and in fact most everyone was somehow related, including the two of them as cousins of some sort.

"Nah. I'm going to drop them off at his house."

"Make sure you say hello to Alicia for me."

"I think he kicked her out."

"Really? And the kids?"

"Don't know."

Danny was off to the king's castle. With the computer towers loaded back in the truck, he followed Route 37 from his home to the res. New York Route 37 ran east and west, the lone road in and out of the reservation. It wasn't the change of scenery that let travelers know they had arrived on the res, though; the trees, the snow, the run-down homes were all the same as in the surrounding towns. The first notice of entering the res was the white Tahoe Border Patrol vehicle that sat on the outskirts of the Mohawk land. Border Patrol always sat somewhere in the vicinity of the res, but they seldom, if ever, crossed the line. This was sovereign land and the Natives were anything but welcoming when it came to outside law enforcement, as evidenced by the signs placed at the perimeter's few access points:

NO NO TAX ON OUR DAMN LAND
YES "TERRORISTS" COME THRU AKWESASNE
THEY ARE N.Y.S BORDER PATROL A.T.F.
F.B.I. I.R.S. ECT. ECT.!!!
THE PEOPLE
THIS IS OUR RECLAIMED LAND

Past the postings of disdain for the outside world was the display of pride and strength felt by the Akwesasne Mohawk culture. The heads of symbolic eagles, feathers, and the faces of Indian warriors were portrayed in bright colors on flags and signs all over the land. These were proud people, though hardened by poverty and their resolvedly insular nature. The Natives had little use for the white men they saw as economic oppressors who had sought to steal their identity and render their entire existence moot.

The Natives only welcomed the outside world when it assisted in bloating their bank accounts. The Akwesasne Mohawk Casino, for instance, was the gem of the reservation. Opened in 1999, the fifty-two-thousand-square-foot casino was as modern and sparkly as any Atlantic City or Las Vegas hot spot. This casino, which was usually occupied by locals, had become the meet-and-greet spot for runners and wannabe dealers. Danny avoided the place, knowing it could only cause him trouble.

There was no real reason for out-of-towners to come gamble in St. Lawrence, located in the middle of nowhere with mediocre accommodations at best. Danny didn't need to get any more sucked into this whole thing than he already was, so he always drove right past the sprawling casino grounds and parking lot. As he passed the tribal police station carrying five computer towers packed with cash, he didn't flinch or even look twice. No reason for worry here. The tribal police looked out for their own and turned a blind eye when it came to Alan Jacobs's business interests, legitimate and otherwise. Heck, Danny thought, although he was never implicated in criminal acts, the chief of tribal police was Alan's uncle! An incestuous world indeed.

Danny drove another mile in and came to Laughing Road, a name striking in its irony since he often felt that laughing was what the world was doing at him, a white man engaged to a Native toting huge amounts of cash to further the Akwesasne cause. Nestled on a wooded lot with a man-made tributary of the St. Lawrence River flowing through its backyard, Alan's ten-thousand-square-foot stone home stuck out like a sore thumb amid the squalor and poverty on all sides. It wasn't that there weren't any nice homes on the res. There were several, owned by other smugglers and dealers. But they were nothing like Alan's, not even close.

He had built a shrine to celebrate his successes with a grand entryway and pristine landscaping surrounded by a ten-foot-high stone wall. The mansion was a testament not only to his own triumphs, but also to all he'd brought to the tribe, which explained why no one begrudged him such an ostentatious display of luxury and wealth. Alan kept his outdoor Jacuzzi temperature at a consistent 104 degrees, while many on the res struggled to pay for the propane to keep any water at all hot in the worst of winter.

Danny pulled up the gate and pressed the button to be let in.

"Yeah?" a voice said through a speaker.

"It's Danny."

"Come on in."

CHAPTER THIRTEEN

The scripted "A" and "J" on the wrought-iron gates parted, inviting Danny onto the property. Danny could never get over Alan's house, no matter how many times he made drop-offs or pickups. Here, the river didn't seem like frozen darkness entrapping him and holding him hostage; it was almost serene and peaceful. During the summertime, the dock that Alan had built on his man-made lake would be surrounded by speedboats, Jet Skis, and tubing toys. Alan's two boys were very lucky indeed, and Danny couldn't help but picture his kids growing up with comparable luxuries.

Alan was currently out on bail, having been arrested on drug charges for marijuana smuggling after being allegedly fingered by either a local law-enforcement officer or a border-control agent who wasn't being paid enough to look the other way. He was potentially facing a long stretch behind bars, which, in Danny's mind, made him much less the kingpin he'd spent the better part of his adult, and young adult, life becoming.

Danny carried the first tower to the front porch and rang the doorbell. Alan answered wearing flannel pajama pants and a New York Giants shirt. Alan, although statuesque, seemed tiny and out of place in the spacious two-story foyer. He was of average size, with a build that was just starting to go flabby in his early thirties. He had Kim's dark hair, and eyes that seemed filled with a vapid look at times, as if they were processing everything he saw in slow motion. He was so unassuming physically, except for those eyes, that it was difficult for Danny to view him as wielding as much power as he did. Alan was out on bail on a charge he and his lawyers were convinced he was going to beat, although Danny had heard that a plea bargain for a reduced sentence on the smuggling beef was being seriously discussed. A large crystal chandelier hung overhead, causing light to dance across the taupe-colored marble floor. All the furnishings looked exquisite to Danny, several steps beyond Kevin and Ashley's place, to the point where thinking of his own slab house made him cringe.

"You can put them over there," Alan said, pointing to the dining room.

The formal dining room was decorated with an ornate Oriental rug, a thick wooden table that sat twelve, and a carved maple credenza. Alan watched as Danny carried in the towers and placed them in the corner of the room as directed.

"That kid moves a lot of shit."

"Yep."

Alan nodded, clearly pleased with Kevin's efforts. "We on schedule for the week after next?"

"Sure are. Kevin said he wants the same as this week."

"Hey, how's Kim? How are your kids?"

"They're good, thanks. How are your boys?"

"Fine, I guess. They're with their bitch of a mother right now. You know how it is."

Danny nodded; he'd suffered through a bad separation from his first wife. They had their first child when they were only nineteen years old. They were young and in love and got married. The next two kids came quickly. Danny was doing everything he could to take care of his family, but they were barely making ends meet. One day, his wife just picked up and left. Danny never was able to find her and they never were able to get divorced, which was why Kim and Danny weren't able to get married. Kim was kind enough to love his children. She became a mother to them. She watched them and cared for them when Danny went to war. So although he remembered what Alan was talking about, he now had a woman he loved and couldn't imagine them separating or his life without her.

Their family was the whole reason he was doing this, taking the risk. But Danny figured Alan was no different. He was still about working and providing for his own and bettering his life. Maybe Alan was no more satisfied than he, thirsting for more no matter how much he had, which was obviously considerable. Danny had never known anyone like Alan before and paid him the deference deserved by a man who could help Danny ascend the same chain he now topped. Beneath the man's calm demeanor and business acumen, though, lurked a ruthlessness and cunning only occasionally revealed in the flash of a gaze, a narrow tilting grin, or an understated comment about someone who had strayed to his bad side. Danny knew from the war what a killer's eyes looked like well enough to know that that description didn't necessarily fit Alan. Alan's eyes gave up nothing, just another mask he wore according to the whim of the moment.

Danny couldn't take his eyes off the furnishings, right down to the marble floor polished to a glow. "I should be going," he said, turning for the door.

"Have a good one," Alan said, attention on the computer towers now. "And tell Kim I said hey."

"Will do."

Danny climbed back into his truck but didn't leave right away. He thought of how hard he worked, the risks he was taking, and how little he had to show for it in a relative sense. He finally drove off, fingers clenching the steering wheel hard. Alan Jacobs's mansion shrank in Danny's rearview mirror, swallowed by the woods as he passed dilapidated Native shacks that reminded him too much of the shoe box that he called home.

No way could he see himself living like this much longer, no way.

2

ICE BRIDGE

In a closed society where everybody's guilty,
the only crime is getting caught. In a world
of thieves, the only final sin is stupidity.

—Hunter S. Thompson

CHAPTER FOURTEEN

Beachwood, Ohio; November 2008

The guy in the blue pickup truck, Danny Simonds, is dead," Detective John Korinek told me over the phone almost a year later, his voice edgy and nervous. "That's the word from the DEA guy Rick Sinnigan in New York."

"Well, now we know why he stopped visiting our guy in Beachwood," I said matter-of-factly. "Sinnigan say how?"

"That he was killed."

"As in murdered?"

"Killed was what he said."

"Gotcha."

The calmness in my voice didn't seem to soothe the less-seasoned Korinek; my response was met by silence on the other end of the line. I didn't know whether Korinek was troubled that the guy was dead or was still under some misconception that New York might steal the case out from under us.

"Did Sinnigan say anything else?" I asked, coaxing Korinek along.

"Yeah. He said that they were aware that Daniel Simonds, the man in the truck, was a drug runner and worked for one of the largest smugglers on the reservation up there in St. Lawrence County."

"Indian reservation, huh?" That made for an interesting twist. I was used to Hells Angels, Russian mafia, and South American drug lords; I'd crossed paths with them all over the years and had taken down more than my share. But I'd never run across a Native American drug ring. This would set forth a whole new set of challenges. Challenges not faced on typical American soil, challenges that could make going after the top of the drug ring more complicated and less financially rewarding for my drug fund. Indian reservations were sovereign land, which meant that the rules I was used to playing by didn't necessarily apply. I wasn't going to be able to just march in and grab the guy or take his house, toys, and money.

"Yup," Korinek continued. "They're aware that this Danny, the dead guy, was running up to Beachwood every other week. Also, they have an informant who claims that two Russian men and a young girl had been coming up that way for the past several months. Can you call the guy?"

I felt more excitement race through me, the pieces of my planned investigation starting to fall together. "Give me Sinnigan's number. Let's get this ball rolling."

I hung up the phone with Korinek and immediately called DEA agent Rick Sinnigan of the St. Lawrence County drug task force. Our brief conversation confirmed what Korinek had already explained. Kevin Sorin and Ashley Schmid, although nameless to the St. Lawrence drug task force, had been pinpointed by an informant on the reservation and in Franklin County, just south of St. Lawrence County. The informant said that he had seen Ashley, Kevin, and Kevin's father, Boris, in the area well after Danny's death. The informant didn't have any valuable information to offer, because he claimed that Kevin and Boris only spoke to each other in Russian, keeping him from discerning the depth of their plans or involvement.

Sinnigan continued to ramble off other meaningless bits and pieces of information, while I politely listened, knowing damn well this was no way to handle a case. It didn't take long on the phone for me to peg Sinnigan as a show horse. It was evident that this guy wasn't going to want me sticking my nose in a task-force case, but I wasn't planning on giving him a choice. I was coming to New York. Now all I had to do was tell my wife.

We live on a horse farm maybe a half hour from the station in decent traffic. We breed Percherons, which are black Clydesdales, very docile, even-tempered animals that have always provided a welcome respite from the rigors of my police work, undercover and otherwise. We've boasted the highest-selling mares in the country for two years in a row. I've always figured that anything worth doing is worth doing to the absolute best of your abilities; I just don't know any other way. The kind of scut work I spend my time on the farm doing—grooming the horses, cleaning the stalls—could easily be jobbed out entirely to hired hands. But that's just not me.

It's the same with my career in law enforcement, particularly fighting the drug war. I never ask anyone, subordinate or otherwise, to do something I'm not willing to do myself. If I write the warrant, I'm going through the door first. I'm not going to write a warrant on the home of a potentially dangerous suspect and send somebody else ahead of me. No. If someone's going to get the first bullet in the vest, it's going to be me. That's what leading by example is all about. It helps me earn respect and that's especially important when I'm working out of state where the other cops don't know me by anything other than reputation, if that. This is a dangerous business populated by criminals who could be facing long prison stretches or even life behind bars. You never know what they're going to do or how they're going to react. And guys, fellow officers, are looking to me for direction. That's what I mean by leading by example, and nobody understands that better than Kathi.

"Kath! Kath!" I yelled her name as I walked around the property.

"Kath!" I called again.

Where the hell is she? It was nearly 5:30 P.M. She was usually out in the barn helping Sarah, our part-time stable hand. Then it hit me: She'd been at a parent/teacher thing for our daughter, something that I rarely had time for, even with the desk job. Damn. I ran inside as fast as I could and found her helping our daughter with her homework.

"Kathi," I managed, gasping for air. Boy, I was really out of shape. "How about I take you to dinner?"

I took her to her favorite restaurant and ordered a nice bottle of wine. Once the waiter poured, I proposed a toast.

"To us. To having the smartest, most wonderful daughter in the world. I love you."

Kathi looked at me lovingly. "What is it that you want, Jeff Buck?"

Man, this woman knew me so well. "I really do love you, Kathi."

"Spill it, Buck."

I told her the story of Ashley and Kevin and everything I had learned so far. "See, this really isn't just a matter of busting drug dealers, this is a matter of national security," I said, grasping a bit.

Her blue eyes got really squinty on me. She took a sip of her wine and then another.

"I love you, Jeff." She paused for a long time. "Getting drug dealers is your passion. And there is obviously a really big problem up there they don't know how to handle."

That was not what I was expecting her to say. For me, protecting the identity and safety of my family were paramount. So in the twenty years I worked undercover, I regularly did what's known in the trade as "heat runs." Normally, that term applies to targets who'd suddenly pull in to a parking lot to check to see if they were being followed. But the thing to remember is working undercover doesn't stop when you leave a bad guy in a bar or any meeting place. I've got to assume he may be watching to make sure I'm legit, could have me followed to see if I'm telling him the truth about where I live, my family, and whatever else my cover includes. So whenever I was rolling home, sometimes at two or three in the morning, I'd pull into a parking lot on a heat run the same way the bad guys do to see if they're being tailed. A necessary precaution in my life as the Dope Ghost.

"Maybe if you go back to work on this case," Kathi continued, "you can teach them a thing or two on your process."

I leaned across the table and gave her a kiss. "Thank you."

"Don't thank me yet. Just so you know, I will be so pissed if you get yourself killed."

To Kathi I wasn't the man who'd brought down some of the largest drug rings across the United States; I was her husband, the father of her child, and a man that she wanted to keep alive and around.

"Kath, I'm going to protect our daughter," I continued. "I'm going to protect our country."

She knew I was sincere. From the moment she'd first met me, Kathi knew that all I wanted was to make the world a better place. But she also knew firsthand how dangerous the people I dealt with could be and how that danger, for an undercover agent, could spring up anywhere anytime. We were in the airport once, about to head out on vacation, when I spotted a target that knew me as Jimmy Morgan, my undercover alter ego.

"Walk away," I whispered to Kathi.

And, always prepared for just that eventuality, off she went to make small talk with a man standing nearby, while I moved off to work the target. Because in this world, you're always working. It never stops. No downtime, even when you're in the airport waiting to board a plane. The ramifications of the cover of someone like me getting blown can be catastrophic. There are no rules in the drug world. Families are considered acceptable targets.

But there were lighter moments for Kathi and me on the job as well. Once I called her out of the blue and told her she needed to accompany me to a Tough Man Contest where I needed to be with a target. Problem was my "work wife," another undercover, was working another case, and I couldn't afford to let the target slip away. I filled Kathi in on her new name, our two fake kids, everything I could think of about our faux, manufactured lives. Only I didn't have time to cover everything, and, sure enough, at one point my target's wife jumped up to accompany Kathi to the concession stand.

"Where do your kids go to school?" the woman asked her, information I hadn't provided.

But Kathi was up to the task. "Doesn't matter where they go to school," she replied, pretending to be in a huff. "Because if they don't straighten out and behave, they're going straight to juvenile detention."

One of the reasons I lasted as long as I did in the undercover world was that I always treated my informants, and even my targets, right. I never lied or broke my promises. I met them for lunch, asked about their families, got invested in their lives the way I do with my friends. Remember Leo Fritz, the informant who calls me every year on Christmas Eve just to thank me? I stayed in touch with another guy, a target, even after I put him away for three years. He's been legit ever since his release and we still get together for a Mexican dinner occasionally. You treat people with respect, they treat you the same way.

Which, of course, begs the question: Why bother? Why bother making a life out of going after weed dealers in an age where marijuana is increasingly acceptable, decriminalized, and even legal on the state level? It's simple: Anyone who asks that question doesn't have their eyes on the bigger picture, the whole picture.

Here's an undeniable fact: The more marijuana use becomes socially acceptable, the more money organized crime will make from it. Kind of like Prohibition, when bars and speakeasies fattened the wallets of countless wiseguys by buying booze from them. You end up with more people getting high and messing up their lives, while a different brand of wiseguys fatten their bank accounts.

People say it's a victimless crime, right? Well, in a word, wrong. Because the low-level dealer from whom a thirty- or forty-year-old business and family man is probably buying kicks that money back up the food chain. All the way up to the Mexican cartels or Hells Angels, who use it to expand their empire deeper into other criminal pursuits, like human trafficking, prostitution, gunrunning, even in some cases terrorism. The guns and weapons used during the biker wars that terrorized Montreal for many years were financed by their drug business. The explosives that killed eleven-year-old Daniel Desrochers in that park in 1995 were financed by the same kind of recreational users who don't think they're hurting anyone. Maybe they're not, but the money with which they're buying the drugs sure is.

And where does that money go? It sure doesn't go to anything good, useful, or productive to society; normally, it doesn't even stay in the country. This is a cash business, and both the decriminalization and the tacit acceptance of weed have given these guys all the more untaxed dollars, which get taken out of the system. I busted a guy once who was doing $4 million of business a month on average. To launder all that, he was building one hotel in Costa Rica and another in Canada, which we ultimately seized when I arrested him. The same guy had opened a bar in rural Ohio that maybe twenty cars passed on average every day—that's it, twenty cars. But every morning he'd have two beer kegs delivered that he'd proceed to let flow until they were empty in order to launder another chunk of his money by saying he sold those two hundred or so cups per keg instead.

Hey, at least he was paying taxes on $1,600 a day.

I busted another dealer in Ohio, back in 1996, who was the ultimate small businessman. Always careful, discerning about whom he did business with, and never tried to climb the food chain to increase his risk of exposure. When I finally arrested him, the Bad News Talk I had with the guy helped me do a dealer in San Diego who was moving twelve hundred pounds a month and another in Florida who was moving two thousand. All because of dealers like my guy moving bits and pieces of their weed, individual parts adding up to a stunning whole. And at the top of the food chain were the kind of organized-crime kingpins the average recreational marijuana user never dreamed he was doing business with.

Buy an eighth or a quarter once in a while? Sure. Help finance a continuing criminal enterprise involved in turning kids into prostitutes and gunning down their enemies? Never.

And that's the point. I don't question that marijuana can help a sixty-year-old woman deal with her glaucoma, or help relieve a cancer patient's pain or even an epileptic child's seizures. But that amounts to a tiny, tiny percentage of weed usage, and, in many cases, there are traditional *legal* drugs that can do the job just as well. Beyond that, a far greater percentage of marijuana use is by recreational users who don't believe they're harming society at all, much less contributing to the proceeds of organized crime. Wonder what those users would think if they saw how the dime bag they bought on a street corner ended up in Montreal forcing an imprisoned twelve-year-old girl to sleep with ten different guys a night? That's not an exaggeration, either. So, tell me, what would they think?

I deal with this every day, and in my experience a large percentage of marijuana users are abusing other drugs as well, like cocaine, heroin, or prescription meds. I'm not talking about weed as a gateway drug here; I'm talking about it being lumped into the bigger pile. The means of the high may be different, but the ends, where the money ultimately ends up, remains the same.

Some who claim to be in the know like to insist that legalizing weed as in Colorado and Washington is the answer, replacing the street dealers with regulated and sanctioned dispensaries. What happens, though, when those dispensaries can't keep up with demand? What happens when they can triple their profits by buying street-level weed in bulk instead of controlled batches from government-sanctioned grow houses? That guy I busted who was building a hotel in Canada to launder his drug money? He was actually smuggling huge wads of cash across the border over Lake Erie in frozen beef. His guys would stop at a campground and build a fire to thaw it out, then get back in the truck and turn the cash over to the company building his hotel.

And when it comes to so-called legalized weed, remember that marijuana is still illegal on the federal level. That federal level, of course, trumps the state level, which explains why legal growers and dispensaries can't open bank accounts, or do business with financial institutions. In Washington State, another challenge has surfaced.

"The immediate challenge," *Time* reported in its July 21, 2014, issue, "is competition. The handful of new, regulated legal sellers will have a hard time luring customers from the hundreds of cheaper medical dispensaries already scattered across the state. Meanwhile, a three-tiered tax system that even Randy Simmons, deputy director of Washington's Liquor Control Board, calls 'terrible and inefficient,' may push smokers and sellers alike toward the black market."

In the article Simmons goes on to say that, "For now, my goal is for legal weed to make up just 13 percent of the overall market for dope in the state."

Where do you think the additional 87 percent is going to come from?

Right now, I'd estimate that there are twenty dealers in the state of Ohio doing $4 million a month out of their homes. Since that's likely a low-end estimate, we're talking about a billion dollars of weed a year being moved just by that level of dealer. *A billion dollars.*

CHAPTER FIFTEEN

Two days after I had my talk with Kathi, John Korinek and Brandon Meyers packed into my Ford Expedition for the eight-hour-and-twenty-minute drive to St. Lawrence County. I had made arrangements to meet up there with Rick Sinnigan and Randy McGuire, a New York state trooper and veteran agent of the Franklin County drug task force. I wanted to make sure that I had all his bases covered as well as jurisdictions.

Travel, of course, was nothing new for me, and it was sometimes harrowing. I was undercover on a case once involving a large-scale drug dealer who was laundering money through Miami and had just purchased a resort in Costa Rica. To nail him I had to take a trip to Costa Rica, where the attorney behind the operation was based, but I also had to take an informant with me. Things got real complicated here logistically, since the key to the operation was the actual transporter I needed to get to sign off on his share of the resort property. That meant venturing into the Costa Rican jungle to reach the village where he lived.

Now, my Spanish is bad at best, but my informant spoke it fluently. He could have been telling our marks just about anything, and I wouldn't know it. This wasn't necessarily a dangerous trip; I just needed to get the paperwork in order to liquidate the property and send the money back home. But it was rainy season in Central America and there wasn't a single minute I wasn't soaking wet. The men who guided me into the jungle carried machetes to slice through the overgrown vegetation, and I was strip-searched once we got to the transporter's home. The thing is anytime you're in enemy territory, especially places like Colombia and even Costa Rica, things can go bad in a hurry and you realize real fast what it feels like to be on your own with no one watching your back and no support from friendly US authorities.

On this 2008 November day, meanwhile, the Beachwood detectives and I discovered firsthand just how painfully long it was to drive from Ohio to St. Lawrence County. I decided that I was going to make the most out of their time. I knew from all the years that cases could take a million different twists and turns. You had to be prepared for every possible move that a bad guy could make; surprises and hiccups could take down years' worth of investigative work. The key lay in thinking ahead, anticipating your adversary's moves, and always remaining a step ahead of him.

The three of us went back and forth repeatedly as to what could possibly happen from any number of angles. There were so many scenarios as to how Ashley Schmid and Kevin Sorin were currently operating, and with Danny out of the picture it was going to be challenging to narrow them down. All we could do now was create the scenes and stories, changing details and endings like a child does in a Choose Your Own Adventure book. Preparation.

Two hours south of St. Lawrence, we were greeted in Watertown, New York, by a sudden drop in temperature and the fall of thick, heavy snow that looked like confetti dropping from the gray sky. We were getting our first taste of the harsh, seemingly endless winter that covered the region like a glove.

"Man, they weren't kidding when they said to watch out for lake-effect snow," Korinek said, staring out the window at the flakes the size of jumbo marshmallows.

"Sinnigan didn't seem much like the joking type to me," I responded, slowing the truck down with the road turning slick beneath the Expedition. "Guess we're going to have more time in the car than we thought. Good thing I didn't tell those guys we'd meet them till eight."

We'd already talked through every situation that we could possibly come up with, so the car fell silent in its steady push through the blanket of white that kept pushing back. If nothing else, it gave me even more time to play through the upcoming events.

We'd driven through miles and miles of a gray drab world encased in the white sheets falling from the sky and had finally reached our destination of St. Lawrence County. It looked like another world, empty and detached from the rest of civilization as if it had fallen off to be forgotten. Almost everything was frozen and what wasn't frozen was dilapidated. There hadn't been any industry or anything remotely passing for a business for at least a hundred miles.

No wonder everyone up here runs drugs, I thought. What choice did they have? I pulled out the directions to River Run, some podunk restaurant where Sinnigan suggested we meet for dinner.

I pulled my Ford Expedition into River Run's frozen muck of a parking lot twenty minutes later. Five-foot-high mud-caked snow piles fenced the parking lot, blocking the view of an adjacent junkyard. Korinek, Meyers, and I climbed out of the Expedition and walked toward the restaurant. Snowy air normally smelled fresh and clean. Not here. Here it smelled like old steel, copper, and rust, courtesy I guessed of the nearby junkyard.

The restaurant itself was a dumpy old diner. The vinyl on the chairs was torn and held together in some places by duct tape. Pieces of the linoleum floor were missing, and everything smelled like cabbage. I hated cabbage. It didn't take me more than a minute to pick out Rick Sinnigan from the Drug Enforcement Administration and New York state trooper Randy McGuire, both from their respective drug task forces. I made a small wager with myself that McGuire was the blond guy with the mop of hair and Sinnigan was the one with the comb-over.

"Rick Sinnigan," Comb-Over said, rising to extend a hand toward me.

I smiled, having won my bet. I knew it. No way someone with as much hair as McGuire could be as biting as Sinnigan had seemed on the phone. And to top things off the DEA man had a weak, limp handshake that was moist with either perspiration or condensation from gripping the icy glass of whatever he was drinking. He breathed heavily out of his mouth, a bit labored as if he was fighting a cold. His nose was red and I waited for him to take out a handkerchief and blow it.

The five of us ordered quickly so we could get down to business. It was obvious that Sinnigan had an agenda. My second impression of him, besides that he was a show horse, was that he was also an "ass clown," a phrase I had coined for the deserving few who could potentially destroy any case that dropped onto their desk. Still, out of protocol I let him take the lead.

"Your Beachwood guys, this Ashley and Kevin, have been making regular runs up here. They're dealing with the Frasers, a couple that live five miles south of St. Lawrence in Franklin County. This Kevin and Ashley show up every other Sunday morning and leave the same Sunday night. The couple that they've been dealing with, Harold and Sabrina, look like a pair of toothless hillbillies. They operate a general store on their farm in the middle of nowhere."

And where are we now exactly? I almost asked him.

"Harold and Sabrina," I repeated instead, glancing out the window at the gray slab of a world, dark and dreary in a way that reminded me of Appalachia without the mountains. Hillbillies indeed. And it was pretty clear that Kevin and Ashley were now buying their weed from these particular ones, and the next logical conclusion in my mind was that the Frasers were somehow connected to the same network as Danny Simonds, Kevin and Ashley's now-departed supplier. "Are the targets actually spending most of their time in your county?"

Randy McGuire responded this time. "Yes. The Frasers have no priors, though. They're not on anybody's radar."

"Well," I noted, "they are now."

"Given that, this is what I propose," said Sinnigan. "Next time your targets come up here to do a deal with the Frasers, we grab them before they land at the house. We know they'll have a minimum of two hundred and fifty thousand dollars on them. We confiscate the money, they're looking at five to ten, and we split the forfeitures seventy-five/twenty-five. Case done."

Sinnigan's thin lips pressed tightly together like a dried-out earthworm, his bushy eyebrows angled in over his sunken eyes as he waited for me to respond. I cut a piece of my chicken parmigiana and chewed slowly, fully aware it was aggravating Sinnigan.

"If I was going to do that, I could do it in Cleveland and save myself the fucking drive," I said after swallowing my food.

An uncomfortable silence fell over the table. No one was expecting me to come right out and take control, least of all Sinnigan.

McGuire tried to clear the air. "Have you ever been up here before?"

"No. Why don't you tell me how business works in your neck of the woods?" I asked him.

"Well, it's an interesting place. The Akwesasne reservation makes for a whole world of troubles that the country has no idea exists."

"How so?"

"Their land straddles New York State, Ontario, and Quebec, and, because it's an Indian reservation, neither government was given the opportunity to set up a border patrol other than in Cornwall Island, where Canada maintains an unarmed station."

"Let's see if I've got this right: People can just come in and out of the country without worrying about checkpoints."

"That's right."

"Even in the post–nine/eleven era?"

Sinnigan shrugged. "There are seven unmanned roads in and out of Canada. Every so often Border Patrol will take a drive up and down the streets, but the Natives make it known that they aren't welcome, sometimes violently. And during the winter there's an eighth road that causes even more troubles."

"An eighth road," I repeated.

"The ice bridge. When the St. Lawrence River freezes. The Canadian growers and Native smugglers and dealers may be less overtly violent than the Mexican cartels, but don't be fooled. A lot of blood has been spilled because of what passes over that water. You think this Danny Simonds was the first?"

He proceeded to tell me about the long biker wars that had plagued Quebec before ultimately being won outright by the Hells Angels. It was the Angels, he explained, who ran the operation north of the border, delivering thousands of pounds of marijuana to the Akwesasne reservation for distribution throughout the region. Picture that operation stretching across the entire border with Canada, multiplied maybe fiftyfold, and I'd have an idea of the scope, and thus the danger, we'd be facing.

"These guys don't give a shit who they kill," McGuire continued. "Nobody up there's been able to touch them in six, maybe seven years;

a couple hundred maybe running the whole damn operation along with these Indians."

"How much product we talking about?" I asked him.

"Nobody's really sure. Best estimates put it at thirty, maybe forty billion annually when you count the whole border with Canada. That's billion with a 'b'."

"I heard you."

McGuire leaned forward, his expression flattening and eyes growing as dull and hopeless as the storm-swept sky outside. "We're talking about the biggest drug-smuggling operation in the country operating right under our nose. The product is grown, or manufactured in the case of pills, across the border in Canada under the supervision of the Hells Angels to be distributed off the res to the Russian mob, like your Kevin Sorin, and then straight to the public. And we can't touch any of them."

I could almost feel the blood coursing quicker through my veins. I'd heard tales of such a massive drug operation straddling the US-Canada border, but up to this point nobody had ever been able to fit all the disparate pieces together. The whole thing reminded me of a line from a movie called *The Usual Suspects*: "The greatest trick the Devil ever pulled was convincing the world he didn't exist." It was the same thing here. The operation had thrived, pretty much unencumbered by law-enforcement elements, because it was insulated by borders, sovereign land, and the intimidation with which the Hells Angels operated throughout Canada. That and no one believed a drug operation to rival that of the Mexican cartels was operating in virtual plain sight on our northern border. The very notion seemed ridiculous. In law-enforcement annals, it was referred to as an urban myth, and that became the operation's greatest insulation. Nobody bothers prosecuting what they don't believe exists.

"Here's how I think we should play it," Sinnigan said, about to repeat the same idea he had before. "We know the runner, how much he's carrying when and where. We take him down, get a nice bust, and net a quarter million or so in forfeiture. How can we go wrong?"

How can we go wrong? Are you serious?

That's what I felt like saying but I pushed my chair back, stood up, and said something else instead.

"I'm going to the bathroom."

A s I was standing by the urinal, Randy McGuire walked in and took the spot next to me, just a divider separating us.

"What do you think of Sinnigan?" he asked me.

"You want the truth?"

I watched him shrug.

"I think he's a jackass," I continued. "Why the fuck would I drive seventeen hours to arrest a guy who was coming to my city anyway? Is this guy stupid or does he think I'm stupid?"

At that point, I was ready to get back in my car and drive home then and there. In my experience, Sinnigan wasn't the typical DEA agent looking to rush a case for a quick money grab. The vast majority of agents I've dealt with are team players after the very same thing I am for the same reason. Sometimes the less patient guys like Sinnigan get frustrated by the pace of a case or lack of confidence in its ultimate result. They feel they're wasting their time or, at least, biding it and look to get out quick with as much as they can grab from a suspect no matter how far down on the food chain he may be. I didn't know how long Sinnigan had stewed on this case before my involvement but imagined it might be to blame for the fact that he clearly didn't see things my way.

Meanwhile, McGuire was nodding, making it pretty clear he thought Sinnigan was an ass clown too. He was a big guy, a real big guy. Randy played college baseball and was actually drafted by the pros, but he was playing on the same field as me now and I could tell he got it. A workhorse, not a show horse.

"That how you see it, Chief?"

"I'll tell you how I see it. I'm not gonna work with Sinnigan because he's gonna fuck us. He'll target my guy in Cleveland, take him out, and there goes my source to climb the food chain. I don't think he gets how big this case can be."

"Tell you what," McGuire responded. "Why don't I pick you up first thing tomorrow morning and take you on a ride through the reservation, introduce you to what it is we're up against?"

"What about Sinnigan?"

"It's Sunday."

"So?"

"He never works on Sundays."

Just as he said that, the men's room door burst open and in came Sinnigan.

"Hey, how's it going?" he asked, stepping up to his own urinal.

CHAPTER SIXTEEN

Franklin County, New York; November 2008

The next morning, Sunday, McGuire picked up Korinek, Meyers, and me at the nicest hotel in the area, a Super 8. We packed into his Ford F-350 pickup, which had been seized in a previous bust, and headed down Route 37 to the St. Regis Mohawk Reservation, home of the Akwesasne Mohawk tribe.

"We're on the same page when it comes to Sinnigan," he said, the truck's heater firing away.

"You made that clear last night."

"But what I didn't make clear is that we don't need him."

"How's that?"

"There are two different task forces operating here; Sinnigan's in St. Lawrence County and another in Franklin County. Since your guys are ending up in Franklin County at the Frasers', we can grab the case from St. Lawrence and we can run it the way *you* want with no involvement from Sinnigan whatsoever. There's a real aggressive DA up there who's got a brand-new wire room he's just itching to use. He'll see this as a multimillion-dollar case just like we do."

McGuire went on to explain that the district attorney for Franklin County, Derek Champagne, was one of the toughest in the country, something that had earned him the rare distinction of being cross-designated as an assistant US attorney as well as an elected county prosecutor. Champagne had recently raised enough money to build his state-of-the-art wire room in the Franklin County task force headquarters in a location kept secret from everyone, even the families of the agents. From what McGuire was telling me, Champagne had the same motives as me: Get the bad guys. Plain and simple. Then use the forfeiture to build more cases and take down even more bad guys.

"I'll sit down with Champagne," McGuire continued. "Lay it all out for him."

"No," I told him.

"No?"

"I need to be at that table too. I need to sit down and let him know what my expectations are. See if Champagne really is like you and me," I added, throwing McGuire a bone to cushion the blow of usurping his authority.

"Not a problem," he said, and I could tell he meant it.

My kind of guy. Super cops don't take down drug networks that cut across multiple jurisdictions and, in this case, actual borders. Super *teams* do.

"I'll set it up," McGuire continued. "How soon can you guys get back here?"

"I'll tell you once we've seen the reservation."

I t's an amazing place," McGuire explained when we were almost there. "Kind of unprecedented, because the four corners of it touch New York and Vermont to the south, Ontario and Quebec to the north."

"Quebec," I repeated.

"Backyard of the Hells Angels who've turned the reservation's water, ice, and land passages across the Canadian side of the border into their personal smuggling routes."

"With help obviously."

"The Indians welcome the money and the business. The Natives have their own insular world apart from the rest of society and so do the Angels. It's been an unholy alliance for years, decades, but the levels it's reached as of late are unfathomable. You know where all that shit coming into Ohio's originating from? You're about to see."

W e drove up and down the unmanned roads of the Akwesasne reservation in upstate New York, where the deep forest of trees and scattered run-down houses made it impossible to tell which side of the border they were actually on. The only markers were the three-foot cement piers that lay crumbled on the ground, courtesy of being ripped out by the Natives, and an occasional speed-limit sign nobody really followed. Located smack-dab in the middle of the reservation was a six-to-eight-mile stretch of border over which more drugs at that time were transported than over any other stretch that thinly separates the United States from Canada. A truly incredible statistic when you consider that the international boundary, as it's called, is the longest international border in the world—5,525 miles including Alaska, and 4,000 even without it.

I guess I could see what had made McGuire so cautious.

"We try this at night, we might never be seen again," he warned. "That's how dangerous this place can be."

As McGuire drove, he had to be careful not to hit the wandering dogs. They had a roaming-dog problem on the res. And there was barely enough money for traditional law enforcement, let alone an animal-control officer.

McGuire also included in the tour a view of the reservation's mansions, the massive homes that were built primarily, if not exclusively, with the profits gleaned from drug smuggling. The largest belonged to Alan Jacobs himself, a sprawling compound built right on the shores of the St. Lawrence, with pristine views of his private dock and, just around the bend in the river, the area known as the Snye. An altogether different world than the one inhabited by guys like Jacobs and his top lieutenants, including his uncle Noah King, who were running the show and fattening their pockets without a lot of thought given to helping their fellow tribesmen.

Plenty of those fellow tribesmen lived in what was essentially the reservation's ghetto, the Snye. Narrow, rural roads, all of them unpaved, sliced through it, lined by dilapidated shack-like homes layered amid the beauty of the riverfront. Elsewhere the parcels alone would fetch six-figure prices. Here the crumbling cottages were occupied by the roughest and most insular of the Akwesasne, from which Jacobs found some of his most able soldiers but also his least reliable. Fearing nothing and hardly averse to violence, the residents of the Snye were better suited to pursuing their own smaller smuggling ventures, which included anything that could be squeezed into a car or truck.

A number of the cottages had abandoned junked cars in their front yards and a few had been converted into storefronts—bars, mostly, to further feed the alcoholism that was rampant here as well as in most Indian reservations. I didn't know a single cop, federal or state, who'd dare serve a warrant up here without an assault vehicle armed with a fifty-caliber machine gun, and I mean that literally. This was, for all intents and purposes, the Wild West transplanted to the North. No law or police to speak of, and the residents could hop in a car or even on a bicycle and be in Ontario, Quebec, Vermont, or New York within minutes. And once they were back home on the reservation it was like returning to some force field–protected zone outsiders could neither pierce nor even see through. What happened on the res stayed on the res, except for the drugs that were being funneled throughout the country.

Here's another thing about these homes that are little more than poorly maintained shacks: Many of their properties also had beautifully built boat sheds sitting right on the waters of the St. Lawrence worth maybe three or four times as much as the houses themselves. Remember, the river doesn't stay frozen all year and there are winters where it doesn't freeze at all. So, many nights if you stand nearby (as I have done), you can hear the near-constant engine sounds of the Natives' go-fast boats traversing the mile and a half, maybe two-mile stretch between the US side of the river and the Canadian side. You get to know the engine sounds well enough to be able to identify one boat from another, making the trip sometimes two or three times an hour.

The Native runners keep their loads light, twenty pounds or so maybe, to stay comfortably below that four-hundred-pound benchmark that will turn possession into a major crime on the off chance they're pinched. It pays to be careful, which also explains why kingpins like Alan Jacobs are always switching up the load drivers on the res and the Hells Angels do the same with their army of suppliers manning the Canadian shoreline. If you're a kingpin, you don't want your underlings becoming so familiar with their clients or each other that they can turn on you. Jacobs knew that personally, because that's exactly how he got his start as a runner. And the same proclivity is what ultimately cost Danny Simonds his life, as it turned out.

It also explains why I can't tell you exactly which of the Hells

Angels were actually supplying weed and pills to Jacobs: The names kept changing. And beyond that, the whole smuggling process is self-perpetuating, virtually automated. The first shipment is fronted on credit. To receive the next shipment, someone like Jacobs has to make good on the last. So one of those go-fast boats, or even a Jet Ski at times, carries cash north across the river in order to secure the shipment that's coming back south.

"What you're saying is, you know this guy Jacobs is a major drug dealer and ordinarily there's nothing you can do about it?" I said, still trying to square things in my own mind.

"Pretty much, yes," McGuire replied. "The problem up here is so overwhelming it's impossible to deal with. There's literally nothing we can do. We figure that over eighty percent of the Natives smuggle some sort of goods across the border, be it cigarettes, drugs, guns, or people."

"People?" Korinek chirped from the backseat.

"Yep. Mostly illegal aliens. One of the fuckers that flew into the World Trade Center came in through this very border."

"Shit" was all Korinek could say in response.

"These Natives rarely make a mistake and they rarely leave the reservation. All we can do is wait for them to fuck up or piss someone off," McGuire continued. "Danny Simonds was one of their rare fuckups."

"How do you mean?"

"Let me show you."

CHAPTER SEVENTEEN

St. Lawrence County, New York; November 2008

Crime originating, or confined to, Indian reservations is hardly a rare phenomenon. Far from it.

As Erik Eckholm reported in *The New York Times* on December 13, 2009, "The Justice Department distinguishes the home-grown gangs on reservations from the organized drug gangs of urban areas, calling them part of an overall juvenile crime problem in Indian country that is abetted by eroding law enforcement, a paucity of juvenile programs and a suicide rate for Indian youth that is more than three times the national average. If they lack the reach of the larger gangs after which they style themselves, the Indian gangs have emerged as one more destructive force in some of the country's poorest and most neglected places."

Emphasis on "poorest and most neglected." As a result, complex organized crime hierarchies have developed on Indian reservations across the length of the entire border stretching between the United States and Canada. Even the lowest-level runners, the way Akwesasne reservation kingpin Alan Jacobs had begun his career, make decent money, especially when "decent" is measured against abject poverty. Given the insular, closeted nature of this world, estimates of actual income, all of it cash, are virtually impossible to glean. Traditional law enforcement is neither welcomed nor allowed on tribal land, and that same *New York Times* article referenced above speaks to the inability, or unwillingness, of tribal police to do much if anything about drug smuggling.

"As federal grants to Pine Ridge have declined over the last decade," Eckholm wrote of a reservation in South Dakota, "the tribal police force has shrunk by more than half, with only twelve to twenty officers per shift patrolling an area the size of Rhode Island."

The biker wars that raged mostly between 1994 and 2002 in Montreal were waged with good reason, specifically control of a drug trade that had grown increasingly lucrative thanks to partnerships across the United States' northern border with Indian reservations. But the Hells Angels' involvement in the drug trade stretches back considerably before that, on both sides of the United States' northern border.

As far back as 2006, *The New York Times* reported on "a violent but largely overlooked wave of trafficking and crime that has swept through the nation's Indian reservations in recent years, as large-scale criminal organizations have found havens and allies in the wide-open and isolated regions of Indian country." That February 19, 2006, article continues, "In the eyes of law enforcement, reservations have become a critical link in the drug underworld. They have helped traffickers transport high-potency marijuana and Ecstasy from eastern Canada into cities like Buffalo, Boston and New York, and have facilitated the passage of cocaine and methamphetamine from cities in the West and Midwest into rural America."

The problem may have manifested itself full bore in upstate New York, but the Akwesasne reservation was hardly alone. It was instead, as the *Times* reported, part of an escalating trend of circumventing drug-interdiction efforts, the bad guys finding a new way to win the war on drugs. Wisconsin's version of the problem lay on the Lac Courte Orseilles Reservation, which formed an unholy alliance with the Latin Kings gang to move crack cocaine into Milwaukee. Minnesota has the Red Lake Nation, where drug shipments rival those originating on Akwesasne Mohawk land. In Montana, it's the Blackfeet Nation. Wyoming has the Wind River Reservation. Washington State features an unholy alliance between another Blackfeet Reservation and drug gangs under the direction of the Mexican mafia. The list goes on.

And on.

"For traffickers of marijuana, cocaine, methamphetamine, painkillers and people," the 2006 *New York Times* article reports, "reservations offer many advantages. Law enforcement is spotty at best. Tribal sovereignty, varying state laws and inconsistent federal interest in prosecuting drug crimes create jurisdictional confusion and conflict."

Writing in May of 2012 about South Dakota's Pine Ridge reservation, Nicholas Kristof, also in *The New York Times*, described it as "a Connecticut-sized zone of prairie and poverty, where the have-nots are defined less by the money they lack than by suffocating hopelessness." His column calls Pine Ridge "a poster child of American poverty and of the failures of the reservation system for American Indians in the West. The latest Census Bureau data show that Shannon County here had the lowest per capita income in the entire United States in 2010," and says, "Unemployment on Pine Ridge is estimated at around 70 percent." Poverty, the column says, "is often part of a toxic brew of alcohol or drug dependencies, dysfunctional families and educational failures. It self-replicates generation after generation."

The factor Kristof's column leaves out is the tremendous animosity Natives hold toward the rest of us, feeling no obligation to obey laws fashioned by those who have so shunned them and their interests. That animosity coupled with the generally lawless nature of reservations like the Akwesasne is a potent and dangerous combination that leads the Natives to embrace any and all alternatives to better their lives. The extraordinarily high proportion of Native Americans who turn to smuggling don't see it as a crime so much as a necessity.

But nowhere was the problem greater than on the St. Regis Mohawk Reservation, where gated mansions dotted the scenery mere spitting distance from ramshackle trailers and slumlike shanties. And no individual was more able to exploit that than Alan Jacobs, the de facto chief whose stake in the casino combined with ownership of a tobacco factory left much of the six-thousand-strong population beholden to him for their jobs and livelihoods. And yet, according to one of the reservation's tribal police officers, as many as 80 percent of the tribe were involved in some kind of smuggling, whether it be people, cigarettes, or drugs.

"The deep loyalty that exists within tribes, where neighbors are often related, and the intense mistrust of the American justice system make securing witnesses and using undercover informants extremely difficult," the February 16, 2006, *New York Times* article says. "And on some reservations, Indian drug traffickers have close relationships with tribal government or law enforcement officials and enjoy special protection that allows them to operate freely, investigators say."

So long as they had to focus their attention on defending their Montreal turf from the Rock Machine biker gang, the Hells Angels could hardly turn to extending their nefarious ambitions. With the Rock Machine vanquished, though, they were free to grow their business unencumbered by either rival gangs or, pretty much, law enforcement. The insular nature and sovereign borders of the Akwesasne reservation made it an ideal route for expansion, especially since a modest relationship had already been established with powerful locals. Partnering with a longtime ally like Alan Jacobs made perfect sense.

The Hells Angels had been wreaking havoc on Canada since the 1970s, but it was the war with the Rock Machine that knocked Canada to its knees in fear of the biker gangs. It was also one of the things that caused the drug trade to soar; the Hells Angels had to fund their war, which would continue until 2002. Indeed, drug smuggling over the St. Lawrence helped fuel the purchase of the vast arsenal that allowed them to eventually triumph over the Rock Machine.

The death of Daniel Desrochers, in 1995, became a symbol of the mounting gang violence in Quebec that triggered an all-out response by Canadian law enforcement, which had up until that point proceeded in fits and starts. That response got a boost in 1997 from new, RICO-like federal legislation aimed squarely at biker gangs, culminating in something called Operation Springtime 2001, which, according to Paul Cherry's excellent reporting in *The Biker Trials: Bringing Down the Hells Angels* (ECW Press, 2005, Kindle Edition), "signaled the beginning of the end of what came to be known as the biker gang war. On March 28, 2001, more than 2,000 police officers across Quebec were dispatched to carry out more than 130 arrest warrants and seize gang assets, including 20 buildings, 70 firearms and $8.6 million Canadian and $2.7 million U.S. The massive police roundup was the result of two police investigations, 'Project Rush' and 'Project Ocean.' Project Rush was put together using what was, at that point, recently adopted federal anti-gang legislation. Investigators and prosecutors built a case geared toward charging gang members with the murder of their rivals, even if they had a limited role in the gang's affairs."

But this did little, if anything, to deter the relationship between the Hells Angels and Akwesasne Nation. The geography made the setting perfect to be exploited. The reservation was divided practically down the middle, and in the center lay a border crossing known as the Kaweh-noke Port of Entry. But it wasn't the kind of crossing you might picture leading into Mexico or even Canada since 9/11. Ever since it opened, the Canadian border agents manning the entry had been unarmed and thus pretty much helpless to stop anyone from crossing the border on the rare occasions when they actually spotted somebody.

"It was a challenge patrolling this Native reserve, to say the least," recalls a Canadian law-enforcement official who once worked as a border-patrol agent on the St. Regis. "If we entered the reserve at night in our marked vehicles, warning gunshots would fly over our heads. We had no choice but to seek permission from the tribal police if we wanted to come in, and we could only travel in unmarked vehicles. But by the time we got the permission we needed, whoever we were after was always gone."

The same official cites rampant corruption on the reserves to explain the insulation of criminals and smugglers that he estimates make up fifty percent of the population. But he goes on to echo what my own research and other media reports pretty much confirmed: that the lives of those living on the res were steeped in poverty and the sole source of income for many was whatever they could scrounge together doing runs for those residing higher up the food chain. The official went on to explain how the liberal nature of "Home Free" Canada makes it very difficult to secure the kind of wiretaps so crucial in making a drug case. And he recalls pursuing Ski-Doos across the frozen St. Lawrence driven by smugglers running cigarettes to the Quebec side of the border and bring-ing back drugs in their place.

"They'd come in convoys of about a dozen, but not all would be carrying contraband, maybe half, and as soon as we closed in on them they'd scatter in a dozen different directions. They'd ride at night with-out lights, almost impossible to catch with a front Ski-Doo leading the way, watching for any sign of us. Most of these mules don't get much of a cut at all, maybe two hundred dollars per run. But for them that's a lot of money."

When Canadian prime minister Stephen Harper announced a change in the policy of arming border-patrol agents, tribes on both sides re-volted. As reported by *Briarpatch* magazine on July 1, 2010, the Akwe-sasne chief called the border agents "a foreign oppressive force who occupies our sovereign community and territory. [They are] unwelcome, uninvited and now carrying firearms. For lack of a different description, that is considered by some an act of war."

Actually, those Canadian border agents never really did carry firearms. Because just as my investigation was hitting high gear, the same *Briarpatch* article reported that the guards who manned the Canada Border Services Agency station near Cornwall, Ontario, had abandoned their post and gone home to avoid an inevitable confrontation. In doing that they'd essentially given up, thrown in the towel. The unholy alliance of Hells Angels to the north and criminal elements of the Akwesasne reservation to the south could now move their product even more unencumbered.

That ice bridge across the frozen St. Lawrence might have been paved with snow but it was made of money, hundreds of millions of dollars of it there for the taking. But the network that would grow into a multibillion-dollar enterprise by the time I got involved offered something else in stark contrast to the part of the drug war being fought on our southern border. As the saying goes, these weren't your father's Hells Angels; the low-level drug dealers selling drugs out of their backpacks and cooking crystal meth in cheap trailers. Not anymore. Instead, on both sides of the border they'd taken their criminal enterprises to the next level by cloaking them in legitimate businesses, headquartered in Montreal in Canada and in Chicago down in the United States, where they actually owned an entire office building. While the country's attention remained riveted on a border with Mexico riddled by drug cartels for which beheadings were business as usual, the war on drugs was truly being lost under just about everyone's radar.

For blame, historically look no further than efforts championed by the United States government dating back to 1830. That's when the Indian Removal Act was passed during the presidency of Andrew Jackson, essentially making lawful the country's efforts to move tribes off their well situated, and thus valuable, ancestral land to replacement territories often far removed from civilization. Not only were members of these Indian tribes unable to reap the benefits of westward expansion then, the problem persists to this day with the land on which they were resettled remaining too distant from reasonable pockets of civilization to take advantage of new economic opportunities as they arise. Quite the opposite, in fact, especially with the move to a more technologically-centered business environment that has left them, literally, in the dust. You want to know why so many Natives resort to crimes like smuggling? Because they don't see another choice, in large part because they don't have one. This lack of opportunity is systemic in nature and has become generational in terms of drug use, alcoholism and substandard education. Where's the motivation to prepare for a future that's impossible to envision?

"It's disheartening," Jeff Faque, undersheriff for Glacier County, Montana, told *The New York Times* about his running battle with the Blackfeet Nation. "I don't think I'll ever see it solved in my lifetime."

Faque's not me. Faque and others like him didn't have twenty years of undercover drug work behind them. And I intended to see the problem that was feeding a steady supply of drugs into my backyard solved.

CHAPTER EIGHTEEN

Franklin County, New York; November 2008

Back on the Akwesasne reservation, McGuire's truck emerged from a densely wooded area and Alan Jacobs's sprawling lakeside home stood directly before us. It was as pristine and lavish as any I'd ever seen up close, including the biggest suburban homes my part of Ohio had to offer. I compared it, in size anyway, to my horse farm. Judging by the layout, the acreage Jacobs maintained on the lakefront equaled mine, and that was saying something given the surroundings.

"Anybody home?" I asked McGuire.

"Alan, for now."

"For now?"

"Jacobs is out on bond. He'd already pled guilty to a marijuana-smuggling beef and was awaiting formal sentencing when the Danny Simonds shit hit the fan."

Jacobs, I'd later learn, had been arrested in 2006 and charged with conspiracy to distribute and possession with the intent to distribute more than a thousand kilograms of marijuana. The *Watertown Daily Times* reported he was "charged in a sealed indictment returned by federal grand jury with conspiring with others who have not yet been arrested to distribute the marijuana, primarily in Albany, Schenectady and Montgomery counties, according to Terrence M. Kelly, assistant US attorney in Albany. The alleged conspiracy took place between September 2002 and the present, according to the indictment."

How does a guy like Alan Jacobs, someone as powerful, untouchable, and insulated from prosecution as a tribal chieftain, get jammed up? The same way every powerful crime boss does: Somebody talks. I was just reading between the lines here, but it seemed pretty obvious that somebody very close to Alan, but lower on the food chain, had been nabbed on a lesser charge and gave the boss up to avoid time himself. I say that with a degree of certainty based on my own experience when it comes to the immense probable cause needed to obtain the kind of federal arrest warrants required for wiretaps and to arrest Jacobs on tribal land.

"You can anticipate that there are people in the indictment whose names have not been unsealed at this time," Assistant US Attorney Terrence M. Kelly said in the same article.

I'd never worked with Kelly, but I'd worked with enough AUSAs to know how they think and react. He had someone on the inside, and I couldn't help but wonder if Danny making the kind of move on Alan Jacobs that ultimately got him killed was somehow related to Jacobs's perceived weakness and vulnerability.

I'd later learn that it was a law-enforcement officer who gave him up. The guy was one of several Jacobs paid off to look the other way and keep him apprised of patrol schedules and routes. But Jacobs must've done something to piss this guy off and ended up getting betrayed when the agent waited until he knew Jacobs had a trunk full of pot before grabbing him and calling in the bust. Could be the guy wanted more money for his efforts and Jacobs wasn't budging on the fee to make him look the other way. To kingpins, that's part of the price of doing business. But there's a limit to the cost they're willing to bear, and guys like Jacobs eventually feel they're too powerful to ever get jammed up themselves. That's normally when they get caught. When they think they're above it all, where nobody can touch them. They've exerted unchecked power for so long that they can't even envision anybody daring to challenge it. All the more reason for Jacobs to take a stand against Danny's betrayal: to make sure his power wasn't further diminished and he wasn't perceived to be vulnerable.

Even though he already knew he was going away on the drug case.

Even though Danny couldn't even put a dent in an overall operation Jacobs figured he could still run from the inside. He was only thirty and was probably looking at five to ten years on the drug charge, meaning he'd still be a young man when he came out, ready to reclaim his throne from the underlings who served in his stead.

Yup, it all came down to power.

"We've got him nailed six ways to Sunday for Simonds's murder. He's going away, the only question being whether or not he pleads." McGuire slowed his truck and looked over at me in the passenger seat. "Look, Chief, don't let that fool you," he continued, about to tell me something I already knew. "Jacobs going away doesn't change a fucking thing. The network he's built won't miss a beat with him gone. They'll move at least as much product supplied by the Hells Angels across the res as before, maybe even more."

"Because with the head guy, the top of the food chain, out of the way, others will feel empowered to branch off on their own."

McGuire nodded. "Exactly, Chief. The guy we're looking at right now to fill Alan Jacobs's shoes was on top before Alan knocked him down. Guy by the name of Noah King."

"Interesting," I said, making a mental note. "One other thing."

"Sure, Chief."

My eyes fell again on Alan Jacobs's mansion, which looked as if it had been lifted straight out of *Architectural Digest*. "Tell me more about Danny Simonds's murder."

CHAPTER NINETEEN

It had been six weeks since Danny Simonds had finally decided to claw his way up the food chain, and it was just three before his murder. Six weeks equated to three runs, three nerve-racking runs undertaken behind Alan's back, Danny having begun to buy from Noah King instead, a contact arranged by his fiancée, Kim. The anxiety ran as thick as molten lava through Danny's veins. He made each eight-and-a-half-hour drive from St. Lawrence to Beachwood with his heart pounding and his breaths growing short and rapid. The possibility of capture, of arrest, had always been there before. But then someone always had his back; at least, that's what Danny was told. His anxiety had little to do with the lack of a chase car and everything to do with betraying a man who, on the res anyway, was someone to be truly feared. No one crossed Alan, no one.

Relax, Danny told himself over and over again, *it isn't like Alan's going to find out.*

There was no way he could. Alan and Kevin didn't routinely call each other. Both of them abided by one of the most cautionary rules in drug dealing: Always use a throwaway phone. (Kevin went through TracPhones on a weekly basis.) They both changed their numbers so frequently that deliveries and current phone numbers were exchanged at the drop-offs, and those numbers would be used only in the direst of circumstances or to cancel an upcoming load. Plus, it wasn't like Alan was going to question what had become of Kevin. Things happened with dealers; sometimes they simply switched to other suppliers; CEOs of the drug world didn't exactly have a customer-satisfaction department checking to see why clients had stopped using their services. The luck of drug dealers was also bound to run out, and Kevin had developed a well-earned reputation as a user as well as a pusher; almost everyone in this world will tell you to never trust a user. Either way, Alan would just let it go. At least, that's what Danny hoped.

Alan had come back from a legitimate business trip to advance the interests of his cigarette factory a few days after Danny took his first trip as a dealer. Alan still hadn't contacted Danny, and Danny knew that he couldn't call Alan with a made-up story of what happened to Kevin. That would look suspicious. Danny would simply have to wait for Alan to say something to him. He didn't know if this was a good thing or a bad thing. But he knew he had to continue to play it cool.

It was the last Friday of April when Danny finally ran into Alan, at Wolf Clan Restaurant. Danny was having lunch with the kids and Kim, who by the hamburger, pizza, and fries she gobbled up was obviously eating for two. The welcome bell on the restaurant's door chimed and Danny felt a shiver run up his spine. He didn't know if it was from the cool April air or his marine instincts trained to sense incoming danger. He glanced toward the door, keeping his head low to avoid eye contact, to find Alan and his mother, Rosalie, entering. The mere sight of Alan forced his heart to skip a beat, but he managed to quickly recover his bearings.

Be cool. He doesn't know anything.

Danny clung to the hope that Alan wouldn't notice him and approach his table. The last thing Danny wanted was to make Kim nervous. He had to convince her every night before bed that they would be safe, but he'd already broken his promise that this was going to be a one-time and one-time-only thing. Fortunately, Alan and Rosalie sat down in a booth on the other side of the restaurant, and Danny breathed a sigh of relief over the fact that Alan hadn't even seemed to notice him.

Alan's mother was forty-five years old, and, in contrast to many of the Natives, she was aging well. She had Alan when she was only fifteen, a common occurrence on the res. She, like most girls impregnated at a young age, never had the opportunity to make much of herself, and she struggled to raise Alan for much of both their lives. Rosalie was now clearly reveling in the nouveau riche lifestyle her son provided for her. And, like her son, she was a shrewd businessperson, especially in how she supervised the day-to-day business at the cigarette factory, freeing Alan to concentrate on his other pursuits.

Danny watched as Alan and his mother ordered food. Hopefully, lunch would prove a big enough distraction for Alan to continue not to notice him. But then Alan stood up, and Danny realized that the food hadn't been a sufficient distraction at all. As Alan approached, Danny felt every part of him seize up. For a moment, his breath bottlenecked in his throat. Then the clog loosened and Danny gulped it down, his heart hammering anew.

"Hey, Alan." His mouth felt as if it were filled with sludge. "It's been a while. How was your trip?"

"It was good," Alan replied, turning to Kim. "How are you, Kim? Getting big I see."

Danny felt an urge to run his fist through Alan's face for that, but knew better.

"Nice, Alan," Kim replied, clearly annoyed. She looked down at her belly. She was getting big for early in her second trimester, but she didn't need Alan pointing it out.

"Have you heard from the Beachwood guy?" Danny asked him. "I could use the money if you got a run for me." He could only hope that he sounded convincing.

"Nah, dude must have gotten popped or something."

"Aw, too bad," Danny said, going along.

"A lot of kids waiting to play in this sandbox, my friend," Alan smirked, confident as ever. "I'm not worried. I'll let ya know when something new comes along."

"Thanks, man. I really appreciate it."

Alan walked back to his mother none the wiser, but the rumblings in Danny's stomach still wouldn't stop.

"Don't worry, baby. He has no idea," Kim consoled Danny.

"I'm just not feeling well," Danny assured Kim.

"Is it because of Alan?" Kim whispered.

"Nah. Maybe something I ate."

They finished their meal and left, but Danny barely made it out to the car before he vomited his lunch in the parking lot. He didn't know which was worse: the pain in his stomach, the embarrassment, or that he'd just scared the daylights out of his poor kids.

Kim rubbed his back as he again spewed up bits of hamburger onto the asphalt. "Let's get you home and into bed," she soothed.

Then she helped Danny into the car and drove home, with Danny dangling his head out the window to keep himself from puking on the upholstery, the cool wind whipping against his face. Twenty-four hours passed and Danny still wasn't feeling any better. He was really sick. Too sick to drive down to Beachwood, for sure, which made this one of those truly dire situations necessitating a phone call to Kevin.

Danny dug through the top drawer of his nightstand, searching for the cocktail napkin where Kevin had jotted down his latest phone number. Once Danny found the number he reached for his own throwaway TracPhone and dialed. The phone rang several times, going unanswered.

Shit, he's not going to pick up!

After eight long rings, someone finally picked up, but all Danny could hear was breathing.

"K?"

No response.

"K?"

Still no response.

"K, it's D."

"What's up, dude?" Kevin asked politely.

Danny wasn't used to setting up deals, especially over the phone. He knew he needed to be cautious. Use the terminology, don't say any names or locations.

"I was wondering if you could come fishing at my house tomorrow. There's no way I can make it there, but I got the fish all ready," Danny said, speaking in code of the duffel bags full of weed he'd be picking up from Noah King instead of Alan.

Noah might've been his nephew Alan's right-hand man, but he was also Kim's uncle and knew Alan was likely going away on the marijuana bust anyway. He saw no harm in cutting Kim's fiancé a better deal to help her out too.

"Hold on."

Kevin pulled the phone away from his mouth to holler for Ashley. "Ash. Ash!" She didn't respond. "Ash, are you fucking deaf?"

"What?" Ashley called back from the other room.

"You want to go fishing at D's tomorrow?"

"Like a road trip?"

"If that's what you want to call it."

"Hell yeah, I do!"

Kevin pulled the phone back to his mouth. "Fishing at your place tomorrow works for us. What time should we be there?"

Danny was relieved that he wasn't going to have to make the eight-hour drive with his stomach in knots. "Why don't we say two P.M. at my pond? That way you can be back home before midnight."

"See ya then," Kevin said, ready to hang up.

"Wait, one more thing. If you want to play it safe, you may want to consider renting a car in Syracuse. Police are pretty easy around here, but the only time they seem to get suspicious is with out-of-state plates."

"Will do, thanks for the heads-up."

The next morning Danny slept in while Kim got Danny Jr. up and cooked breakfast. Danny woke to the smell of eggs, bacon, and fresh-brewed coffee. Standing in the doorway of the kitchen, he watched Kim sip her coffee and cut up Danny's food and pictured her doing the very same thing in a real kitchen in a real house.

"Feeling better?" she asked.

"A little."

"Try to eat something. You look like you've lost five pounds from that flu."

Even though Danny couldn't eat much, he still enjoyed his Sunday breakfast with Kim and the kids. He spent the morning hanging out in his pajamas, just like Kevin and Alan Jacobs himself. A real drug dealer. It was nice not to be up at the crack of dawn to begin his run.

It wasn't until noon that Danny made his way to Noah's house to pick up the drugs. It was a dreary, drizzly day, typical of spring in St. Lawrence. A wet haze coated the air, so thick that Danny couldn't see past the end of his truck. What a great day *not* to be driving to Beachwood! The weather was Kevin's problem today. Danny greeted Noah on his front porch and the two men conducted their now normal exchange of cash for drugs. Danny really liked working with Noah, since Noah treated him with respect like a friend instead of making it abundantly clear he was merely a peon and a replaceable one at that. He knew that it might have had something to do with Kim in the beginning, but now it was about appreciating the volume Danny was moving for him.

Noah King knew their business together was helping to cement his place as Alan's successor at the top of the food chain at the same time it fueled Danny's rise.

"I ran into Alan the other day," Danny said, almost confessing the truth of his anxiety to Noah, something he hadn't even shared with Kim.

"Yeah?" But Noah's tilted head and cocked eyebrows actually said, *Why the hell are you telling me this?* It wasn't that Noah didn't know Danny had lied to him about not stealing Alan's client; he just didn't know why Danny would want to talk about it with anyone at this point.

"He didn't seem to know anything."

"Sure. Alan would never think you'd double-cross him," Noah said, his eyes boring into Danny's. "He doesn't think you're that big of a dumb-ass."

On that note, Danny grabbed the duffel bags off the porch and carried them to his truck.

"You take care of Kim and those kids, you hear me?" Noah yelled as Danny got into his truck, and Danny waved in acknowledgment, trying to smile reassuringly but failing.

As Danny drove back to his home he made a decision: This was going to be his final run. He was done, spent. He'd made more money than he would've ever seen in his lifetime otherwise. Quit now and he could start a better life for his family. Get out clean before his luck ran out. He had gotten greedy and took comfort only in the fact that he was getting out in time to make the fresh start he so desperately craved. He just needed a little more luck, just a little more.

As he made his way home through the cotton-thick fog, Danny found himself feeling free and satisfied for the first time since embarking down this potentially treacherous road. One last deal and he was done. And he wasn't even running to Beachwood. What could go wrong?

CHAPTER TWENTY

Franklin County, New York; April 2008

Kevin and Ashley's rental car kicked up the gravel in Danny's driveway at twenty minutes past two. The older kids had made it to friends' houses, but Danny Jr. was still at the house. Danny wasn't fond of the idea of having him there while he "worked," but there wasn't much of a choice.

"Could you please take Danny Jr. somewhere to play?" Danny asked Kim.

"Of course. Come on, buddy, let's go watch Elmo in Mommy and Daddy's room."

Kim swooped Danny Jr. up in her arms and carried him off.

Ashley and Kevin looked like a real-life Bonnie and Clyde as they approached his tiny house. Danny could see the two bickering out on his front lawn.

"I don't see why we can't stay and make it like a vacation!" Ashley yelled at Kevin.

"Because it's business, not a vacation. We're in the fucking middle of nowhere!"

"There's gotta be something to do!" she spat back.

Ashley hadn't been many places, so even St. Lawrence in all its drab dullness seemed exciting to her. She'd grown up in a town neighboring Beachwood and had always longed for what those snotty Beachwood girls had. Her father, Richard, had been laid off from his job three years prior to Ashley finding Kevin, and her family's sole income right now came from her mother, Mary Louise, who worked at Walmart. To Ashley this might as well have been New York City with gray air instead of gray buildings.

"What the fuck, Ash? Can we please just go and do what we came here to do, and get the hell out of this shit hole?" Kevin's last comment was made with his eyes drifting toward Danny's house.

"Fine," Ashley muttered, pouting the rest of the way to the front door.

Before Kevin could even knock, Danny swung the door open. "How was the trip?"

"Long. I forgot how fucking long it was."

Ashley shot Kevin a curious look. She didn't know he had been up to St. Lawrence before. Kevin wished he could've taken the line back. He was a lockbox of secrets and even Ashley didn't have the combination, nor did she seem to care. The only person who had any inkling of what truly went on in Kevin's world was his father, his true partner in the business no matter what Ashley thought. His father's language barrier made it easy to keep Ashley out of the loop without her knowing there was any loop at all.

"Your packages are over there," Danny said, pointing to the hockey bags next to his distressed living-room sofa, a stark contrast to the designer brand he'd shared with Kevin along with a beer.

He didn't mean to seem inhospitable but didn't want these two punks sticking around any longer than they absolutely had to. Didn't want criminals in his living room or around his kids, the sense of irony lost on him. Plus, the sooner Kevin got the drugs out of his living room, the sooner this whole mess would be over with once and for all.

"Cool," Kevin said.

Each bag that Kevin carried out of the house felt like a hundred-pound dumbbell being hoisted over his shoulders, a labor with which he seemed distinctly uncomfortable. While Kevin loaded the rented Taurus, Ashley gazed around the small living room. Danny could see the high chair and toys resonating in Ashley's slow-functioning brain.

"You have a kid?"

"I do. Several."

Danny had never shared personal information about himself with Kevin or Ashley, or with anyone for that matter; there was no reason to.

"Awwwwww," Ashley chirped, picking up a picture of Danny Jr. "He's soooo cute! Is he here?" She spun around in a circle like the baby was hiding in plain sight.

"Uh, well . . ." Danny was going to lie but the infectious little giggles of a child emanated throughout the house from upstairs.

"I want to meet him!"

Danny figured it was best to have these guys on his side and what harm would a quick meeting do anyway? "Hey, Kim, could you please bring D.J. down?"

Kim descended the steps, baby boy in her arms. "Hey there. I'm Kim," she said, her hand extended toward Ashley before she reached the floor.

"Ashley. It's nice to meet you. And aren't you the cutest thing?" she said, cooing over D.J. as she released Kim's hand.

While the girls were getting to know each other, Kevin came in to grab the last hockey bag.

"This is my fiancée, Kim, and son D.J.," Danny told Kevin.

"Nice to meet you," Kevin said politely, clearly disinterested.

He heaved the last bag off the carpeting, feeling his back strain. The task wasn't as easy for Kevin as it was for Danny, but Danny had no reason to lend a hand; it wasn't like Kevin offered to help when Danny brought the stuff to him. When the last bag was loaded Kevin came to get Ashley.

"Let's go. I want to get back on the road."

"But I'm having fun! I want to stay!" Ashley protested, back in vacation mode.

Danny felt his breathing tighten anew. They couldn't stay. He wanted them back in Beachwood and out of his life now, immediately.

"Not a good idea. You're best off traveling Sundays," he advised. "The DEA and drug task forces don't work Sundays or holidays, lucky for us them being lazy pricks. Plus, there's not much to do around here."

"We're going to head straight back," Kevin agreed, his comment aimed at Ashley.

"Well, travel safe," Danny told him.

"What about the next load?" Kevin asked, not wanting to leave without making the necessary arrangements.

Danny hoped he would've forgotten. "I'm going to have to call you. Leave your new number."

Kevin wasn't crazy about the idea, but wasn't in a position to argue. Danny grabbed a blue pen from the coffee table and scratched the number Kevin recited on his hand.

"I'll call you."

Ashley and Kevin walked out the door and out of his life. And when it closed behind them, Danny wiped the blue ink off of his hand.

I don't see why we can't go to the casino," Ashley protested. "Come on, it'll be fun!"

"Really?" Kevin snapped back at her. "You don't see why? We have two hundred fucking pounds of weed in the car. That a good enough reason for you?"

"Fuck you! That sign said the casino is on the reservation. It's not like anything will happen."

"I know it's on the res, but no fucking way!"

"Fine. Then see if I give you any ass. You'll beg and plead and I am going to tell you no fucking way!"

Kevin considered this for a moment. The very thought of consummating another deal, two hundred pounds of weed just a few feet away, made him horny and, since he was too paranoid to dare get close to another girl, all he had was Ashley. They were in all this together, and that meant she was the only woman he could possibly trust.

"Okay, fine."

"Yay! Thank you! Thank you!"

Kevin turned the car around and headed back east on 37 to the Akwesasne Mohawk Casino, the only building on the reservation more grand than Alan Jacobs's house. As the green Taurus turned left into the parking lot, Ashley began to chirp and squawk. Kevin couldn't understand what she was saying, but even he found himself excited to be out in public in a place no one would know him.

"We can stay there!" Ashley said, pointing to the only hotel on the casino's grounds.

"We can hang for a while but no fucking way are we staying. Not with all this shit in the car."

"Fine!" she replied, pouting and crossing her arms tightly over her chest, a sign that she was about to give him the silent treatment.

Kevin pulled in to a parking spot, got out, locked the car, and then checked the locks again. The casino before him was new and clean and decorated like one straight off the Vegas Strip, just smaller. Upon entering, he saw loopy flowers were stitched into the black carpeting. There was a sports bar with dozens of televisions and three places to eat. New felted card tables and flashing slot machines looked like something out of a movie to Ashley. Her gaze moved from the flashy lights to the sparkly chandeliers, while Kevin remained unimpressed, starting to wish he'd stuck to the original plan.

"Let's get a drink," Kevin said, and gestured to the sports bar.

Ashley nodded and followed him; she was always up for a drink. The two took a seat at the bar. Kevin ordered a beer and Ashley a vodka and soda. Kevin stared at the television while Ashley talked at him, her words not registering much. He'd become an expert at the "smile and nod." He would let Ashley talk and would smile and nod at the appropriate points, which was good enough for her. Ashley was in the middle of a story about her sister and some drama she'd had at the hair salon when Kevin heard someone yelling his name.

Who could know me here? he thought.

"Kevin. Dude?"

The voice came again. Kevin looked around, distracted by the dinging sounds and moody half-light. Approaching him from across the casino floor was none other than Alan Jacobs, the man himself.

"That you, Kevin?" Alan asked, a handshake's length away.

"Hey, man. How are you?"

"You know someone here?" Ashley asked, confused by the strange turn of events.

"Ashley, this is Alan. This is the main fisherman."

"Not to you anymore, I guess," Alan said, his stare hardening a bit. "Since you stopped buying two months ago."

Alan's mind was racing. Something felt very wrong here, the only conceivable connection being Danny Simonds. But there was no way Danny would fuck him, no fucking way he would be that stupid.

"What are you doing here, Kevin?" he continued.

"Came to pick up a load from Danny. He said he was sick."

"From Danny, huh?" Alan felt his blood pressure rise, his face flush, and his breathing quicken as his face bent into a sneer. *That fucking little punk fucked me over?*

Kevin could see the anger that Alan wasn't bothering to hide, and something that felt like ball bearings rumbled around in his gut. "Dude, I had no clue."

"You sure about that?"

"Yeah, man, I swear! See, it was like this—"

But Alan cut him off. "No worries, man, we're good."

"You—"

"All good, like I said."

He forced a smile Ashley's way as he slid off, cell phone already in hand. Because things weren't all good at all, not even close.

Nobody fucks over Alan Jacobs!

The phone rang, answered by a groggy, drugged-out voice. "Yeah?"

"Hey, Wildcat," Alan said, "I need to see you. We gotta teach somebody a lesson."

CHAPTER TWENTY-ONE

The Beachwood detectives and I headed home after our tour of the reservation, only to return to New York the following week for our meeting with district attorney for Franklin County, Derek Champagne. We met Champagne at the Franklin County task force headquarters to see firsthand this new wire room. The Franklin County drug task force, like most task forces, was composed of ATF, DEA, state troopers, and local police, each of whom brought different experiences and techniques to the table. The only divisions of law enforcement that were unique to this DTF were members drawn from the tribal police up on the Akwesasne Mohawk reservation and the border patrol, a must for this particular part of the country since they're the only LE (law enforcement) who can work that territory. It's too insular, never mind downright dangerous, for any outsider to expect to be able to accomplish much. That's how the principals like Alan Jacobs can start their criminal careers carrying hockey bags full of weed on snowmobiles across frozen rivers and work their way to the top of the food chain.

"Chief Buck, nice to meet you," Derek Champagne greeted me when I entered the Franklin County task force headquarters, a simple office building that looked modular in design. "I've heard great things about your work."

"Likewise," I said, shaking his hand.

Derek Champagne was a stereotypical Irishman with strawberry-blond hair, freckled skin, and the smile of a schoolboy. I could immediately tell he was a good ol' boy who'd grown up in the sticks and somehow developed the schmoozing abilities of a real politician, coupled with the drive and verve of a true crime fighter. In other words, another workhorse. He'd been the district attorney for Franklin County since 2002 and prior to that had done a stint as a United States customs officer, experience I imagined he was putting to good use now. Like me, he didn't crave the limelight or see his antidrug crusade as a stepping stone to advancement or higher political office. As near as I could tell, he just wanted to put bad guys away.

Also like me.

Champagne introduced himself to everyone and took his seat at the head of the conference table to hear what the new arrivals from Ohio had to say. The wire room, what I really wanted to see, was located in the back. This meeting would be all about laying out the ground rules, determining how everything was going to work.

I was glad Champagne had heard of me, or maybe he'd just done his homework, because that meant he knew I had high expectations about what we were getting into. This meeting was all about figuring out if we really knew what the fuck we were doing here, if this was the dead bang case it certainly seemed to me. But it was also multi-jurisdictional, and that can make things very delicate to handle. I was coming into somebody else's territory to talk them into handling the case the way I wanted to handle it. These guys, the workhorses as opposed to the ass clowns and show horses, are power brokers. They don't like someone from another state rolling in to tell them how to do their jobs. Before I could get them to hear me out, they had to see that I knew what the fuck I was doing.

I'd come prepared, armed with paperwork designed to impress; the cliché that you never get a second chance to make a first impression was never more true than in the world of drug investigations. As soon as I got back home after leaving the reservation on Sunday, I'd started the process of creating several files, now housed in large black binders, of all of the information and intelligence we'd gathered on Ashley Schmid, Kevin Sorin, and his father, Boris. I'd spent countless hours writing search warrants for bank accounts, property searches, and phone records. Left no stone unturned, at least the stones I could see at this time. Convincing a department to exhaust such resources on marijuana wasn't always an easy task.

Marijuana is the number one cash crop in the United States and

Canada. But a federal indictment for a pot dealer or distributor required the target to have in excess of four hundred pounds of marijuana in his possession at the time of the seizure to meet the federal thresholds. Short of that, feds don't see pursuing a case as a worthwhile endeavor or investment of their resources. The upshot is that law-enforcement agencies seldom, if ever, have the protocol to put up the money to go after the drug dealers who primarily sell weed. I disagreed with this train of thought and I was willing to put my money where my mouth was when it came to catching dealers.

"In all my years in the prosecutor's office, I have never seen such organization and detail. Most of you guys come in with notes scribbled on napkins," Derek Champagne said with a chuckle.

Paperwork was a huge part of law enforcement and also shunned and disliked by virtually everyone. But my mantra centered around details and organization. I kept all my ducks in a neat row throughout the entirety of every case I took on. It was key to an indictment, to getting the bad guys. There was no reward in catching the bad guy just to watch him go free in court owing to bad paperwork that could sabotage a case right from its inception. Most lawyers hired by drug dealers, regular Rambos in the courtroom, were prepared to seize whatever advantage they could, and I wasn't going to leave them any.

Then, to his credit, Champagne yielded the floor to me. He and everyone else in the room remained silent while I laid out my thoughts, that we were going to go up on a wire with our targets, build the case from the bottom, or middle, up. They'd failed to take down the kingpins like Jacobs and the Hells Angels north of the border because they'd failed to successfully work somebody like Kevin Sorin. That made Beachwood the key to toppling the whole empire, because the closer you got to the source the less chance you had of finding your Leo Fritz, as you recall from the Brancel case. You think the Mafia is bad when it comes to the *omertà* code. Try the res or a biker gang.

"This would be a great opportunity to take my new wire room on a maiden voyage!" Champagne said eagerly, waiting until I'd finished before commenting. More points in his favor.

"That's what I'm talking about. I could set up surveillance in Cleveland and take care of writing the warrants in my jurisdiction, and your agents could use my affidavits as probable cause for our warrants in the Title Three," I said, using the technical name for securing a federal wiretap.

"That's great. Once we're set up, we can take things from there if you'd like."

"I want to be involved through every phase of the case," I told him, leaving no room for negotiation. "I'm willing to commit the funds for the investigation and two guys at all times to work the wire and do all surveillance in Ohio, as well as to and from New York," I added, figuring this would be the absolute best way to keep the daily intel information from the wire fresh and communicated in real time to the surveillance units who were working the Ohio portion of the case. Eliminate the middleman, in other words.

"You're willing to send two guys up from Ohio to work the wire?" Champagne asked me, not used to such an extension of resources. "Are you sure? It's a long haul for you guys and the best accommodations we have to offer is that Super 8 you're at now."

"I'm sure, but under one condition: I don't want this to be just a money grab. I can do that in Ohio. If we come here, I want to get the source of supply. I want the guys at the top. I want to provide you with a case solid enough to take off the big shots on the res and the HAs on the other side of that frozen river."

"Canada's got that working on their own right now. Something called Operation SharQc."

"As in *Jaws*?"

"Spelled with a 'q-c' at the end. It's an acronym for something but I forget what it stands for." Champagne stopped, then started again. "You know how big this is, right?"

"I've got a pretty good idea, yeah."

"When I started, a big case used to be two million dollars' to three million dollars' worth of drugs. The usual now is anywhere from forty million to a hundred and fifty million dollars."

A hundred and fifty million in drugs coming across the border in a single case? Jesus Christ . . .

"One last thing," I said. "We split the forfeitures fifty-fifty after case expenses."

"Sounds fair to me." Champagne pushed his chair back and stood up. "Now, how about we check out that wire room?"

Task force headquarters was a four-story building that looked utterly innocuous from outside. There were a ton of offices along the halls, more than enough for every officer and also support personnel. The wire room was located on the far left of the ground floor, the entrance set off by itself at the end of a corridor and easy to miss if you weren't looking for it.

It was state-of-the-art and then some. And it had to be, because this was where we were going to make our case. I don't mean to make getting to the top of the food chain sound simple, because it's anything but. I started looking around at the high-end electronics and machines placed neatly at high-tech stations and thought of Kevin Sorin. A twenty-two-year-old kid with no job living in a $600,000 house with a quarter million in furnishings. This room was going to help me nab Kevin, and then Kevin was going to take me where I needed to go.

The wire room was probably twenty-five by thirty-five feet, ringed the whole way around by counters. On one side of the room, I counted six stations from which suspects would be monitored and scrutinized. Each station came complete with two computers with accompanying monitors that would home in on the phone numbers of our targets. All audio is recorded automatically and the conversations are transcribed on screen in real time. The endless man-hours you put in are spent listening to every phone call, first to mark it pertinent or nonpertinent. If it's nonpertinent, a personal call, or privileged like a call from a lawyer, you shut the call down right away.

Across the room, on the other side, sat an array of printers, fax machines, and cubicled slots with chairs sitting at the ready for task-force personnel to write out reports that were mostly of a surveillance that would chronicle our targets' movements. Not every member of the task force actually works the wire. In my experience, task forces work best when everyone's on the same page and privy to the same information. Ego has to be left at that door. Successful drug operations are all about sharing.

Derek Champagne caught me staring at a series of big-screen television monitors perched on the short side of the room. You normally needed one to view video-surveillance tapes, but I counted four here, all fresh out of the box.

"I saved the best for last," Champagne told me.

"What's that?"

He led me over toward the televisions, like a kid on Christmas morning. My kind of guy. He was full of energy and impressed me as the kind of guy not scared off by long hours or long odds. Champagne didn't have a first gear; he started in overdrive.

"Since this case deals with border issues, we had to bring in Homeland Security," he told me.

"And that's a good thing?'

"Sure is. Because it gives us access to a surveillance tool most task forces can only dream of: drones."

"You're kidding."

"Not at all. We have the ability to utilize all the assets that come with having Border Patrol on our task force. We can follow targets and they'll never know we're even watching them."

I pictured call monitoring taking place on one side of the room while, in real time, we were following the same target on one of the televisions. We'd be able to hear and see him at the same time.

"We put a green box on the target's car or face," Champagne continued, "and the drone will stick with him until told to break off."

"Amazing," I said, not bothering to hide how impressed I was. "What do we have to do to get started?"

"Get you sworn in, Chief."

Champagne made arrangements the following day for the three of us, along with those officers who'd be working the wire, to be cross-designated so we could work in New York, but in the meantime we had to get to know the guys we were going to be working with. And the way narcs bonded was over pool, darts, and alcohol: shots, beer, whiskey—you name it.

That night the three of us from Ohio met Randy McGuire and two other guys from the task force at a hole-in-the-wall bar in Potsdam, a working-class hamlet in St. Lawrence County. I figured the bar was even more run-down than the houses I'd glimpsed in St. Lawrence County and counted maybe fourteen teeth between all the clientele. But the place had a pool table, a dartboard, and plenty of beer and shots. All we needed.

The youngest of the three task force members was Pete Banks, an officer with the St. Regis Mohawk Tribal Police. Banks may have had the least amount of experience on the team, but, thanks to his knowledge of the reservation, he carried as much weight as any of the officers with years of service under their belts. Pete knew the ins and outs of the res, information that would be vital if our plans were to succeed. He could literally drive by every house and tell you who lived there and what type of goods they were smuggling. Pete was a boyhood friend of Alan Jacobs; they had been best friends, to be exact—that is, until junior high, when Alan sold his soul to the Hells Angels.

Matt Flanders was a New York state trooper who'd moved up to Franklin County two years prior. He was a good family man who was forced to deal with a wife extremely unhappy over his lengthy assignment away from home. Now in his late thirties, Flanders had already racked up a lifetime of experience working drug cases in South Florida. I liked him immediately, the two of us sharing the kind of bond only narcs understand.

The six of us talked and swapped stories over Budweisers and shots of Jägermeister, each telling of tales of heroism and defeat.

"This is the greatest business ever," Flanders said, his words muddled together by the booze.

"I'll drink to that," I said, hoisting my glass, which had come out of the wash so dirty that I'd wiped it down with a napkin before filling it from the pitcher of Bud.

"So why'd you get out?" Flanders asked me. "Trade in the Life for a desk?"

"I needed a break."

"Why?" Randy McGuire coaxed.

"What do you mean?"

"Something had to push you out. Come on, Chief, spill," Randy egged me on, the alcohol clouding his eyes.

I told him the story about Curtis, my lungs burning after chasing him down, the sense that I'd just gotten too old for what was increasingly a young man's game.

"The jackass falls five stories and keeps running?" Randy McGuire asked once I'd finished my tale, his bellowing laugh filling the bar.

"You bet he did. Very moment I tackled him, I knew I was done chasing drug dealers. I'd had enough hundred-hour weeks away from my family," I said, thinking of my daughter growing into her teens. I wanted to be there for her a lot more than I'd been so far. "I was out." I waited for the table to go silent again before continuing. "But you know what?"

"What?"

I guzzled some beer. "I'm glad to be back."

CHAPTER TWENTY-TWO

And now that I was back, I needed to understand the entire scope of the problem. I knew I had a Russian OC (organized crime) guy, Kevin, in Beachwood who every week was moving a couple of hundred pounds of weed that was coming in from upstate New York. Connecting the organization Alan Jacobs had set up on the reservation wasn't too far of a stretch, but I didn't know for sure where Jacobs was getting all that weed he was putting out in the streets. Who, in other words, were his suppliers at the top of the food chain? Derek Champagne had mentioned the Hells Angels out of Montreal, which made perfect sense. But I needed the whole picture filled in to get an idea of exactly what I was facing.

So after being formally sworn in, I made arrangements to head north over the Canadian border to sit down with an old buddy of mine I call Frenchie, kind of a Canadian Dope Ghost who worked for the Ontario Provincial Police, or OPP. We first met at a local bar in Cornwall, a mom-and-pop joint not too far from the northern side of the Akwesasne reservation, and took a corner table before the place had filled up for Monday's Karaoke Night. Frenchie was younger than me, around thirty, with scruffy hair and beard, all part of a lived-in appearance that made him look like he'd just come from Woodstock. The bar was located in a shopping plaza among a combination of chain stores and local shops, the kind of place where you feel comfortable as soon as you walk in.

To get more comfortable, we ordered drinks and appetizers. If that sounds familiar from past instances I've related already, that's because it is. In the world of law enforcement, particularly the undercover part

of it, there's no better way to break the ice than doing so over drinks
and food. You need to establish a relationship of trust quick, fast, and
in a hurry. No time to waste trying to convince the other guy you're
the bigger dog, because you've both got the same booth. I came accompanied by Beachwood detective John Korinek, and Frenchie brought
a pair of other OPP cops he was working with.

"How'd you know?" Frenchie wondered, once we got down to business.

"How'd I know what?"

"That we're getting ready to take the HAs down. And I mean, *down*.
Operation SharQc."

I told him about Derek Champagne and how I was now working on
my own case on the Akwesasne reservation.

"Then I guess we're partners." He grinned. "Sort of, anyway."

He explained that "SharQc" stood for *Stratégie Hells Angels Région
Québec*. Years before I'd committed myself to taking down the distribution network in St. Lawrence County being operated through the reservation, my counterparts in Canada were in full swing pursuing the
suppliers.

Right from the start, it was clear that Frenchie had aimed his laser-
like focus squarely on the Hells Angels and, like me, wasn't going to
stop until he brought them down. I had worked a case up there with
the OPP back in 1993, so we already knew each other by reputation.
And this meeting took our interagency task force across international
borders, at least in a figurative sense.

Scratching at his beard, Frenchie explained that his team had been
up on the HAs with wires and surveillance for ten months and he had
absolutely no doubt that 100 percent of the weed coming across the
reservation was supplied by them. That was the hardest thing for me to
grasp in all this, the notion that I was dealing with a huge area that
had no boundaries, no borders. The reservation was utterly a world
unto itself. This was a huge operation for my Canadian law-enforcement
brethren, going back two or three years, and it had succeeded in identi-
fying the Montreal HAs as the kingpins behind a smuggling operation
that may have exceeded a billion dollars per year. And they were going
to start making arrests soon.

You see, in Canada, just like in the United States, everybody wears everybody else's dope. Put ten guys together and no matter what part of the food chain they inhabit, each has to carry the full weight. That means a small-time street dealer moving maybe ten pounds a week, even a month, goes away for the same term that the kingpins running a billion-dollar operation do. In other words, I'd be able to provide Frenchie with the evidence that could put his HAs away for life, never mind fifteen to twenty.

It was right about then that the evening's karaoke entertainment started, with a squealing rendition of the Starland Vocal Band's "Afternoon Delight." We had to raise our voices a bit over the music, but I knew from Frenchie's face that I had him, that we were indeed cut from the same cloth. He impressed me as professional all the way, no bullshit and a workhorse for sure as opposed to a show horse. He'd been fighting the same battles I had for not quite as long on different turf. And the other thing that impressed me was he'd done his homework. He knew my history and reputation, knew I was no bullshit too.

"You're a long way from home," he said at one point.

Yup, my kind of guy. Nothing like the show horses out there who lack the ambition to see a case all the way to the top. Uh-uh. Frenchie wouldn't be satisfied unless he took down the whole HA network and seized all the assets that went with it. He was smart enough to realize that the biker wars had spawned any number of undercover officers with that very goal, many of them succeeding on various levels. But no one had ever succeeded on the level Frenchie and the OPP were after this time, and they saw our task force as a means to help them do that.

"Right now, all I've got are the broad strokes," I told him, referring to the network operating south of the border. "Give me a little time and I'll fill in the blanks with surveillance, subpoenas, tax records, and mail covers."

He grinned at that, recognizing the importance of mail covers from his own experience. What we do is write a subpoena ordering the local postmaster to photocopy all the envelopes going to a certain address. Opening those envelopes requires a different subpoena, but all we need to know is what they say on the outside. That will tell me where my targets do their banking, who their investment companies are. And the best time to do a mail cover is July, because that's when all the property-tax bills go out. With those in hand, I'd know what real estate my targets owned. I'm looking at assets and expenditures all the time. And the best mail to actually subpoena full out is, say, an American Express bill. Because that tells me where they fly, what hotels they stay at, what airlines they use, what restaurants they eat at, and what cars they're renting.

That's the thing about a drug investigation. Seventy-five percent of the time I'm doing an undercover, I don't even carry a damn gun. The vast majority of the drug dealers I've arrested and put in prison don't carry guns either. Normally, they're family guys who live in the suburbs down long driveways with Volvos or minivans tucked away in the garage. You don't stay in this business long, on either side of it, if you rely on bullets instead of brains. That's why the Hells Angels out of Quebec went mostly legit.

Operation SharQc, Frenchie explained, wasn't so much indicative of a new initiative as a continuation of an old one. The RCMP and police across Canada, especially Quebec, had been at war with the Hells Angels in particular and biker gangs in general going back decades. The difference now was that they had a huge number of suspects in their sights, seeing this as the opportunity to break the gang's back for good. And that's why Frenchie now figured he needed our task force's help. Past operations, while successful, had pretty much yielded them only underlings and a few token big prizes.

There was so much at stake this time, though—so much money, thanks to the staggering amount of product making its way south through the Akwesasne reservation—that this was a real opportunity for the RCMP to nail the kingpins at the very top of the food chain. Frenchie made that clear to me, along with the fact that any intelligence provided by the task force I'd formed would be ultimately crucial to his team building their case and taking down as many gang leaders as possible.

The most important thing Frenchie could offer me was success. Because that success would help ensure that the distribution network that had been feeding drugs through the reservation for so long would be down for a long time, if not for good. There are several ways to judge the success of a drug investigation, not the least of which is how long it takes to replace the flow out into the streets. When the price soars, making the product less accessible, you know you've made an impact, since higher prices are tied directly to a supply diminished by your efforts. And the thing that made this particular investigation so important south of the border was the expansiveness of its reach.

Ohio was hardly the only place affected by the weed and pills coming over the St. Lawrence River. Danny Simonds had been only one runner, Kevin and Ashley only a single pair of large-scale dealers. The reach of the weed provided by the Hells Angels of Quebec and then funneled through the network erected by Alan Jacobs stretched south and farther west as well, reaching all the way to Florida and California. That's what made the investigation so big in my mind, just like Brancel and Heckman before it. As for Alan Jacobs, I didn't give him much thought at this point. He was yesterday's news, a jammed-up kingpin about to be usurped and replaced by whoever was next in line; Noah King, in this case, who we were targeting.

The key for us was not to move until Frenchie was able to take down his Hells Angels targets in a coordinated strike meant to scoop up the lot of them at once. That's the way it works. A drug investigation is a bottom-up operation through the exhaustive months and often years of accumulating evidence and building a case. But it's a top-down operation when it comes to the final takedown. Otherwise, the higher-ups vanish into the ether when you bust their underlings. The number one thing that came out of my initial meeting with Frenchie, in addition to our agreement to share intelligence, was a more tacit agreement that I wouldn't move on my targets south of the border until he moved on his to the north. A coordinated strike, in other words, as part of Operation SharQc.

Frenchie explained the problems he'd long faced north of the border, which were vast and complicated. The unholy relationship between Indian tribes and the Hells Angels up there had been going on for a long time, perpetuated to some extent by the country's frontier and wilderness aspects; wide swaths of land there were often uncovered by anything other than tribal authority. In his mind that reality, coupled with the tobacco trade that was often the only legitimate industry on reservations, had combined to make Indian tribes ripe for criminal activity and left them vulnerable to relationships with gangs that ran the gamut from the Hells Angels to the Italian mob and even Asian street gangs. Frenchie ran off a litany of busts involving gangsters and illegal tobacco smuggling and sales. He mentioned one recent bust where two dozen Natives were arrested along with a couple of dozen Kahnawake Mohawks for their association with a cigarette and methamphetamine ring around Quebec City. Given the vast size of his country, much of it filled with mere pockets of civilization amid veritable wilderness, I didn't envy Frenchie's plight at all.

The existence of Operation SharQc kept me from needing to work informants and expand my investigation north of the border. A big plus given all the challenges of crossing international borders, not the least of which was language. The Angels and many of those they did business with called French their primary language. While I'm sure many of them spoke English as well, we would still have been required to recruit informants and drug officers not stymied by the language issues. In cases this big, you don't have a lot of choices of who to take on your team, and the language issue would have shrunk the list even further.

Frenchie and I parted company after agreeing to maintain regular contact and also to put liaisons from our respective task forces in touch with each other at the proper times. We shook hands and his grasp was as firm as mine, our stares holding as long as our grips.

"When do you think you'll be ready to move against the HAs?" I asked him.

"I don't know, not yet anyway," Frenchie told me. "But you'll be the first to know."

The whole drive back to Franklin County, something was plaguing me and I couldn't wait to meet up with Randy McGuire in our wire room.

"Hey," I told him, "you never finished the story."

"What story?" he asked me.

"Last week. About how Danny Simonds got himself killed."

CHAPTER TWENTY-THREE

Two weeks had passed since Kevin and Ashley picked up the last load from Danny's house. The time had gone by peacefully, Danny mostly staying at home with his family. He and Kim had found out that the baby inside her growing belly was a girl. Danny had convinced Kim to use the recent profits to fund a move to Syracuse, where he would get an honest job as an electrician.

It was Monday night and for the first time in months everything outside wasn't frozen. The snow had completely melted and tiny buds were forming on the trees. Kim was in the kitchen cleaning up from dinner, while Danny played video games with the kids in the living room. Danny knew that he'd always given everyone the love that they had needed, but now he was finally going to be able to give them the things they wanted as well. This move would get them out of this place that he had been trying to escape his entire life. Kim was hesitant to leave. Like most Natives, she liked the security of being near the reservation and her people and family. It took a lot of convincing on Danny's part to get her to leave this frozen land and this waste of a life. But she knew that the only way that they would have a chance to show their kids a quality life was to escape the ice. So that, along with the fact that his days as a runner were over, left him sleeping considerably easier at night.

Bryan "Wildcat" Herne, Brian LaTulipe, Chad Edwards, Anson Edwards, Kaientanoron "Nolo" Swamp, and Derek Cooke gathered at the mansion on Laughing Road at the behest of Alan Jacobs. These were the six most trusted of Alan's cadre, the few anointed as part of his inner circle. All five men had grown up with him on the res, and they'd followed him diligently and loyally. The kind of mission they'd been summoned for today was rare, since few had ever dared cross Alan before.

"Whatever happens, *do not* kill him," Alan instructed, after laying out his plan. "I don't need that kind of trouble. Just take whatever money you can find. I don't care if you have to tear the house apart in the process but I want no casualties. You guys got that? Am I making myself clear?"

"What about his family?" Brian LaTulipe asked, after they'd all nodded.

"Everyone will be sleeping. Just stay quiet. The wife and kids will stay upstairs."

Brian didn't question how Alan knew what he did, and he would never second-guess him. He seemed to remember that Alan and Kim, Danny Simonds's fiancée, were related somehow or other.

Alan didn't want Danny hurt; he just wanted to teach Danny a lesson, make an example so the world he inhabited would understand that no one fucked with Alan Jacobs. Violence could end up being counterproductive, explaining why most of the men like him, kingpins, avoided casualties at all cost. Violence drew attention, and attention increased the chances of getting caught tenfold. Alan wasn't about to screw up the good thing he had going because a single runner had ripped him off, especially while his lawyers were trying to plea-bargain down his sentence as low as possible on the marijuana beef. Of course, he might yet beat it free and clear, but he was getting himself prepared to do a brief stretch inside. He could do a year, even two or three, holding his breath. Even run his operation from behind bars. Prison wasn't going to stop him and neither was Danny Simonds.

Before the five men climbed into Wildcat's black pickup truck and Nolo's black Yukon, Alan handed Wildcat a .22-caliber pistol.

"I thought you said not to hurt the guy," Wildcat said, the gray metal gun weighing heavy in his hand.

"I did. This is to scare the shit out of him if he gets out of bed, nothing else. You hear me? Just find his stash and bring it back here. You got it?"

Wildcat tucked the gun into the waistband of his Lee jeans. It felt cold against the bare skin of his abdomen, sending a shiver down his spine.

"Yeah, I got it."

"Grab the cash and get back here," were Alan's parting words.

The two black trucks left the king's castle and headed toward Danny's residence off the res.

All of the little ones were asleep. Kim and Danny had just gotten into bed. Danny rubbed his hand across the tight skin of Kim's pregnant belly. He pushed up her nightshirt and began kissing her belly button. He was slowly making his way up her soft skin when he heard the familiar sound of gravel crunching in his driveway, sending goose bumps up his flesh.

Lying beside him, Kim felt a stillness spread over Danny's muscular frame. He slowly rose from the bed and walked toward the window. Kim didn't even have to ask to know something was wrong. Danny peered out the window to find Alan's five men getting out of the two cars.

"Get the kids and hide in our closet!" he ordered, processing the information the way he had in Afghanistan. "Use the phone on our nightstand and call nine-one-one. Whatever happens stay quiet and stay in the closet, you understand?"

Fear had taken her voice and it took all Kim's strength to nod and lead her family from their room into hers. Danny had a keen ear open, listening to make sure his family had made it safely to the closet and timing how many steps the men were from breaking down his door. From the clumsy sounds of their approaching footsteps, he figured he had eight seconds to hide in the front hall closet before they broke the door down. The closet was his best bet to utilize the element of surprise.

Danny tiptoed into position and secured himself among the coats and clutter, squeezed against the door so he could burst out in a single quick motion. He could hear the wood panels of his front door cracking with every kick. It took the men a ridiculous three minutes to break it down. The whole scene would've been humorous if Kim and his kids weren't upstairs in danger. He'd recognized Wildcat through the window but the darkness hid the other intruders' faces, though he could probably guess who they were.

"Just find the fucking money," Wildcat ordered, stomping around the living room and fumbling for a light switch.

Danny stiffened in the closet. There was no fucking way they were taking his money! He had worked too damn hard and risked too damn much for that money. That money represented his way out, the future for his family, and he didn't intend on giving it up. Plus, these assholes had invaded his house, *his* home! He felt something almost inbred kicking in inside him. He felt violated, the rage that set his heart pounding starting to trump whatever fear he'd felt.

Danny listened for a matter of minutes as the motley crew of thugs scoured his home. For a moment he thought they might give up and leave. Then he heard Wildcat's voice again.

"Check the bedrooms."

Instinct took over, a father's protective mentality kicking in. Danny burst out of the closet and, in a single fluid motion, pounced on Brian LaTulipe before he could make it to the second step. His fist slammed into Brian's jaw and he felt something crunch on impact with his knuckles.

Anson came running to Brian's rescue and tried to pull Danny off. But Danny, a trained marine who'd fought and killed for real, whipped around and smashed his elbow dead center on Anson's face. Anson's tooth caught on Danny's long-sleeved shirt, and, as Danny tugged his shirt free, Anson's tooth came with it and blood spewed from his mouth.

Danny saw the remaining three men as nothing more than dark shadows splitting the darkness, coming at him from three different angles. He whirled toward the nearest, Chad, taking him down with a swift kick to the groin and a foot sweep that yanked his legs out from under him. The coffee table broke his fall when his skull hit the wood with enough force to crack it. Before Chad had even hit the floor, Danny spun and launched a boxer's jab toward Nolo, feeling his nose compress, mashed inward against his face under the force of the blow.

"Let's get the fuck out of here!" Brian LaTulipe yelled, stumbling toward the remains of the door they'd kicked their way through.

"Fuck this shit!" Nolo screamed, blood gushing through the fingers that had jerked up to his nose.

All five men fled from the house. Danny should've just left it at that; he'd won, after all, beaten back the assault, defended his family and honor. Five against one. . . . They had fucked with the wrong guy. But he couldn't calm the adrenaline rush still surging through him and ended up chasing the thugs into the night. The tables had turned, the hunters becoming the hunted. At that point Wildcat did the only thing he could think of to protect himself and his crew: He pulled the cold hard pistol Alan had given him from his jeans, hoping the sight of it would stop Danny in his tracks.

"Go back in the fucking house, Danny!" Wildcat roared, holding the gun in his shaking hands.

"Fuck you! No one fucks with my family!"

He wasn't thinking anymore, functioning at a level where he couldn't control the rage that had consumed him. Break down his door? Endanger his wife and child?

Were they fucking kidding?

Danny charged Wildcat, the leader, the one who needed to be put down. Alan had sent his thugs to make an example of Danny, and now Danny was making an example of them instead. Make sure Alan knew never to fuck with him again. Wildcat saw him coming, steam rising off Danny's skin in the cold dark, and did the only thing he could by pulling the .22's trigger. The barrel kicked upward, more kick than he'd expected from a small-caliber weapon.

Realizing he couldn't reach Wildcat before he fired, Danny had swung around at the last instant and the single bullet, as a result, hit him in the ass. The sting of the bullet knocked Danny to the ground. He lay there thrashing about and feeling for the wound, while Alan's five thugs piled into their two trucks and screeched out of the driveway, kicking up gravel in their wake. Danny tried to stand to chase after them, but the wound to his butt had caused his leg to go numb on that side. He watched in agony as the two black trucks tore down the road, took a corner hard, and disappeared. Danny realized sirens were blaring, his brain not processing the sound until then. He managed to sit up on the ground, as an ambulance and two police cars roared into sight.

The sounds of sirens, meanwhile, let Kim know it was safe to come out. She and the kids made their way down the steps. Kim could see that Danny was lying on the front lawn. The kids ran out the shattered front door and to Danny's limp body. This while Kim ran to the floor-board where Danny hid his two duffel bags of pot. She lifted them from their hiding spot and ran outside dragging one of the bags toward the woods as fast as she could. Then she ran back inside and did the same with the other. Danny and his children lay aglow in the spill of the re-volving lights watching as Kim worked frantically.

She was out of breath when she reached Danny.

"Oh, my God," she gasped, when she saw the blood flowing from his left butt cheek. Then, quickly recovering her senses, "You're going to be okay," she soothed. "You're going to be fine."

"I know. It's just my ass," Danny said, and forced a smile so Kim wouldn't be worried. All of the kids were sitting around their father, tears running down their faces.

The two SUVs arrived back at Alan's house at 1:30 A.M. to find Alan waiting up for them. If they were dogs, they'd have had their tails between their legs. Alan could see that the copper-colored skin typical of their Native heritage had gone pale white, like someone had sucked out the pigment. Then Alan saw how beaten and bruised they looked, blood staining faces as well as clothes.

"Where's the money?" he asked, not believing one man could have done this much damage. No way. "Tell me you got the fucking money."

"We had a problem," Wildcat tried to explain.

Alan looked at the men gathered before him, his men, coughing out blood, a tooth missing from one and a torn scalp that had bled down-ward to make another's face look like a Halloween mask.

"What the fuck happened?"

"That fucking asshole is a monster!" Nolo answered.

"You're telling me that prick beat the fuck out of all five of you?"

Ashamed, Wildcat could only nod.

Alan tried to calm himself. "I ask again. Did you get the money?"

"No."

"What the fuck? Are you fucking kidding me?"

Incensed, Alan took a step toward Wildcat, still not believing things could have gone this bad. Then they got worse yet.

"Er, I accidentally shot him," Wildcat said.

"You *what*? How do you accidently shoot somebody? He better not fucking die! *Fuck!*"

"No, I shot him in the ass. But what if he talks?"

Alan looked at the brute, his chief enforcer reduced to a quivering mass of molten flesh swimming in his oversized clothes. Standing there still breathing hard like he was going to have a heart attack. Alan could've called the Hells Angels in on this, but didn't because he wanted to avoid exactly what had happened. Oh man . . .

"He won't talk," Alan said, his mind working again, trying to convince himself that this whole thing might yet work in his favor. "If it's just his ass, he'll have learned his lesson for sure." Then he lost it anew. "*Fuck!* Why the fuck did you have to shoot him?"

CHAPTER TWENTY-FOUR

Franklin County, New York; May 2008

The Tri-Town Volunteer Rescue Squad arrived on the scene of Danny's house in the village of Stockholm and got Danny situated in the van. "He's lost a lot of blood. We've stitched him up but we're best off flying him to Vermont," the EMT told Kim.

"Whatever it takes," Kim told him. She gave Danny a passionate kiss on the mouth. "If you think that bullet hurts, wait until you get home," she said, sounding more loving than ominous.

Danny shrugged. "I love you, babe."

"Love you, too."

Since Franklin County had far from adequate health care, all gunshot wounds and any major injuries were transported to the closest hospital with a properly staffed trauma center. Danny was life-flighted to Fletcher Allen Health Care in Burlington, Vermont. He arrived at three A.M. Tuesday morning. The Tri-Town EMTs had alerted doctors there that Danny had been stabilized and sutured after suffering a gunshot wound, so he was simply admitted but not actually examined beyond a cursory check of the dressing. The rest, it was thought, could wait for morning, when the center would be fully staffed, just a few hours from then.

Danny lay in the hospital bed, feeling weaker and weaker. He figured it must have been from the exhaustion and stress. Battle fatigue, he remembered somebody calling it in Afghanistan. Leave the needle in the red too long and the batteries end up drained.

Just before dawn Danny slipped off to sleep thinking of his family and his future. He felt strangely content, almost blissful.

A nurse rushed into his room just before seven o'clock after the life monitor he was hooked up to began to squeal at her station. She found him unresponsive and not breathing. The nurse immediately signaled a Code Blue, but it was too late; Danny had bled out from the gunshot wound to his buttocks and could not be revived. The small-caliber bullet had nicked an artery, but no one had done the kind of testing that would've revealed that to be the case. He was pronounced dead at 7:10 A.M.

The police found the money that Alan Jacobs's thugs had failed to find beneath the Stockholm home's floorboards, the money that Danny had earned running drugs. The money he'd risked his life for to do better for himself and his family in his climb up the food chain. A sobbing Kim watched the cops pack it into cardboard boxes and haul it away.

Kevin Sorin and Ashley Schmid got the news in Beachwood three days later. Out of respect, they made the trip up to St. Lawrence County to attend Danny's funeral.

Half of St. Lawrence County showed up to pay their respects to the fallen marine and local hero. He had served his country and had been a role model for most of his life. The locals didn't begrudge the actions that had ultimately led to his death, because they knew the way things were here, knew good options were few and far between. Kim sat in the front row, little Danny Jr. on her lap, her baby belly a sight that added to the dreary day's sadness even as it made Danny's plight all the more tragic.

Kevin and Ashley waited to go through the receiving line. Passing along their condolences to Danny's immediate family, none besides Kim having any notion of who they were. Kevin was hoping to move through the line quickly and head home. It was Ashley who'd wanted to come, not him.

He had leaned into Kim for a quick, perfunctory hug when she whispered in his ear, "Don't leave yet. I need to speak with you."

Her words took him by surprise, but he would wait and hear what she had to say. When the dozens of mourners finished paying their respects and the crowd began to dwindle, Kim approached Ashley and Kevin.

"Are you guys still interested in fish?" she asked awkwardly.

The product of another bust packed into evidence bags.

Gazing across the St. Lawrence River from the Akwesasne reservation to Canada across a plowed ice bridge.

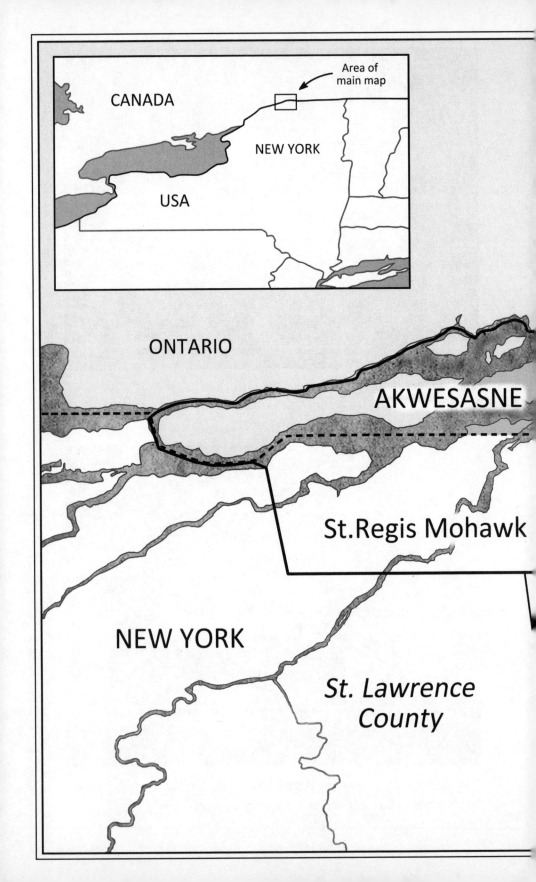

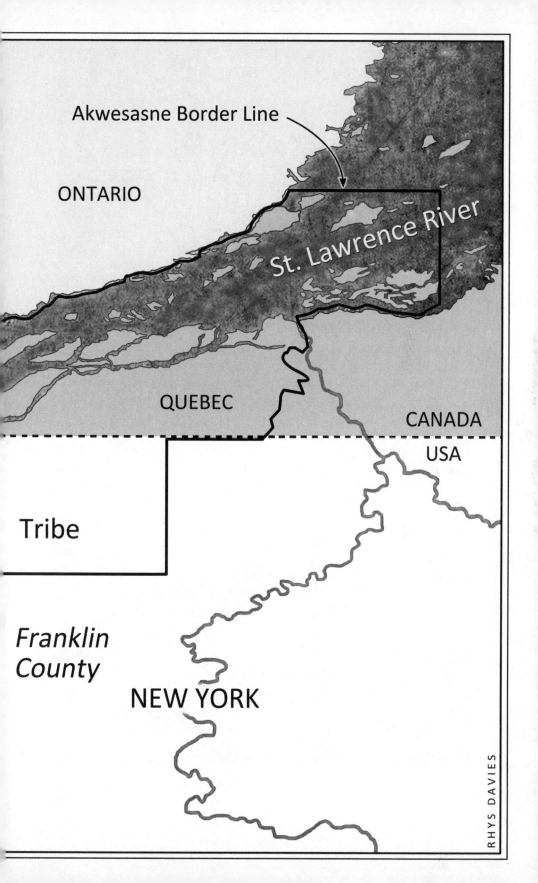

A sign greeting visitors to the St. Regis Mohawk Reservation.

The sprawling mansion belonging to drug kingpin Alan Jacobs on the reservation.

The Franklin County wire room where the drug task force was headquartered.

More product from other drug busts by Jeff Buck packed into evidence bags.

The sole marker for hundreds of yards denoting the US-Canada border, illustrating how porous that border is.

YES "TERRORISTS" COME THRU AKWESASNE
THEY ARE N.Y.S. P BORDER PARTROL
A.T.F. F.B.I. I.R.S. ECT. ECT.!!!
...THE PEOPLE

A welcoming sign that encapsulates how the Akwesasne people feel about non-Natives and how outsiders are greeted on the reservation.

Jeff Buck pictured in his undercover guise of the "Dope Ghost" on a Harley with his daughter.

A colonial home that now serves as headquarters for the Reminderville, Ohio, police station where Jeff Buck still serves as chief of police.

"Is the world still rotating?" Kevin responded. "Of course we are."

"I have a load that you can take with you today," Kim said. "I then have someone I can hook you up with for future runs. Come with me."

The police had seized all of the money that Danny had earned, leaving Kim on her own with absolutely nothing to feed her baby and growing children. So when she heard that Kevin and Ashley were coming to the funeral, she figured she would unload the hockey bags that she managed to hide before the cops came after Danny was shot. She had also called Noah King, both her uncle and Alan's as well as Alan's de facto replacement at the top of the food chain, to have him set her up as the dealer for Kevin. During the course of our case, I heard rumblings from some on both sides of the law that Kim had actually set Danny up. While I've never seen any firm proof of that, any evidence at all really, it's a kind of betrayal common in the drug world. It's quite possible that Kim tired of Danny's promises to provide a better life for her and their kids and decided to cut her losses by selling him out to Alan Jacobs, intending to go into business for herself. As it turned out, she was probably none too pleased by Danny's plans to move the family to Syracuse and go "legit," especially after she'd set him up with Noah.

Viewing her simple home on Porter Lynch Road in contrast to the mansions on the res where she was born made that seem a possibility at the very least. When you've worked drug investigations as long as I have, nothing surprises you about the potential targets you're pursuing. Not all in that world start out that way, but that's how they all seem to end up, as if the whole nature of the business encourages it. The line spoken by Eve Arden's character in the 1945 film *Mildred Pierce*—"Personally, Veda's convinced me that alligators have the right idea; they eat their young"—has never seemed more applicable than in the drug world.

Either way, Noah King felt horrible for Kim's situation, but there was no way he was going to allow his niece to get involved in this mess, not after everything that just happened. However, he knew he had to do something, unable to escape the guilt over being a party to Danny's death. So he decided a fair compromise would be to use a middleman and give Kim a referral fee, so to speak.

"Kevin, this is my uncle Noah," Kim said, introducing Kevin to Noah.

Noah felt no need for formalities. He felt uncomfortable enough as it was, doing a deal like this at a funeral. Noah had liked Danny. Something about the whole situation was rubbing him the wrong way. Even the way Kim was reacting—it just didn't seem right to Noah. He was going to get right to the point and get the dirty work done.

"There's a white couple that live just south of St. Lawrence, in Franklin County," Noah told Kevin on Kim's behalf. "They can supply you with whatever you need. It's the same fish that Danny was getting you at the end, coming in from over the border."

"Cool. Thanks."

"The thing is you're going to have to pick it up from them. They don't deliver."

"Hey, no problem," Kevin said appreciatively, none the wiser.

"Their names are Harold and Sabrina Fraser." Noah reached into his pocket for his cell phone. "Let me give you their number. . . ."

3
THE KINGPINS

What are kings, when regiment is gone,
But perfect shadows in a sunshine day?

—Christopher Marlowe, *Edward the Second*

CHAPTER TWENTY-FIVE

MILDRED: What are you rebelling against?
JOHNNY: Whaddaya got?

—*The Wild One* (1953)

California and Montreal; 1948–1990

Although some of the Hells Angels' history remains a disputed mystery to this day, the gang's origins appear to date back to 1948 in Fontana, California. Formed from the remnants of another gang, called the Pissed-Off Bastards, they took their name from a fighter squadron known for its daring exploits in World War I as well as the just-concluded World War II. It was a group of veterans from that war, coming home displaced and disenfranchised, who found the action and freedom they craved by joining biker gangs. Motorcycles were cheap and the open road beckoned, the route these men returning home chose to ride into their futures.

It wasn't until nine years later, though, in 1957, that Ralph "Sonny" Barger founded the gang's Oakland chapter and set the gang on the road to infamy that persists to this day. Violence became their calling card, defining the colors they wore and the reputation they built for retribution, revenge, and all-out domination of any scene or road they inhabited. The first turning point was their disruption of the annual American Motorcycle Association race in California in 1957, followed in 1963 by their violent takeover of the town of Porterville that many say was the basis of the classic Marlon Brando film *The Wild One*.

But the biggest turning point came when three hundred Angels roared into the coastal town of Monterey in late summer of 1965. It was there, after a wild weekend of partying and violence, that four Angels were arrested on rape charges. The gang couldn't afford lawyers to defend them, so they took to selling speed to raise the money they needed. The case never went to trial; the bikers arrested weren't even charged. But they'd finally landed on law enforcement's radar, including that of California's attorney general, Thomas C. Lynch.

Meanwhile, drug dealing was so easy, and so lucrative, that the Angels just kept doing it. These outlaw bikers—who somehow saw themselves as latter-day incarnations of Western frontier heroes in the tradition of Billy the Kid and Jesse James, riding choppers instead of horses, now complete with the overwhelmed sheriff in Thomas Lynch—had found the ideal way to finance the sustenance of their life-styles. They went from being a loose amalgamation of disparate groups to a highly organized, centralized gang that began to spread from coast to coast. They looked at the road and embraced a twisted romantic notion of the new America, carving out their own version of the American dream.

"When you're asked to stay out of a bar you don't just punch the owner," Hunter S. Thompson observed in his seminal *Hells Angels: A Strange and Terrible Saga* (Ballantine Books, 1966), "you come back with your army and tear the place down, destroy the whole edifice and everything it stands for. No compromise. If a man gets wise, mash his face. If a woman snubs you, rape her. This is the thinking, if not the reality, behind the whole Hell's Angels act."

Until then, the Angels had stuck to their roots in California. But their growing popularity among a disaffected, rebel element of the postwar generation, together with Barger's vision for expansion, spurred them to grow to ninety-two chapters in twenty-seven states. Barger foresaw a modern-day outlaw gang that would trade the badlands of the Old West for the fledgling interstate highway system, allowing members to move unencumbered and undeterred through the nation.

"When we award charters in new states," Barger wrote in his quasi-biography, *Hell's Angel: The Life and Times of Sonny Barger and the Hell's Angels Motorcycle Club* (Fourth Estate Ltd., 2001 edition), "it's always done by national vote. When a prospective club lets us know they want to become Hell's Angels, we'll check them out to see if they're stand-up people. We'll send officers out to meet with them, and in return they'll send guys out to meet with us. We might invite them to a run or two, and likewise we'll send some of our guys to party with them.

At some point—time varies—we'll vote on whether they can become prospects. Eventually we'll vote on their membership status. The same process that lets in individuals applies to entire new chapters as well. . . . Once we sanctioned each official Hell's Angels charter, it became *their* responsibility to keep anybody from starting up an illegal charter in their part of the country."

But Thompson himself presents a wholly different take on the Angels, based on his time spent living in their midst to research the book that launched his career:

> *California, Labor Day weekend . . . early, with ocean fog still in the streets, outlaw motorcyclists wearing chains, shades and greasy Levi's roll out from damp garages, all-night diners and cast-off one-night pads in Frisco, Hollywood, Berdoo and East Oakland, heading for the Monterey peninsula, north of Big Sur. . . . The Menace is loose again, the Hell's Angels, the hundred-carat headline, running fast and loud on the early morning freeway, low in the saddle, nobody smiles, jamming crazy through traffic and ninety miles an hour down the center stripe, missing by inches . . . like Genghis Khan on an iron horse, a monster steed with a fiery anus, flat out through the eye of a beer can and up your daughter's leg with no quarter asked and none given; show the squares some class, give em a whiff of those kicks they'll never know. . . . Ah, these righteous dudes, they love to screw it on. . . . Little Jesus, the Gimp, Chocolate George, Buzzard, Zorro, Hambone, Clean Cut, Tiny, Terry the Tramp, Frenchie, Mouldy Marvin, Mother Miles, Dirty Ed, Chuck the Duck, Fat Freddy, Filthy Phil, Charger Charley the Child Molester, Crazy Cross, Puff, Magoo, Animal and at least a hundred more . . . tense for the action, long hair in the wind, beards and bandanas flapping, earrings, armpits, chain whips, swastikas and stripped-down Harleys flashing chrome as traffic on 101 moves over, nervous, to let the formation pass like a burst of dirty thunder. . . .*

Melodramatic, perhaps, but accurate in depicting this criminal scourge that had appeared on the scene to battle local authorities ill equipped to match their firepower, and national authorities ill prepared at that time to deal with an organized menace that stretched across the entire country. Almost from the beginning of Barger's reign, the Angels' business model was defined by drug dealing. Initially, they played the role of mob hit men and enforcers, providing muscle for drug dealers they would later usurp and replace. After all, why take a small cut of the action when you can own it all? Barger knew full well that the field was there for the taking, no rival gang anywhere near capable of matching the Angels in terms of firepower or muscle. And these Angels of the sixties, the seventies, and even the eighties had another advantage: They weren't at all reluctant to use that firepower and muscle when it came to claiming and solidifying territory from coast to coast.

The same kind of scourge arrived north of the border a bit later, in 1977 specifically, when a small group of Hells Angels in Quebec essentially seized control of a much larger gang known as the Popeyes. The gang saw Canada, rightfully, as an untamed frontier, even back then known for producing some of the best weed anywhere, best known now as BC Bud. The drug trade up there wasn't centralized, and was pretty much there for the taking from several disjointed outlaw gangs that lost members to a combination of desertion, attrition, and constant battles with each other over territory. The precise role Sonny Barger played in all this was in dispute both before and after his release in 1992 from Phoenix Federal Correctional Institution, where he did a three-and-a-half-year stint for conspiring to violate federal explosives, firearms, and arson laws, and it remains in dispute today.

Barger flouted his parole by immediately associating with fellow ex-con Angels as soon as they picked him up at a California airport upon his release. And he was known to have long coveted the methamphetamine business on both sides of the border. It also made perfect sense, although it was never proven, that the increased scrutiny given the gang in the United States through undercover stings like Operation Roughrider would lead Barger to turn attention north to Canada. After all . . .

"It didn't take long for the Hells Angels in Quebec to establish a reputation for murder and intimidation that far exceeded that of any other outlaw biker gang in the world," Julian Sher and William Marsden wrote of those early days in their *Angels of Death: Inside the Biker*

Gangs' Crime Empire (De Capo Press, 2006), a definitive treatment of the era. "With its dozens of boutique gangs, Canada was fertile ground for a typical Hells Angels consolidation. Ruthless and determined, the Hells Angels, from the moment they established themselves in Montreal in 1977, began muscling their way to supremacy in a province whose biker gangs had been mere gofers and assault troops for more established and better organized crime syndicates. The Hells Angels, on the other hand, had no intention of being anybody's patsies. They were all business. Their product was drugs, and their goal was to make money."

And make money they did, first under the auspices of Apache Trudeau. Trudeau was an able leader when pickings were easy and the Angels had the field all to themselves. But Trudeau proved unable to keep his own soldiers under control, and other chapters quickly tired of his weak leadership style. After his top lieutenants were killed in the infamous March 1985 Lennoxville, Quebec, massacre by those now-rival chapters, Trudeau turned tail and ran to the cops for protection in return for information on the gang's membership and methods. What he didn't tell the authorities, because he didn't know, was that the bodies of his late associates had been wrapped in sleeping bags and dumped in the very St. Lawrence River that would later help make the gang a veritable fortune. (Ironically enough, the same fate was suffered by Frank Quellette, the HA responsible for the death of Daniel Desrochers, in 1998, though his body wasn't recovered from the St. Lawrence Seaway until April 15, 1999, wrapped in plastic this time.)

As 1990 dawned, though, new rivals like the Rock Machine surfaced, smelling blood in the water. The biker wars, which had begun in earnest with the massacre in Sherbrooke, exploded across Quebec, centered in Montreal. The Hells Angels of Quebec found themselves in need of new wartime leadership—their own version of Sonny Barger, so to speak—and they found him in one Maurice "Mom" Boucher.

CHAPTER TWENTY-SIX

I never met Alan Jacobs. Nor did I ever meet the Hells Angels kingpins from whom he was buying the weed that fueled his smuggling operation. But I'd met plenty of others in my time and they're all the same, believing themselves to be invincible. They often spent years achieving and amassing vast amounts of power in building the kingdoms over which they preside. And like all kings they believe themselves to be insulated from pursuit and investigation by people like me. The power goes to their heads and they make mistakes they believe themselves immune to.

In the case of Alan Jacobs and the Hells Angels out of Quebec, it was a marriage of splendid convenience. A perfect storm of being in the right place at the right time, right from the very night it all began.

St. Regis Mohawk Reservation, New York;
March 1994

Like most kingpins, Alan didn't start off planning to be bad. It all started over a Nintendo Game Boy.

Alan's mom, Rosalie, was only fifteen years old when she had him. From what his mom had told Alan, his father was a few years older and had lived on the other side of the border. He had promised Alan's mom great things the spring Alan was conceived, but by the time winter came and the snow began falling, so did a reality of truth upon Rosalie. She was forced to drop out of school and take a job in a small Laundromat on the reservation, hardly unusual on the res and pretty much the norm. She worked for minimum wage while Alan spent his days at her parents'. One thing she knew for sure, she was going to bring her son up right. When he had kids, he was going to stick by them, take care of them. She would see to it! She gave him a lot of love but she couldn't give him a lot of things or a lot of her time. So he, like many of the kids on the reservation, would be free to run around and do his own thing once the bell rang signaling the end of the school day.

Which brings us to the Game Boy—veritable gold for a poor kid on the res.

"Dude, I just want to see it for a minute. Ain't like I'm gonna break your shit," a twelve-year-old Alan said to a kid named Elan, trying to grab the Game Boy from him.

Alan would never speak that way in front of his mother, but when he was around the cool kids he did everything to fit in.

"Back off, Snye shit," Elan snapped back.

Alan felt a burning in his belly. He hated being referred to like that, dismissed because of the station in life he'd been born into with virtually no chance of separating himself from it. No wonder almost everyone on the reservation smuggled something for the sake of survival. Some worked on their own and others worked for the rich dealers who lived more inland on the reservation, dealers like Elan's dad. At the time, Elan's dad was probably the most well known smuggler on the reservation, and he actually never smuggled a thing. He used other Natives, who were lower on the food chain, to do his dirty work. He then used the poor white men who lived off the res to do his running.

That's why his son Elan had a Game Boy.

Alan's family was one of the few living on the Snye that didn't smuggle. In fact, they were actually one of the few families on the entire reservation that didn't smuggle. They were also among the poorest. Alan was teased about it often, usually by Elan. Elan and Alan were cousins, Elan's father and Alan's grandfather being brothers. Hardly unusual, since just about everyone on the reservation was related in one way or another.

"Stop being a dick, Elan," a female voice said.

"Alan being saved by a girl." Elan tried to get out his words through his laughter.

"Knock it off or I'll tell Uncle Noah!" Kim Cook, future fiancée of

Danny Simonds, snapped in her typically sassy fashion, stopping just short of Elan.

"Knock it off or I'll tell," Elan said, mocking her. Kim's mom and Elan's father were brother and sister. Kim's mom worked for Elan's dad, Noah King. Noah made sure to let everyone know that he was the big boss, even though he was just ten or so years older than Alan. Early to midtwenties, though the boy couldn't say exactly.

"Let's get out of here," Alan said to his cousin Kim.

"Whatever, losers," Elan said.

Alan and Kim began walking down the street toward her house. "I'm going to be like Uncle Noah one day," he said, biting his lip. "That will show them. Treat my grandpa and me like crap." He kicked a stone hard. "They'll be sorry. Man, will they ever. . . ."

"You don't wanna be like that, Alan. You're better than that. You're smart. Really smart. You could do something amazing. You could make Uncle Noah look like Snye shit," she said, laughing. "Really."

Winter always came quickly in Franklin County, and when the river froze the road across the river opened and the Snye became busier than usual. Alan didn't have cable, so at night he would watch the headlights zip across the river; it seemed more like a four-lane highway some nights than a once fast-moving body of water.

Even at the age of twelve, Alan dreamed of being on the ice. He didn't care what he had to have strapped to his back as long as it would give him the money he needed to buy what he wanted. How else was he going to become as big as Uncle Noah?

Alan's opportunity to become an ice runner came just shy of his thirteenth birthday. However, it wasn't from a family member, since none of Alan's own family would use children to smuggle. It was only the bottom-feeders that would resort to using children as runners.

Alan was cursing the snow and the Snye while walking home from school one cloudy afternoon, the muddy snow creeping into his worn-out boots, when his opportunity came.

"Hey, kid, you want a ride?" a young Native in a res rocket yelled out to him.

Alan didn't have to give it a second thought and hopped into the souped-up pickup truck. While he knew it wasn't the safest move, it wasn't quite like on the white-person land. Kids weren't typically taken to be held captive and molested. That wasn't the thought that had the ball of spit welling up in Alan's throat. It was that Alan knew there was no turning back. In climbing into the passenger seat of that truck, he had committed himself to becoming the kid with the Game Boy instead of the one trying to snatch it from another's grasp.

"What's your name, kid?" the driver asked, flicking a lit joint out the window.

"Alan," he replied, trying to sound tough.

"I'm Sam Fields, Alan. This is Wildcat," Sam said, pointing to the scrappy Native seated in the middle seat. "Do you know why we stopped to pick you up?"

"I think so. You need runners to get cigarettes to Canada," Alan said, keeping eye contact at all time. He could hear his grandfather's words echoing.

Always look a man in their eyes when you speak no matter how scared you are, never drop your lids, because the moment you do is when they will take a bite out of you.

"How old are you?" Wildcat asked.

"Old enough to get the job done," Alan said, puffing up his chest.

"You're small."

"I'm light, which means more product can be packed on a snowmobile," Alan said, adding "Right?" to at least appear deferential.

"Sounds like you will work out perfectly, little man. Meet us at the northernmost tip of the Snye tomorrow at sundown. And dress warm," Sam said as he pulled the truck over to the side of the road just a few homes down from Alan's house.

Alan could feel the surge of adrenaline running through his veins. No longer was he going to be just the kid whose family lived on the river and didn't smuggle. He was going to be a runner, in charge of his own future and destiny. No longer a Snye shit.

The next night Alan met Sam and Wildcat at a rendezvous point. The headlights of the snowmobiles, trucks, and other ATVs were beginning to clutter the muddy swampland cutting through the darkness of the frozen river. Sam had two snowmobiles set up, one for Alan and one for Wildcat. Large packs hung over the snowmobile and the compartments were full of cigarettes.

"Listen here, kid, all ya have to do is follow Wildcat. Once across the river it's only a half mile down the road. Get in, get out, get back," Sam explained.

Alan threw one leg over the snowmobile. His energy was running as high as the revving engine.

"Ready, kid?" Wildcat asked.

"You bet."

Wildcat took off across the ice and Alan followed. Ice chips flew up from beneath the blades, causing a storm of crystals around Alan. He'd never felt so free.

When the duo hit the hard, iced-over land of Canada, they took the half-mile ride to meet Benny, Sam's Canadian partner. Benny was sketchy, even more so than Alan was used to seeing around the Snye. He had a scar that cut right through his eye. The reflection of the light of the snow made Benny's dead eye glow. It sent a shiver down Alan's spine.

"Who's the newbie?" Benny asked.

"That's the kid," Wildcat said, gesturing toward Alan.

Alan stood as tall as he could manage, helped a bit by his boots. "I'm Alan."

Benny gave a nod and Alan relaxed a little. Then Benny filled up Wildcat's packs with money from the deliveries from the night before.

"He know what happens to kids who fuck up?" Benny asked.

"He's cool," Wildcat told him, slapping Alan on the back hard enough to rattle his ribs.

"I'm only asking," Benny persisted, his one working eye still fixed on Alan.

"I'm cool," Alan told him, and in that moment he was. Cooler than he'd been in his entire life.

It was almost one A.M. when Alan and Wildcat hit the American side of the reservation again. Sam was sitting inside the truck, smoking a joint, waiting on them. Alan and Wildcat stopped their ATVs behind Sam's truck. Sam stepped out of his truck.

"How'd it go out there?" he asked.

"Great!" Alan said excitedly and without thinking.

"Sounds like you had fun," Sam said, rubbing his hands together for warmth.

"It was awesome, except Benny's an asshole."

"You're smarter than I thought, kid."

Sam smiled. It was always good to start 'em young. Get them to be your mope. This was what Sam needed, especially while he was starting out. As the trio loaded the ATVs back on the truck, though, something told him this kid was different. Smart, yeah—maybe too smart eventually, but just what Sam needed right now.

"Will you be helping us out again tomorrow, kid?" he asked.

"Sure will," Alan answered.

"Same time and place," Sam replied, getting into his truck.

Sam put his car into drive and took his foot off the brake and then stopped and rolled his window down.

"Kid, I almost forgot." Sam reached into his pocket and pulled out a bill. "For tonight's work."

Alan stood alone in the darkness trying to see how much money he had made. *Is that a fifty-dollar bill?* He'd made more in a few hours than his mom made in days!

Alan met Sam, Wildcat, and Benny the next night, and the next. Winters would fade into spring. The runners dashed across the ice even as it was cracking beneath their heavy snowmobiles. It became a game to see who could challenge the ice, who was more fierce than the angry freezing water below. Over the next two years, he and Wildcat became known as the craziest of the bunch, pushing it the longest into the season. Every year there were casualties, but that was the way it went.

Alan had been pretty happy with his fifty-dollars-a-night pay, but he knew there was more waiting for him. His opportunity came almost to the day of the two-year anniversary since he'd started running. He met Sam and Wildcat in the usual spot, but on this night there was one snowmobile and no Wildcat.

Before Alan could ask why, Sam was already answering. "Wildcat is too sick to run tonight, so you're going at it alone. You okay with that?"

Alan was thrilled. This was his chance to prove himself. "All good, boss."

Alan pulled in ten minutes ahead of schedule, even before Benny had arrived. He was smoking a cigarette as Benny's truck pulled to a halt.

"Where's Wildcat?" Benny asked, walking toward Alan.

"Sick. Hungover or some shit, probably."

Benny glanced down at his watch.

"You want to come with me for a drink? Seems you have some time to kill."

"I would but I got orders and don't wanna fuck with Sam. You understand," Alan replied.

"You seem to want to get ahead in this business," Benny observed.

"Whatever it takes, Benny."

"Yeah? So do you want to be Sam's bitch or your own man?"

"What do you think?"

"Then spare some time," Benny said, walking toward his truck. "And have a drink with me," he continued, giving no heed to the fact that he was talking to a fifteen-year-old kid.

Alan followed behind him. The two rode in silence until Benny pulled in to an old dive bar on the Canadian side of the reservation. The parking lot was filled with snowmobiles and beat-up pickup trucks with chains around the tires. Even from the outside, Alan could tell he was going to be out of place. The bar was filthy and run-down. The lighting inside was dim and the air smoky.

Benny sat down on one of the very few empty barstools, gesturing for Alan to do the same. "Want a drink?"

"Nah. Not while I got Sam's shit with me," Alan replied, staring at the clock on the wall.

"Relax, kid."

"You said you could make me my own man?"

"Right down to business. I like it," Benny replied, gulping his beer. "I've noticed that you ride back totally empty after each run. A waste of space, don't you think?"

"Yeah." Alan had a feeling he knew where Benny was going with this but had to be cautious. "So?"

"Here's what I am thinking. While I am giving Wildcat the money, you walk to the back of my truck, grab a couple packs of pot, whatever I have for the day, and carry it back with you to the res. You sell it, and bring me back the money. I'll pay you ten percent of everything you bring in." Benny took another swig of his beer. "Not a bad gig."

"Why haven't you made the offer to Wildcat?" Alan asked cautiously.

"Wildcat is Sam's bitch. You, kid, on the other hand, are your own man."

Alan knew better than to show his poker hand and his excitement to this guy. "Maybe I want to stay that way."

"Come on, Alan," Benny said, addressing him by name for the first time ever, "step on up. You don't want to be a low-level cig runner forever, do you?" Benny was almost taunting him. "That'll kill you even faster than smoking the fucking things."

"Ten percent?" Alan asked, wondering if he should push for more.

"Ten percent, kid."

"I'm in," Alan said, extending his hand to Benny, figuring there'd be time to push for more later, after they'd worked out the details of how to keep Sam and Wildcat from becoming any the wiser about his little side deal.

He had to race across the ice, but even at full speed he reached the Snye on the other side of the frozen St. Lawrence late.

"What took you so long?" Sam asked, as Alan flew onto shore.

"Benny was all sketched out that Wildcat wasn't there. Gave me shit," Alan replied, hoping his lie would pass muster.

"Dude is pretty strange" was Sam's only response.

"Hey," said Alan, "it's business, right?"

And from that point in 1994 on, it was.

CHAPTER TWENTY-SEVEN

E very army needs a general, and the Rock Machine had lost theirs when Salvatore Cazzetta went to prison. That gave Cazzetta's opposite number in the HAs, Maurice "Mom" Boucher, just the opening he needed, as the rival gangs declared all-out war on each other.

Boucher had joined the Montreal chapter Angels in 1987 after completing a forty-month sentence for sexually assaulting a teenager. Before that he'd built a notorious reputation for spearheading the murders of five members of a rival Angels chapter when he was riding with the HAs of Lennoxville, Quebec, in 1982. Interestingly enough, the incident ran him especially afoul of none other than Salvatore Cazzetta, who, as a result, would end up founding the Rock Machine, against which Boucher ultimately declared war. Even more notable, ironic, or prophetic even, was that these five bodies too were dumped in the very St. Lawrence River the Angels under Boucher's command would later run dope over.

Cazzetta and Boucher had actually been friends and associates at one point while riding with a white-supremacist motorcycle gang called the SS that was based in Pointe-aux-Trembles. And, as reported in Murderpedia, Boucher initially invited Cazzetta to join him at the top of the Quebec Hells Angels chapter once he'd seized control there. The interesting thing here, as Murderpedia also reported, is that, like Alan Jacobs, Boucher's childhood was steeped in poverty, with turning to a life of crime being seen as the only way out:

*Born in Causapscal, Quebec, Canada, he was raised in poverty
in the Hochelaga-Maisonneuve section of inner-city Montreal,*

where his family moved when he was two years old. Boucher dropped out of school in grade 9 to work odd jobs. Unhappy with his income and desperate to support his drug habit, he turned to crime. He was arrested for three break & entries in the fall of 1974 and served nearly six months in detention. In November of 1975, Boucher performed an armed robbery, but was caught and sentenced to 40 months in prison.

In 1994, Boucher dispatched his HA soldiers to take over territory then controlled by Cazzetta's Rock Machine. Boucher wasn't interested in buying them out or consolidating in an orderly fashion. And when the Rock Machine resisted, the all-out war that would ultimately claim the life of eleven-year-old Daniel Desrochers broke out.

A similar childhood experience wasn't the only thing Boucher shared with Alan Jacobs either; he also enjoyed a comparably delusional view of the extent of his own power. Just as Jacobs was brought down by greed and the belief that he could order an attack on an underling (Danny Simonds) with impunity, Boucher believed himself capable of intimidating the entire Canadian justice system. That was precisely his intention when he ordered the deaths of three prison guards to, in large part, discourage the use of the kind of confidential informants who are the key to making any big drug case stick.

After Boucher was initially acquitted in 1998, though, it was just such an informant that led to Boucher's rearrest and ultimate conviction in 2002. "The key witness for the prosecution was Stéphane Gagné, nick-named Godasse, who was involved in both murders," Murderpedia reported. "He testified that Boucher ordered him to carry out the killings and was later congratulated by Boucher himself. After 11 days of deliberation by the jury, Boucher was found guilty of attempted murder and two counts of first-degree murder. Boucher received an automatic life sentence, with no possibility of parole for at least 25 years."

Boucher didn't tolerate competition or what he perceived to be disloyalty any more than Alan Jacobs had. "He expected full loyalty from his drug dealers," writes Paul Cherry in *The Biker Trials: Bringing Down the Hells Angels*, his superb 2005 study of the era, "and he asked them to adhere to the same structure and rules expected of him as a member of the Hells Angels when he created his own gang in 1992, calling them the Rockers. And when he felt other members of the Hells Angels' Montreal chapter were not bloodthirsty enough for his war, he created his own chapter in 1995."

Unlike Alan Jacobs, though, Boucher was the very definition of a career criminal, and those crimes tended toward the brash and violent. And whereas Jacobs resisted using any drugs himself, by all accounts Boucher was afflicted with a serious drug problem that led to him being arrested in three separate robberies in the fall of 1974, just after he'd turned twenty-one. Bold smash-and-grabs mostly with window glass and alarm systems viewed as minor inconveniences.

"The first arrest came on November 5, just after midnight," Paul Cherry writes. "Boucher smashed the front door window of a neighborhood grocery store in Hochelaga Maisonneuve, the low-income Montreal district where he had grown up. He grabbed twenty-three cartons of cigarettes and headed out. But his actions had set off an alarm heard by two cops in a nearby patrol car. When they pulled up to the front of the store, the officers saw Boucher standing in front of it. A green plastic bag filled with cigarette cartons lay at his feet."

Boucher had dropped out of high school and tried his hand at construction for a time before that first arrest in the fall of 1974 ushered in his chosen career. His criminal escapades were marked by escalating risk and violence, moving from smash-and-grabs to his preferred form of armed robberies. Boucher didn't shy away from violence; he embraced it, and eventually used the proclivity to fuel his relentless, mercurial rise through the ranks of the biker world, particularly with the Hells Angels, which proved to be the perfect vehicle for him to exercise his increasing penchant for brutality and bullying.

The Montreal chapter of the Hells Angels was the first one ever established in Canada, and by the time Boucher joined it upon his release from prison it was a decade old. But the gang had been decimated by defections and incarcerations, making Boucher the ideal candidate for a leadership position. And, never one to disappoint, Boucher embarked on a crime spree to both satisfy his urges and make his bones with the gang. One of those guys who delighted in the fact that no matter how far you were willing to go, he would go farther. No exceptions. Boucher was a true sociopath without conscience or morality, to the point where he seemed to revel in his teenage son following in his criminal footsteps.

By 1994, though, he had a lot more on his mind than the petty crimes his son kept getting pinched for. The arrest and incarceration of Sal Cazzetta, head of the Rock Machine, created a void Boucher intended to exploit by wiping his rival biker gang off the Montreal map. This after they had spurned his overtures to turn over their entire drug business to him. Again, there was no equivocating with Boucher. His goal was nothing less than control of Montreal's entire drug trade, and nothing less would suffice.

CHAPTER TWENTY-EIGHT

Twenty-four thousand seven hundred, twenty-four thousand eight hundred, twenty-four thousand nine . . ."

Alan's stacking of hundred-dollar bills into neat piles was interrupted by a knock on the door.

"Hold on a minute," he called.

But the door started opening anyway.

"I said hold on," he snapped, trying to hide the wads of cash under his sheets and pillow.

"Don't worry, it's just me. Plus, it isn't like I don't know what you're up to," Danny Simonds's future lover Kim said as she walked into Alan's bedroom and sat down on the floor. They weren't just cousins; they were friends, too.

"How did you know? I've been covering my tracks. I'm not even buying any of the shit that I want, that I need," Alan said, gesturing to his worn out shoes. "Who told you?"

"Derek. No way that fool could afford a new ride without mooching off of someone. And the only one willing to give him a chance was someone desperate and oh so very sleepy during class," she joked.

At fifteen, Alan couldn't drive and would have to resort to selling all the pot to kids or other Natives on the res. But he knew that was bad for the business he was planning on building. Good thing, lucky thing, that Benny had given Alan a chance a year ago, just like Alan had given his cousin Derek a chance. He was a little crazy and not so smart but very trustworthy, and that was what Alan needed. He used Derek to take the goods off the res to the poor white folks who lived just beyond it. They never had money to feed their families, but always seemed to find money for drugs. In return, Alan gave Derek a small percentage of the proceeds, which he inevitably wasted on obnoxious decals and louder speakers for his car.

"Derek is a trustworthy fool," Alan said, confiding in Kim.

"And you're a fool to be messing with this shit," Kim snapped at him. "What if your grandfather found out? You're better than this, Alan! You're way too smart to get caught up in this shit!"

"My grandfather won't find out. I'm doing this smarter than everyone else. I'm not in it for the short term, I'm in it for the long. I've got a plan. Trust me, Kim," Alan told her.

"I miss you, Alan. I miss my friend," Kim said, climbing onto the bed next to Alan.

The years had been good to Kim. Her coppery skin seemed to always have a summer glow, even on the coldest grayest days of the St. Lawrence winters. Her long thick black hair fell perfectly in place every day. Her eyes were black like the deadly patches of ice on the St. Lawrence River. Sometimes animals got stuck on those patches of black ice and had to choose between freezing to death in the water or waiting to starve, clinging to the false hope that the patch might miraculously join up again with the larger swatch leading to land. That's what Alan feared more than anything, metaphorically.

Black ice. An apt metaphor as well for pretty much every drug dealer I've ever put away, big and small.

Alan shook off his lustful thoughts over Kim, his cousin, and sprang off the bed. Sharing a bed as well as blood was hardly unusual on the res, but he had already resolved to be different. A man with a plan that had no room for such a proclivity.

"I know what I am doing and I really have to finish up," he insisted.

"I really hope you do, Alan, I really hope you know what you're doing," Kim replied as she tossed her raven-colored mane over her delicate shoulders.

Then she gave Alan a kiss on his cheek and left.

Alan went back to counting. He already knew that Wildcat wasn't riding with him tonight and his lone nights always gave rise to bigger opportunities. Alan met Sam at the usual spot, at the usual time, with a backpack full of Benny's money on his back. Sam was leaning up against his truck smoking a joint.

"Want a hit?" Sam asked fifteen-year-old Alan as he drew closer.

"Nah, man. I'm good," Alan replied, making his way toward the snowmobile on the back of the truck. Not mixing business with pleasure was another part of his plan. Rule number something in the world of a kingpin: You don't use your own supply.

Sam came to help him get it off the truck. "You still don't smoke?"

"Not my thing," Alan replied, pulling the ATV down the ramp.

Then he turned his attention to a nearby snowmobile and started pushing it down to the river.

"Seems like this will be one of the last ice runs this year," Alan heard Sam say into the darkness. "I'm already seeing cracks in the shallow parts. I'd watch out for patches of black ice, if I were you."

"I always do," Alan said back to him, knowing the irony would be lost on Sam. But he also sensed something else couched in his words: Sam was on to him and his true plan. Alan would do the drop as usual but he would have to skip bringing anything back today. He couldn't risk it with how sketched-out and suspicious Sam was getting.

Alan hit the frozen river running, zipping across all of the hairline fractures that were forming in the ice. Like every night he rode without Wildcat, he had beat Benny there on the other side of the St. Lawrence. When Benny showed up, Alan quickly unloaded everything and gathered up the money before telling Benny he wouldn't be bringing a load back with him tomorrow.

"Sam knows and is going to lose his shit if I have a load with me," Alan told Benny.

"Sam is not my fucking problem," Benny said, getting into Alan's face, intimidating the kid with his size. But what Alan remembered most was how much his breath stank, a combination of dead fish and stale tobacco. It hit him like a gale-force wind.

These two years had not been as helpful to Alan as they had to Kim. He was still small in comparison to his friends and puberty still seemed to be taunting him. That meant he had to be doubly tough to avoid being taken advantage of.

"I think it's time we go for another drink. Remind you of how things work," Benny said, his tone not leaving Alan much of a choice.

Alan knew he was better off dealing with Sam being angry than Benny. You could fuck with Sam. Benny might've had breath that smelled like ass, but his eyes held a glint of madness and restrained rage. So Alan got in Benny's truck, already contemplating just how he was going to get out of this one. Since carrying product back with him today wasn't an option.

Benny pulled up to a different dive bar and got out of his truck. Alan knew his role was to follow, and he did. He just wanted to get this over with. The bar was full of burly, overgrown white men. These weren't the typical poor white toothless saps that Alan was used to seeing around. They were a different type. At a closer look he noticed they were all wearing the same heavy black leather vests with the death's-head insignias on the back:

Hells Angels.

Alan's heart started pounding. *Why the hell did Benny bring me here?* Carrying back with him was looking like a better option, after all. Maybe ambition really was going to be the death of him. Dealing with Sam on the south side of the river would be a whole hell of a lot easier than dealing with shit that included the Hells Angels on the north. He stuck close to Benny until they found a spot at the bar.

"Hey, Whiskers. Two tequilas," Benny said, waving at the bartender.

Whiskers brought over the two drinks, "Frank is looking for you," he told Benny. "Said if you walked in to send you right over. Orders."

"Hang here, kid. I'll be right back," Benny said, walking toward the door.

"What? You're leaving me here?" Alan asked nervously.

"Thought you were tough," was Benny's only reply, before he disappeared out the door.

I am so fucked, Alan thought as he sat back down, studying the distance to the door in case he decided to make a run for it.

When he turned back around, two leather-vested HAs had taken the barstools on Alan's right. The boy kept his eyes on his drink, doing his best to ignore them. Stirring the straw ever so slowly. The two men began to talk. Alan realized he'd been holding his breath and sucked some in. He knew that they weren't there to bother him now.

"That blaze was a good one," the larger man said to the other. "They could see the flames for miles," he added proudly.

"Ey, didn't take that house but fourteen months to rot out," the bearded man replied.

Alan knew right away what they were talking about—the grow houses scattered through Quebec where the Angels grew their weed. These guys were the top of the food chain. Get in with them and he'd no longer have to worry about Benny or Sam or being a bitch to anyone. He'd be at the top of the food chain too, no longer needing to rely on losers on both sides of the St. Lawrence. Suddenly those precarious patches of black ice seemed very small indeed.

But how the hell was he going to break into this conversation? These guys weren't Natives. These guys were *Hells Angels*, known for being cold-blooded killers. If things went wrong with them, they would go really wrong. It wasn't as simple as an ass-kicking. Forget being stranded on black ice. Fuck up with the HAs and you ended up dead beneath it.

Alan knew moments like this don't come along but once in a lifetime. He also knew that he was taking one hell of a gamble. He lifted his tumbler of tequila to his lips and threw it back. The burn caused him to choke, catching the attention of the Hells Angels next to him.

"You okay, kid?" the one guy asked.

"I'm good," Alan said, trying to hold back his cough, "all good."

The man was beginning to turn back to his conversation and Alan knew that he would lose his opportunity and had to act fast.

"But if you don't mind," Alan managed to push through his sore vocal cords, "I got something I want to talk to you about."

The man looked around, shocked at being addressed like that. "You talking to me?"

"Yes, sir, I am," Alan said, and swallowed hard, hoping to get enough saliva to wash over his throat.

The large man elbowed his bearded buddy to turn around and look at the kid. The two Hells Angels sat in amusement, shaking their heads that a boy, an Indian no less, had the balls to talk to them.

"I overheard you and I thought maybe I could be of assistance," Alan continued, nonetheless.

The two men looked at each other and at first Alan thought he was in trouble, but then they started to laugh. Just a chuckle at first, but then loud. Really loud.

"I'm serious!" Alan insisted to them, louder than he'd intended.

"Okay," the bigger HA said, swiping the tears of laughter from his eyes with a sleeve, "and just how are you going to assist us?"

"By cutting out whatever half-wit middleman you're using on this side of the river," Alan said boldly. "You work directly with me. One less hand in the pot, so to speak."

The HAs clearly didn't know how to respond.

"What's your name, kid?" the big guy asked.

"Alan."

"I'm Roger. You serious, Alan?"

Alan nodded.

"Then follow me. Let's talk a little business."

Roger slid down from his stool, the other HA left to work his beer alone. Alan stayed where he was.

"There a problem, kid?" Roger asked him. "'Cause if you want to assist us . . ."

"I'm sort of waiting on someone and I have to get back to the river," Alan stammered.

"Doesn't work that way, Alan. Now follow me."

Alan followed Roger out to his truck in the parking lot. Roger got in the truck. Alan debated running but figured a bullet could outrun him, so he got in.

"You want to assist me, right?" Roger asked again.

"I do. I'm tired of being someone's bitch," Alan told Roger.

"You sure you know what you are doing, kid? Working with us isn't the same as being a bitch for someone. Once you're in, there's no out." Roger's eyes gleamed. "Except dying. So this is one last shot at an out I'm giving you. Think hard, real hard, about what you say next."

Alan sat still and silent for a moment, the other side of the frozen river seeming farther away than it had ever been before. He thought about Benny and Sam. He thought about his uncle Noah. He thought about what this could mean. No one on the reservation had ever dealt directly with the Hells Angels before. There was always a northern middleman and here he was fifteen years old, all hundred scrawny pounds of him, about to make a deal that could change his life.

Or end it.

"I'm in, Roger," Alan pronounced.

"There's some rules."

"Rules?"

"Like procedure. 'Fore we get started, I'm going to need your address and the names of all your family members. Nothing personal, kid. Just procedure. For security reasons. You understand."

Alan didn't. He swallowed hard. He'd heard the stories. This was part of the Hells Angels drill. It wasn't enough for them to make you suffer if you didn't toe the line; they would take down your entire family. They needed to know where to find you and your loved ones. There was no disappearing on them. If you thought of running they'd go after your family, your loved ones, whoever you cared about the most. Sometimes they took pictures without you knowing and flashed them if you ever fucked up.

"You okay with that?" he heard Roger asking him.

"Sure," Alan said. "Sure."

Roger explained how the runs would work. The HAs would start off fronting him $10,000 worth of pot. He'd have three days to bring the money back. If he proved he could do that, he'd be able to escalate and move up the ranks.

"How soon—" Alan started. Then, words veering in midthought, "When do I start?"

"How about tomorrow night? That's as good a time as any."

Not so simple, Alan thought. First he had to get rid of Sam and Benny. And he'd have to buy his own Jet Ski and snowmobile before tomorrow night.

"Yeah," he said to Roger, nodding, "that sounds good."

Benny was back in the bar when Alan walked back in.

"Where the fuck were you?" Benny snapped.

"Me? Where the fuck were you? I was supposed to be back an hour ago. Just give me the money and take me back to my ride!" Alan snapped, perhaps emboldened by the new partnership he'd just cemented.

Maybe it was the new strength in Alan's voice or maybe it was the fact that Sam really was going to be pissed, but Benny actually acquiesced.

With nothing more owed to Benny, Alan only needed to finish this run to Sam. Thirty-five minutes later Alan stopped the engine behind Sam's pickup truck. Alan started loading the ATV before Sam got out of the car.

"What took you so long?" Sam asked, sounding suspicious enough to make Alan wonder if he could possibly have known something about what had gone down on the other side of the frozen river.

"Benny is just a crazy fucker. Said I had to go with him to this bar to get the money. Tweaked out and left me forever," Alan said while tying down the snowmobile.

Sam lurched forward and started to pat Alan down.

"Hey, what the fuck? What are you doing, man?" Alan snapping, pushing the guy off him, remembering how bad Benny's breath had been when he'd gotten this close.

"Nothing, nothing," Sam said almost apologetically when he realized Alan was clean.

Alan pulled the backpack off his shoulders and tossed it at Sam. "Well, here's your fucking money. I'm done, man, fuck you!"

Alan hopped out of the truck. As he walked away, down the dark street, he couldn't help but smile to himself. That had worked out even better than he had hoped for. Starting tomorrow he was in business for himself, working directly with the Hells Angels. First step in building his own empire on the St. Lawrence River.

CHAPTER TWENTY-NINE

Montreal; 1995

The Hells Angels, as it turned out, played a crucial role in that empire. A relationship born that frigid night in a bar on the Canadian side of the border prospered and grew over the years. Alan Jacobs wasn't the first Native from the res to be employed by the HAs as a dealer, but he was certainly the most ambitious and capable.

Perfect timing for Boucher, whose Angels had been coming under increasing scrutiny from Canadian authorities in the wake of Daniel Desrochers's tragic death. That one incident of collateral damage represented a seismic shift in the attitude of Canadian law enforcement to the biker wars and a sea change as to how LE would approach the violence that up until that point had been about little more than bad guys killing each other.

"I'll tell you honestly," André Bouchard, the Montreal homicide commander at the time, told Julian Sher and William Marsden for their definitive study of criminal biker gangs, *Angels of Death*, "the department didn't give two shits. They're killing each other. I give a hell if some guy pops somebody who just got out of jail? No. We didn't give a shit."

Until Danny Desrochers died in a Montreal hospital a few days after being hit by shrapnel from the Jeep that blew up outside the Rock Machine's headquarters.

Having pretty much vanquished the Rock Machine and all other criminal competition, Boucher unwittingly left himself law enforcement's primary target for its self-described war on the bikers. With revenue decreasing north of the border as a result, he had no choice but to try increasing his business south of the border. The early smuggling success achieved by Alan Jacobs proved the prototype, and, for his part, young Alan was more than happy to enlist some of his most trusted friends and associates on the res, many of them relatives, in the effort.

Although there is no evidence or indication that Jacobs and Boucher ever met, they were fueling each other's interests and solidifying their power in their respective domains. On the back of those early night-time runs across the frozen St. Lawrence River, Alan built an empire of legitimate businesses fueled by the cash profits from his drug running. The more runs he did and the more runners he enlisted into the cause, the better he did. And under the radar mostly.

Not so with Maurice Boucher. By the time he was found guilty at that second trial in 2002, the Rock Machine had been eliminated from the scene save for a few stray elements. And the HAs barely missed a step without him. Remember Sal Cazzetta? Arrested in 1994 on a pit-bull farm for attempting to smuggle two hundred kilos of cocaine into Canada through the United States, Cazzetta was extradited to Florida and convicted. He spent three years in the US penal system, earning a high-school degree, and then was transferred back to Canada to serve out the remainder of his sentence. After serving two-thirds of it, he was paroled and released from a medium-security penitentiary in June 2004.

And here's the thing: Upon his release from prison, he changed his colors and joined the very Hells Angels he'd sworn off years before, in large part to fill the void left by Boucher's incarceration. This in spite of the fact that his original incarceration in 1994 left a similar void in the Rock Machine that, partly anyway, led to Boucher declaring all-out war on his Montreal rivals. And by 2004, with the Rock Machine and all other competition vanquished, Cazzetta had pretty much adopted Boucher's attitude that the HAs wanted to control distribution of all drugs through the city; no room for competition in Cazzetta's or Boucher's world.

As the now titular head of the Montreal chapter, Cazzetta found himself presiding over an empire that in large part was fueled by the same profits from running drugs across the res that had doomed his original gang to extinction in the first place. The Angels might be at war with the Royal Canadian Mounted Police and the Ontario Provincial Police, along with their various local counterparts, but they weren't at war with anyone in the United States. So for the HAs and their new leader, Cazzetta, the pipeline over the St. Lawrence became all the more vital, a reality further supported by the increasing power Alan Jacobs gained thanks to the profits he was reaping by transporting their weed into my backyard.

Criminals are nothing if not opportunists, and Cazzetta saw a golden opportunity here, just like Alan Jacobs did the night he first approached those HAs in that bar. But kingpins like this seem to have something else even more prevalent in common: They always get caught.

By guys like me.

CHAPTER THIRTY

Franklin County, New York; 2004

Alan Jacobs was smart enough to avoid contact with Sal Cazzetta and any other Hells Angels directly. He left that task to the army of runners who performed the same task he had as a boy atop the frozen St. Lawrence. If anyone got pinched, it would be them, but that was unlikely at best given the peculiarities of the reservation that stretched across both borders. Alan's tribal leaders, as well as their Hells Angels counterparts, were wise enough to know a good thing when they saw it, and his was better than good; it was perfect, an inexhaustible supply of product on one side of border and an inexhaustible supply of runners, dealers, and distributors to move it on the other.

Jacobs built an elaborate network of distribution while the Angels further expanded their supply chain to meet the new demand. What do you expect, given that there weren't many other options available on the res? Smuggling, even for a kid, provided the opportunity to make more money than most of the Natives would see in a lifetime. What separated Jacobs from other kids on the res who ran cigarettes over to Canada was his ambition, along with his work ethic.

As a boy, Jacobs always enjoyed what he was doing, and he reaped the rewards of his hard work. He was able to move out of his parents' home and into his own at the age of eighteen. He bought himself a shiny new black Ford Expedition with twenty-four-inch chrome wheels—what law enforcement called a "res rocket"—and used it to expand his own smuggling enterprise. Where most parents would question the success and inexplicably newfound fortune of their teenage son, Alan's mother did not. Nor would any of the elders on the Akwesasne reservation. Smuggling was a way of life, a means of advancement that had survived for generations and was sometimes the only means available for Natives to truly better their lot in life. As many as 80 percent of the Natives smuggled *something* into or out of the country, whether it was cigarettes, illegal aliens, or drugs, which was what Alan Jacobs found himself doing very early into his career.

It took Alan several years, but soon he was running one of the largest smuggling rings in the country, the envy of his peers and rivals alike. They'd never dare cross him, for one reason primarily. He'd earned the trust and respect of his own people, who became increasingly beholden to him over the years, along with the hardest organization in the world to crack: the Hells Angels motorcycle gang, which pretty much controlled the drug business in Canada.

The thing about Alan was that he thought big. The world was his to do what he wanted with, and what he wanted more than anything was to be head of one of the largest criminal enterprises in the country. He thirsted for something that he could brag about to everyone as it gave him the power to help his people. But help also implied a form of control, and, no doubt about it, Alan Jacobs visualized himself as a kind of Indian "Godfather," presiding over those he might cajole even as he held them under his thumb.

His benevolence and generosity would know no bounds, so long as it helped further tighten the hold on power he so desperately craved. He had a network of thugs and enforcers to summon when needed, and the services of the Angels to be called upon only in the most dire of circumstances. Jacobs wanted people to kiss his ring, and thanks to his now long association with the Angels, that ring was twenty-four-karat gold and diamond-studded.

Similarly, Alan knew the rules for running drugs that had gotten him this far and promised to get him further: You never brag and you never share with anyone outside your circle. With some of the profits gleaned from his smuggling operations, he opened a cigarette factory. Jacobs Tobacco Company, operated in a newly built ultramodern 47,000-square-foot building on the res, boasted all the latest equipment and made Alan a truly beloved, if not revered, figure among the tribe. He was putting food on Mohawk families' tables and helping them keep the heat on through the winter. Jobs available at the factory drastically cut the reservation's massive unemployment, and Alan was sure to pump funds into building and improving more schools along with any number of civic projects. Doing his part for his people by effectively owning them.

And, of course, the cigarette factory also proved to be substantially lucrative for the smuggling enterprise. Drugs aren't the only things smuggled across the border; so are people, guns, gas, and any type of contraband that can bring in a buck. But cigarettes are number one. Every day, twenty thousand cartons cross the Akwesasne reservation into Canada, which amounts to over $300 million a year. (In a September 2011 interview with CBC News out of Canada, Derek Champagne put that estimate much closer to $1 billion per year, the same figure he estimates is amassed by the drug traffic coming in over the res.)

Alan saw this happening while he was just a young boy. He saw the dollars lining the pockets of the smugglers, and he saw opportunity. By the time he was in his early twenties he created his own line of cigarettes, which he sold only on the reservation. That was the way to make real money. The United States wasn't allowed to tax Native Americans for their own brands of cigarettes sold exclusively on the reservation. This allowed Alan to both sell at a lower price and put an extra one to two dollars per pack in his pocket. The profit margin was even higher with the cigarettes he smuggled into Canada. Canada taxes cigarettes at such a high rate that they could cost up to fifteen dollars a pack. Alan was able to sell his smuggled cigarettes at such a reduced price by Canadian standards that people would come in droves to the reservation to buy them.

Now not only was Alan making money by having people smuggle cigarettes to Canada, he was making the money on the cigarettes themselves. Real entrepreneur that he was, he'd effectively cut out the middleman, and his house was a testament to the heights to which he had risen. You would think that this would have been enough for Alan, but most of the true kingpins of the drug world have a legitimate business, because while it is about the money it's also about the power. The more money, the more power. They can never have enough of either.

It wasn't uncommon for Natives on the reservation to have children while never getting married. Alan Jacobs was one of those who never wed, which was probably for the best. He was well known among the Mohawk, and the ladies loved him. He'd grown from an undersized boy with dark brooding looks that made him almost pretty into a handsome young man. His full head of dark hair, his copper-colored skin, and his midnight eyes made him extremely attractive, but those same eyes held a surety and arrogance in their glare Alan didn't bother to hide. Thing is, though, Alan had earned the right to boast of his power and success, because—on the res, anyway—he had his hands in everything.

Between Jacobs Tobacco Company, Jacobs Construction Company, and Jacobs Paving Company, Alan employed many of the Natives in legitimate businesses. Other than his tobacco company, Alan used those businesses to launder the massive amounts of cash his drug distribution brought in. For Alan Jacobs, though, even that was easy to justify. Look at the number of Natives he employed, providing them with income and decent lifestyles, lifting them from the poverty that might've otherwise claimed them. So the reservation was dependent on him in ways that made him a revered figure among the Akwesasne people.

It was good to be king, but his reign was over by the time of my involvement, just like Maurice Boucher's was. But there's always someone else ready to step up and seize the throne, and I was more than happy to set my sights on them instead.

4

DOPE GHOST

A person is born with feelings of envy and
hate. If he gives way to them, they will lead
him to violence and crime, and any sense of
loyalty and good faith will be abandoned.

—Xunzi

CHAPTER THIRTY-ONE

Ten months after Alan Jacobs sent Wildcat and four more of his thugs to deal with the Danny Simonds problem, my Firestone Winterforce snow tires glided across the thick ice like a well-trained ice skater. Winter had not yet released its stranglehold on the St. Regis Mohawk Reservation. If there was one place where hell could freeze over, it was here.

I finally regained control of my truck. It made sense that all the res rockets still had on their equipment snow tire chains. I pulled in to a parking spot across from the office building that was task force headquarters.

"Welcome to our new home, boys," I said to Mike Hughes and Joe Miles, the young patrolman I'd chosen to work the wire room up here.

Of course, none of this ever would've happened if I didn't have the support of Reminderville's mayor, Sam Alonso. He's a big supporter of eradicating the drugs from his community and has always given me a lot of latitude to make that happen over the years. He gets the big picture and has always granted my requests to pursue big cases outside my jurisdiction. Mayor Alonso could just as easily have ordered me to focus my efforts elsewhere. Instead, he's always had my back, just like I always have my men's backs. The same goes for Keith Winebrenner, the sergeant in charge of the Beachwood narcotics unit at the time and the town's current police chief. Without his foresight to see the end result of a large-scale drug investigation, and the latitude he was able to give us to follow the case from his home turf, there might never have been a case at all.

Multi-jurisdictional drug investigations, meanwhile, are like multi-legged stools, and that means they tend to collapse if one of the legs gives way. Mike would be working our leg, and I felt very good about that. He was ready for the responsibility, even if he didn't have a total grasp of how big this case really was. It was big for us, sure, but it was also big for the state of New York, the DEA, and now Border Patrol too. Because of his cross designation as an assistant US attorney, Derek Champagne was the perfect man to run the show. Sort through the competing agendas and keep everybody happy.

"About fucking time," Mike said. "I'm glad I'm just staying here. I can't imagine doing this drive all time. My ass isn't made for this."

"You better get a pillow for that sensitive ass of yours because your ass will be doing a lot more sitting in this wire room than it will be in the car."

"But at least I'll be in the action."

Mike's response was that of a soldier ready to face the enemy on the front line.

Miles started laughing so hard that he choked on the sip of water he had just gulped back. "Oh, Mike, this is definitely your first wiretap."

"What's that supposed to mean?" Mike asked defensively.

This was his first wiretap. I had hired Mike right out of the academy. I knew he had potential, but I'd never put him in a wiretap, because I'd never had an opportunity. I had been out of the drug business since Mike came on board. Now that I was back in, I knew he'd be good at it despite the lack of action he was about to experience. There really was a lot of sitting and waiting involved. But once you caught a call you had to be on your game. You had to listen. But more than that, you had to know what to listen for. Because these guys were paranoid by nature, you had to learn their code. And while there wasn't any gun-slinging action, it took a deep understanding of the drug trade and the bad guys to work the wire right and not fuck everything up.

No one would have guessed that this simple building now held one of the busiest drug task forces in the country. Inside those walls, the DEA, the ATF, Border Patrol, tribal police, and various entities of local law enforcement had come together to stop one of the largest smuggling operations in the country. At any one time there could be hundreds of pounds of pot, thousands of different types of pills, cocaine, and whatever other substance might have been confiscated in the past week, sitting behind heavily padlocked doors waiting for cases to be adjudicated, after which they would be disposed of.

Randy McGuire met us at the door. "Glad you guys made it back," he said, chewing on a toothpick. "Wasn't sure if I was really going to be seeing you again so quickly, but I'm glad you all are here! One thing, though, Chief."

"What's that, Randy?"

"I'm still hungover from our night on the town."

"You young guys just don't know how to hang."

It felt good to be on that front line again. Getting away from it makes the problem seem even more enormous from a distance, and I could see how law enforcement tended to avoid even dealing with it. The problem was just so big. It almost seemed pointless to take down one group of dealers, because there was always someone to take their place. But I never looked at it that way. You had to do it. One less bad guy on the street was one less bad guy, along with the drugs that came off with him.

McGuire walked us around an area in the DTF headquarters that we hadn't seen before. The walls were covered with maps of the reservations. Homes of the known smugglers were circled, roads that led in and out of the country were highlighted, and there were "X"s marked on places where runners would most likely meet the Natives, at the hefty price of a hundred dollars per pound. Faces covered the walls. Untouchable Native faces. Natives who rarely left their sovereign land. They'd learned never to be caught with the dope themselves. It was the runner's job; that's what they got paid for, to take the risk. That explained why DTF knew their homes, knew when they had the drugs and pretty much everything they were up to, and still couldn't do anything about it. I was here to help change that.

At first glance, the wire room was clearly a disappointment to Mike Hughes. I think he was expecting something out of *Star Wars*. It looked more like an office than the futuristic control room he'd pictured. Because he'd never worked a wiretap before, Mike had no idea how advanced this facility was and the magic it would allow us to perform by negating many of the bad guys' advantages.

McGuire sat down at one of the computers. "Don't look so bummed out," he said to Mike, echoing my thoughts. "It may not look impressive but this is the most advanced tracking and monitoring system out there."

And here's how it works: We start with warrants for all the phone numbers we want to be up on. A central computer is then programmed with all those numbers, and when any one of those numbers gets called, it rings on our computer just like it does on the other end of the line. The left-hand side of the screen displays the numbers we're up on, and the number that's ringing lights up. The right-hand side of the screen, meanwhile, then has the actual conversation transcribed line by line, accompanied by our notes as to whether the specific part of the conversation was pertinent to our case or not.

That's what happens when we've got only one line running. In this case, though, we were up on nine lines total, and numerous times more than one conversation on a line we were up on would be going on. In those instances, the officer assigned to that number would put on his headphones. We'd listen in real time, not via tape, because some of these calls are constitutionally protected—conversations with a lawyer, for example. A more leisurely conversation wouldn't necessarily interest us, but we stay on the line anyway in case something pertinent and germane to our case ends up getting raised. You literally never know and have to be patient. And it can get chaotic because at times you have more than one conversation going on simultaneously in real time, which is why you need so many computers and so much manpower.

Now the waiting would begin.

B uck! Hey, Buck! Get your ass in here," Miles yelled from the wire room the very next day while I was in the map room with McGuire.

McGuire had gotten everything fired up and ready to go. He had given my guys the rundown and now all that was left was to program in the number he'd be watching and begin the listening process. That was the fun part, representing that all the details had been taken care of, all the warrants and paperwork in place. It meant we were up and running with no more bureaucracy between us and the bad guys.

I rushed inside with McGuire to find Miles and Hughes squeezed in front of the main computer, which was monitoring all the numbers we were up on.

"What have you got?" I asked Miles, as Hughes moved aside to make room for me and McGuire.

"We're up on a call from Ashley to an unidentified female," Miles said, pointing to the scroll of the conversation rolling on the opposite side of the big screen.

ASHLEY: *Seriously. No fucking way. No fucking way. How dare you fuck me over like that, bitch.*

SECOND FEMALE VOICE: *Ash, why are you losing your shit? I have no idea what you are talking about. Is it that time of the month?*

ASHLEY: *Bitch, what do you mean you don't know what I am talking about? I totally left my favorite skirt at your house and when I picked it up there was a fucking stain on it. A stain. Which means you had to wear it. Unless your couch stained it or something.*

SECOND FEMALE VOICE: *Chill out, Ashley, did you ever think that you maybe got a stain on it? You had to have swallowed at least six oxys before you stripped out of the skirt and left in your underwear before you decided you didn't like the color blue.*

PAUSE.

ASHLEY: *Oh, I didn't think of that.*

SECOND FEMALE VOICE: *All the guys in the room kept hoping your underwear was going to be blue. (GIGGLES)*

ASHLEY: *Were they really?*

McGuire shook his head, grinning.

"She is something special, isn't she?" I said, chuckling.

As I continued to watch the words scroll down the screen, I learned just how right I was.

CHAPTER THIRTY-TWO

Franklin County, New York; March 2009

When you work a case as big as this, or any case really, getting to know your targets is the first priority. You need to know them as well as they know themselves—maybe even better, since ultimately you're going to confront them with stuff they may have forgotten and they won't believe you know. You've got a very small window to convince them to turn, because the drug world operates on a very narrow clock and even stricter timetable. Runners and dealers are often supposed to call in every two hours or even more regularly. When a call doesn't come in, the next rung up the food chain knows something might be wrong. So think about what happens when some local LE sweats a suspect for eight hours, hoping to get something out of him. By the time he finally gives up, all the numbers he's got have been disconnected, because the guys above him are smart and experienced enough to know he's been taken off the streets. So the LE did it all for nothing.

I never do anything for nothing, and I knew Kevin Sorin was the weak link in this case for the same reason I knew Leo Fritz was my guy on the Brancel case: because he was vulnerable, gave me something I could exploit, which I fully intended to do working the Ohio leg of the stool. That didn't mean I had to turn Kevin into an informant; he'd never even get to hear the Bad News Talk. Kevin was ripe for the taking because I could see him making mistakes and me capitalizing on those mistakes.

I didn't view guys like Kevin as losers so much as victims of circumstances. They normally didn't intend to get in so deep, but they're up to their waist before they even know it. A lot of them, like Kevin, are young and thus prone to making more mistakes and bad choices, end up getting carried away. And thinking about that made me compare it to my own youth.

My dad started out working two jobs while going to school at night to earn a master's degree and become a teacher, and he landed a job teaching English at my high school in Akron, Ohio. My father was a stickler for discipline, and my mother followed his lead. He would say that he had seen enough kids go bad and he would not let his kid follow the road to nowhere. He was teaching during the sixties and early seventies, during the era of the revolution of peace and love and pot and acid and all the illegal substances.

LSD was the pill of choice. Kids would walk around school in a haze. I just didn't want to be like that. I don't know if it was that I heard the lectures so much at home or if it was a personal opinion, but I never once did drugs. I always kept my nose clean.

That made me pretty much the exact opposite of Kevin Sorin, who would become the centerpiece in my part of the investigation. That's the thing about these guys. With few exceptions, in my experience, the dealers are also users, and that makes them the best subjects to target. They're not always thinking straight, and sometimes their decision-making process is rooted in making sure they score their own supplies first and foremost. Beyond that, after they've had some success without detection for a while, a bulletproof mentality begins to set in. They figure because they haven't been nailed yet, they never will be. That vulnerability is what makes them the best subjects to target on the food chain, the perfect foils to take us up to the next level and beyond.

And Kevin was no exception, his entry into the world that would ultimately bring him across my path dating back to Beachwood in 2005.

CHAPTER THIRTY-THREE

How much do I owe you?" Kevin asked Ivan Ivashov.

"Four hundred dollars," Ivan replied, looking around nervously, "and I am giving you a deal. The guy I got it from said it is some primo potent shit. From fucking Canada, man."

"Better be for this much."

Kevin handed Ivan the money, walked back to the waiting car, and climbed in.

"You got it?" Mark Ververka asked, anxious to calm his nerves.

Only nineteen, Mark had been experimenting with substances for nearly five years now.

Kevin nodded. He had the smoothness and ease of a young James Dean, and was almost as good-looking, though his features were more Slavic. He also had the same nicotine habit. A nineteen-year-old high school senior who'd never really fit in or assimilated into that culture, any more than his parents had into American culture in general.

"My house?" Mark said.

Kevin offered up the same nod.

Mark lived with his parents in Willoughby. His parents had given him the basement of the house to call his own. It got him out of their way while providing a way for them to know he was safe and monitor his behavior a bit. They knew about his drug habit, but passed it off as normal behavior, because they were afraid to acknowledge the severity of his problem and, perhaps, their role in it.

The two boys made themselves comfortable, opened a beer, and turned on *Saturday Night Live*. Kevin pulled the bag out of his jeans pocket and began inspecting his latest purchase.

"Bowl, bong, or blunt?"

Kevin didn't respond.

"Dude!"

Still no response. Something from inside the bag of pot had gotten Kevin's attention.

"Hey asshole, do you want to smoke out of a bowl, bong, or blunt? Pick one."

"Check this out" was Kevin's reply, as he pulled a tiny ripped piece of paper from in between the thick furry buds.

Kevin had a faint Russian accent that he tried his best to hide. His parents had immigrated to the United States when Kevin was ten years old and his brother was seven. Kevin and his brother had tried to learn English even before the family had decided to move. He especially was determined to fit in. His parents, on the other hand, had come to this country and never once tried to learn the language. That embarrassed Kevin, but it demonstrated their reliance on the Russian community (as insular and tribal, in many ways, as that of the Akwesasne Indians who'd end up determining Kevin's ultimate fate) for work and socialization. His parents had no desire to assimilate into their new world. This was very typical of first-generation Russian immigrants. As a result, however, they weren't giving their kids the opportunity to enjoy what the rest of the kids in their school had. This wasn't quite the American dream that Kevin had anticipated, since the inability to interact with Americans his own age was denying him the kind of social opportunities and growth he might have otherwise enjoyed. His parents simply didn't trust residents of their new country and remained dependent on fellow Russians who felt exactly the same way.

"Bowl or bong?" Mark asked.

"Someone left a piece of scrap paper in the bag," Kevin told him.

"What do you want to do, roll a joint with it?"

"Stop being such a fucking tweaker and hold the fuck on. There's a number on it."

"Big whoop-de-do. We are smoking out of a bong. I've made the decision."

Mark went and pulled the bong out of the cabinet. He then yanked the bag out of Kevin's hand and packed the bowl full of the sticky green leaves. He held a lighter against the removable pipe and sucked hard.

The tube filled with smoke, and, as he pulled the pipe from the cannula, the thick gray smoke billowed into his lungs. He dropped into the couch and slouched comfortably, coughing out the remnants of the smoke.

"Okay, now I can listen to you. What were you saying about some piece of scrap paper?"

"Fuck you, dude. None of your fucking business."

"Seriously, do you have to be such a dick?"

"Fine, but whatever happens, it's mine. Got that?"

Mark rolled his eyes. "Whatever, dude. What's the big fucking deal anyway?"

"Because this phone number must belong to the supplier or something. Area code's five-one-eight. How many times we been dry the past few years?"

"Too many," Mark said, nodding.

"Maybe this is the ticket to no more dry spells." Kevin held the scrap of paper before him. "You think I should call it?"

"Dude, that number was not meant for you."

"I'm going to call it. What the fuck we got to lose? Maybe whoever answers tells us to go fuck ourselves. Maybe they don't."

Kevin pulled his phone from his pocket and dialed the number on the piece of paper.

"Yeah," a voice answered on the other end.

"Yeah, hi. I got your number, umm, from a bag I bought."

A pause followed and Kevin figured the click of the guy hanging up on him wasn't far behind. But the voice returned instead.

"Bag of what?"

"Weed."

"Good shit?"

Kevin glanced at Mark slumped on the couch, his eyes already gone glassy.

"Oh, yeah."

"This isn't my usual guy?" the voice said, in something between a statement and a question.

"No, my name is Kevin."

"You calling me from Cleveland, Kev?"

"I am."

"How do I know you're not a cop, Kev?"

"Uh, because I'm not." He almost found the question funny.

"You're telling me you're not a cop. But if you were, you'd have to tell me the truth. It's the law."

"Hey, I'm not from this country. I come from Russia."

"But you're in Cleveland now."

"Yeah," Kevin said, leaning forward. "And how'd you know that exactly?"

"Because that's where I delivered the weed you're smoking. And I'm always looking for new connects in the city. We talking about a bulk shipment of fish?"

"We are," Kevin said in return, quickly latching on to the lingo this guy was using from wherever he was. Upstate New York, from the area code.

"Okay, my man, sounds like a plan. I'll be in town next Sunday. Plan on thirty pounds of fish at thirty-two hundred dollars per pound. That is my minimum. I have your number. I will be in touch. The deal is sealed, bro, and there's no backing out. We clear?"

"We are."

"Don't fuck me, bro, or I'll take your balls." Then the voice laughed. "Nah, I'm just messing with you. Next Sunday. Be ready."

Then the click came.

Kevin was trembling when he pocketed his phone. His breathing had gone shallow.

"Like you said, dude," said Mark from the couch, "it's all yours."

"Just hand me the fucking bong."

Next Sunday came quickly, and just like the caller said, he was in touch. The call came around six P.M. and the voice laid out a set of instructions, which Kevin jotted down on the back of a pizza box.

"I'll meet you in the parking garage of Beachwood Place. I'll be across from Nordstrom in the furthest parking spot in the back. I'm in a blue pickup truck. Be there at seven. Don't be late. Do you understand?"

A simple "Yes" was all Kevin was able to get out before the caller hung up.

Kevin sat on the couch watching the clock. From his parents' house in Solon to Beachwood Place would take him twenty-five minutes. That meant he needed to leave at six thirty. Incredibly, in his first foray into drug dealing he'd already presold eight pounds of the thirty pounds of weed he was about to pick up at $3,800 per pound, a tidy $4,800 profit that still left him $25,600 tucked in the duffel bag.

Forty-eight hundred fucking dollars for barely a week's work! Fuckin' A, man!

Now, that was the American dream!

Kevin knew he'd be able to sell a good amount of the supply, but eight pounds in ten days? That was crazy, it was nuts. The city was really in need of a dealer.

I could fill that need, Kevin thought.

His contact was selling the goods for $3,200 a pound, but Kevin still wanted to up the margins and negotiate this guy down. If he could get him down to $2,900 a pound, he would make an extra $6,600 on the remaining twenty-two pounds he had to sell—almost $25,000 from one random phone call to a number plucked from a bag of weed. Now all he had to do was get to Beachwood Place and do the deal.

Kevin's 1994 green Ford Taurus pulled in to the quiet parking garage, passing a few Mercedeses and Lexuses parked in the front. In the last parking spot near the wall, hidden in the shadows, was the blue pickup truck, just as the voice had said. Kevin pulled up next to the truck. Inside was a good-looking guy with a crew cut. The driver didn't look much older than Kevin. He didn't seem threatening or intimidating. And he was alone. What happened to soldiers in the drug trade traveling in armies?

"You must be Kevin," the guy said, without ever making eye contact.

Kevin got out of his car, leaving it running in case he needed to make a quick getaway. He walked closer to the guy's window.

"I am," Kevin said, breathing easy now. "Who are you?"

"I'm Danny. You have the money?"

"I only have twenty-five thousand six hundred on me, but I'll get the rest no problem. I just need the stuff."

Three years before the drug world would cost Danny Simonds his life, he barely regarded Kevin at all until he finally turned and made eye contact. "Okay, I'll take what you've got. You have twenty-four hours to get rid of the rest of the fish," Danny said, looking away again, "and get me the rest of what you owe."

"Come on, dude. That's one day."

"Call it a test, *dude*," Danny said, seeming to mock Kevin a bit. "If you want to deal for us, you need to prove you're up to it."

Kevin thought about his American dream. He thought about the cash he could make in such a short period of time. More than he'd ever imagined. More than his parents would see in a lifetime working odd jobs for Russian friends who couldn't even speak English. Maybe he even visualized the kind of lifestyle getting into the drug business could provide. The kind of house, car, and toys that his association with this runner named Danny, born this very day, would ultimately yield him.

"Thirty-two hundred a pound is too much," he heard himself say, like it was someone else talking. "Especially if you're giving me only a day to unload the whole supply. Twenty-nine hundred is more fair."

Then Kevin waited as Danny considered the offer.

"What do you say?" Kevin added, when Danny continued to remain silent.

Danny's face was expressionless. Kevin had no idea what to read from that.

"That's fine," Danny said finally. "But for that price you'll have to move fifty pounds and the amount is not negotiable."

"The deal was for thirty."

"You just changed the deal."

Then Danny took a pair of sunglasses off the dashboard and climbed out of his truck. He took the bag of cash from Kevin's grasp.

"We good?"

"Wait, you're leaving?"

"Our business is done. Fish are in the back."

"You brought all fifty pounds with you?"

Danny smirked. "Guess I was a step ahead of you. You can handle the loading. I'm going to the mall. See you back here in twenty-four hours."

Danny walked off, leaving Kevin standing next to Danny's truck wondering what he'd just gotten himself into.

How the hell am I supposed to sell forty-two pounds of pot in twenty-four hours? I am so fucking dead!

Kevin loaded the duffel bags packed with weed into the trunk of his Taurus and headed toward Mark Ververka's house. His friend was playing a video game and smoking a joint when Kevin pulled in to his driveway.

"I've got forty-two pounds of weed in the trunk we have to unload," he told Mark.

"What? No fucking way, dude! Seriously? Sweet!"

"Not sweet. I have to sell it all by tomorrow. I owe the guy, like, fucking a hundred and twenty thousand bucks or . . ." Kevin let his words trail off, unsure of the rest himself.

"Are you fucking kidding?"

"No, asshole, I'm not. This is like fucking Donnie Brasco. Fucking white dude works for someone who wants their money in twenty-four hours. Now start calling people. We need a place to store all this shit."

"We?"

"I'll cut you in, bro."

"How much?"

"Name it."

"Fifty-fifty."

"Too much."

"Then you name it."

They settled at seventy-thirty. Kevin and Mark created a home base at the Super 8 motel in Beachwood. They waited until it was late and carried in the pot. They called everyone they knew and told those people to call everyone they knew. Kevin guarded the home base, while Mark worked as a runner. And Kevin put his younger brother, Alexander, to work, figuring he was doing the kid a favor, giving him a chance to make a few bucks. Kevin and Mark called everyone that they ever bought pot from, dating back to middle school. A bunch of the numbers had been disconnected. A bunch of them were answered.

Kevin found that he was good working the numbers. He was meticulous in a way he'd never been before. Fuck school—this was the real deal, the real thing. He kept detailed sheets of who bought what, a future business blooming right before his eyes, with him as the boss. Divvying the shit up and paying a sliding commission scale to his people first day out. The more they moved, the better they did.

The American fucking dream. Oh yeah . . .

The stack of pot dwindled quickly and the stack of money grew just as fast. As the sun began sucking up the last of the night, all the pot was gone and Kevin fell onto one of the twin beds laughing. He wasn't quite sure how they'd done it. It felt surreal; shit, maybe it never happened at all and he'd just hallucinated the whole thing. As if to reassure himself it was real, Kevin counted the stack of money: $168,000. He pulled out the $121,800 for Danny. Then he started laughing. And laughing some more.

He had just made $46,200 in one night, *one night*!

What nineteen-year-old could say that, never mind one who was a Russian immigrant?

It made him want to sing the fucking "Star-Spangled Banner."

Oh say can you see, by the dawn's early light . . .

Kevin forgot the words after that.

He waited anxiously for seven P.M., couldn't wait to show Danny that he was worthy of dealing for him, as if the stranger's approval meant something. Kevin started thinking of the last time an adult had approved of anything he did, including his parents. Then he quickly stopped bothering.

They met in the same parking garage, just a few spaces down from where Danny had parked the day before. He was waiting for Kevin in the shadows of the garage. Kevin pulled up next to him and stepped out. Danny sat in his truck with the driver's-side window down.

Kevin handed him a Dollar Store handle bag. "Your money's all there, dude."

Danny peered inside the bag. "No shit . . ." He peeled some of the bills back, doing a rough count.

"It's all there," Kevin said defensively.

"I have no doubt. You in for more?"

"You bet your ass. Just name the time and the place."

"First things first. You need to come to the res and meet Alan."

"Alan? . . . Res?"

"I'm just the runner. Alan's the head honcho. He lives on an Indian reservation in upstate New York. Runs the operation from there. If he is going to front you that much shit, he's gonna want to meet you. Check your schedule."

"I'm available."

"When?"

"Anytime."

"So you're in."

"I'm in.

Franklin County, New York; March 2009

Kevin was in all right, and before long he'd be in over his head. Dealers and runners can take all the precautions and safety measures, pay all the bribes, they want. But nobody remains untouchable for long, never mind for good. Danny Simonds learned that the hardest way possible, and Kevin Sorin was about to learn the same lesson.

A drug investigation is about going after the weakest link possible. You gather evidence in large part through surveillance, OnStar, and investigative techniques, make your case, and then grab the suspect in order to float a deal in front of him. He gives up everyone he knows and he does less time, maybe none at all.

But Kevin's profile, and predicament, also exemplified something else I'd seen in any number of drug dealers I'd come across, namely that it's an intoxicating world (no pun intended). Kind of reminds me of the great line from the Eagles' classic song "Hotel California": "You can check out anytime you want, but you can never leave."

Kevin might have tried to check out of the life on any number of occasions, but he never did leave either.

CHAPTER THIRTY-FOUR

T he room was spinning, faster and faster and faster. Once the room got up to a good speed, the internal drums started beating. That was how Kevin's mornings always started. He began to take it as a sign that he'd actually lived through the night. He'd survived another night of pills, coke, ecstasy, and alcohol.

Reason for celebration in itself.

He turned toward Ashley, who was passed out in the bed next to him. He wasn't sure if she was dead or not. He was always worried that her hundred-and-five-pound frame wouldn't make it through one of their nights of partying. Who was he kidding, they weren't even nights of partying anymore; they were *days* of popping oxy, just so the withdrawal didn't set in. Best he could figure, they were running a tab of about $20,000 a week on pills.

As in $80,000 per month. As in nearly $1 million a year. Eating up a sizable share of his income from dealing.

The thought made him want to throw up. Either that or maybe it was the heroin he smuggled back with him on his last run. Hard to tell which, a combination even.

"Ash, get up," Kevin said as he nudged her limp body, "get up!"

It was Sunday and time for another run, the endless days that had begun at Danny Simonds's funeral when Kim had put him in touch with the Frasers to replace the product he had been getting from Danny. He had to make all the drives himself now, because, according to Noah King, the Frasers didn't deliver. In point of fact, the Frasers didn't deliver because they couldn't; as non-Natives living off the res, they lacked the credibility that Noah required for him to front them the dope for an extended period. Picking up his money two or three hours after he dropped the weed off for the Frasers to sell was one thing; fronting it for the several days it would take some driver hired by the Frasers to get back and forth to Beachwood was something else again. So if Kevin wanted the weed, he had to come and get it; it wasn't coming to him.

He wasn't sure how he could possibly make it all the way to St. Lawrence County. Maybe he'd crash into a tree and kill them both. That was a good way out. He'd been thinking about it a lot lately—getting out, that is, though not necessarily via some car wreck. Trouble was he knew it wasn't possible. No one gets out. Not when you are in as deep as he was. One of those crazy Natives would come down here and do him in just like they did Danny. He'd rather get done in by a tree than a crazy Indian. Maybe today would be the day. Seemed to him that Ashley might have been a step ahead of him.

"Ash, get up! Time to go!"

Ashley threw her bony arm into the air and waved it around.

"What the fuck is that supposed to mean?" Kevin asked her.

"Water," was the only word Ashley could muster through remnants of crystallized cocaine on her tongue.

Kevin tossed a bottle at her. She flipped over just enough so she could pour the water into her mouth, never even opening her eyes.

"Can't go," she said, and flopped back onto her belly.

Kevin grabbed the water bottle off of the bed, turned the cap, and poured it all over his zombie of a girlfriend.

"What the fuck?" she said, jerking upright.

"Get your ass out of bed. Get dressed. We're driving up to St. Lawrence. Now! My dad is already in the driveway."

Ashley knew when not to push things too far, and when it came to Kevin's business, being too late would be pushing it too far. She fumbled out of bed.

"You almost ready?" Kevin yelled to her five minutes later, while she stood leaning against a wall, collecting her balance. The room seemed to be tilting from side to side.

"Hold your fucking horses," she yelled back, the rush of adrenaline from getting pissed at Kevin bringing her back to life. "I'm coming."

"Bring the oxy. I'm carrying the cash to my dad. He's in the driveway."

Kevin quickly put the cash, packed into hollowed-out computer towers, in the trunk of the rental car his father was driving and sent him on his way. There wasn't much to talk about. Having done this run almost every week for months now, they had the drill down. He needed his dad on the road ahead of him to run interference and ensure that Kevin wouldn't go down with the money if he was pulled over. His father had the insulation that comes with being adult, mature in appearance. Guy like him gets stopped, cop writes a ticket. Young guy like Kevin gets stopped, maybe because somebody's been warned to look out for him, cop gives him a much closer look and maybe notices the stale odor of weed in the car. Probable cause for a search.

Paranoia, typical of any drug dealer but especially one who sampled his own product as much as Kevin did.

Although it didn't seem like a completely normal choice to most to make his father the chase car, it did to Kevin. He needed someone he could trust. Someone he could control. Someone who would never run away with the cash, which was held in the chase car. And who would never turn on him if he got caught. Ashley was not that person. Plus, his dad needed the money. His parents had migrated from Russia to give their kids a better life, right?

Well, based on Kevin's current economic standing, they'd certainly done that much, albeit not on their own behalf. They never even took the time to learn to speak English. Their opportunities were pretty bleak. This was Kevin's chance to give his parents a better life. He honestly believed that. Call it payback.

Kevin beeped the horn for Ashley. Finally she sulked out of the house. She didn't look like the same girl he had met years before. The drugs had started to take a toll on her. Her once-glowing skin had become gray and ashlike. She was nothing but bones, her skin sagging over them like stretched-out cotton. Today she was looking especially pale and listless. She sat down in the passenger seat next to him. She looked like a lump of laundry: a baseball hat, a Juicy Couture tracksuit, and oversized sunglasses. Kevin wondered if he'd ever find her even remotely attractive again.

"Let the journey begin," Kevin said as the red Honda with New York plates, courtesy of Hertz in Beachwood, pulled out of the driveway.

Kevin made a right out of Bryden Road onto Richmond Road, made a left onto Chagrin Boulevard, and started out down 271 North. Ashley was curled in a ball, headphones shoved into her ears, attached to an iPod full of teenybopper music lulling her back to sleep.

Kevin picked up his burner phone and dialed Harold Fraser's number.

"Yeah," a gruff voice answered.

"Be there by seven or so," Kevin informed him.

"How much fish you wanting?"

"Usual."

"Okay. I'll be waiting."

Kevin hung up the phone and turned on the radio. Smooth sailing from here. Or so he thought.

CHAPTER THIRTY-FIVE

Because what he didn't know was that while he was running up to New York, my team and I were busy running the plates on every car that had ever been in and out of his driveway. We had contacted LEADS (Law Enforcement Automated Data System) for an offline records check to identify all the various locations where the vehicles were being operated, as well as when they were checked or stopped by law enforcement in the past twelve months.

We had also sent out subpoenas for Kevin's and Ashley's checking accounts, phone records, credit cards, and any other paper trail we could find for them, as well as for Kevin's parents, Boris and Loudmilla Sorin, and Ashley's parents, Richard and Mary Louise Schmid. We had already seen that Boris was helping his son, and we had a sneaking suspicion that he wasn't the only parent endorsing a child's illegal career choice.

Upon research of the parents, we found out that Kevin's unemployed father had two vehicles in his name. His mother was employed in a low level at Key Bank, but she had four vehicles in her name. They lived in a middle-class neighborhood in Solon, Ohio. Neither of his parents had a criminal record, or any visible or viable source of income that could possibly explain their housing and their ownership of six cars.

Sometimes a paper trail is just that. You just have to learn how to follow it.

Ashley's parents appeared to be a bit more dysfunctional, both having criminal records. Both had been arrested on numerous charges. Richard currently owned a small business and Mary Louise worked at Target, in the eyeglasses department.

But with everything I had under way on my end Kevin could breathe easy today; he was safe. I wasn't grabbing him now. There wouldn't be much sense in that. I was making a historical case and that meant going as deep into the network and as far back in time as I possibly could. That's the very definition of "ironclad" in court. And to achieve that benchmark I'd need as much evidence as I could get. That would take time and mean following him on several of these runs. Watching how he moved the money. Letting the information we gathered now lead us on to even more information. It was about following clue after clue.

And I needed to make sure the targets wouldn't walk, and it didn't hurt that there was always a larger grab at the end. You always want to get these guys on a money day. That was my plan. Because whatever we seize goes into the drug fund. And right now, with his average money grabs, as far as I could tell, we were looking at some pretty big numbers. No way was I giving that up for a quick pop. I had big plans for Kevin in the end.

Kevin made it safely to Harold and Sabrina Fraser's house right on time. Harold heard the cars pull up the gravel driveway. He was waiting for both Boris and Kevin on the porch of his cabin. Harold liked to bullshit with Kevin. Kevin always thought it was because he really didn't like his wife, Sabrina, since other than drugs and the local general store they ran together as a front for their real business, Harold and Sabrina had absolutely nothing in common. Harold and Kevin spent most of their time talking about the "work," the weather, or some other bullshit topic Harold could dig up. This usually made time for Sabrina and Ashley to bicker about anything and everything. Rarely did it get physical, but there were always threats. What you learn about mopes like them is that they hate themselves more than anyone.

And they never change. They just keep on keeping on. Call it the allure of the business and being addicts themselves—the worst of all possible combinations.

Boris was always the mule, with Danny out of the picture. Kevin would pack his father's trunk with the drugs collected at the Frasers', because he knew it was best for his father to carry. Cops and Border Patrol were far less likely to pull over a guy in his fifties than they were a couple of twentysomethings. Beyond that, Kevin was always craving and needing pills on his way back. Coming all this way only to face the realization that he had to turn around and repeat the process was becoming more and more daunting with each run. He knew that this couldn't go on much longer. All it took was a good look at Harold and Sabrina to know that his lifestyle couldn't have a happy ending under any circumstances. Death was more becoming than turning into isolated hillbillies as they had. Hell, they looked more like meth users than high-end dealers.

Something made Kevin study Harold in more detail on this unseasonably cool day with a bite in the air and the overcast sky falsely promising snow. Harold's face looked like a mesh mask pocked with acne-like scars and webbed with red spider veins. His eyes were slow and lifeless, his teeth brown and rotting, and his lips dried and chapping.

Is this how I'm going to end up?

Standing on the porch of Harold's house, surrounded by the frosty winds so known to St. Lawrence County, Kevin decided that he was going to rehab and taking Ashley with him whether she liked it or not.

CHAPTER THIRTY-SIX

W hen was the last time you took any substances?" Shawna, the intake coordinator at MDS Drug Detox, asked Kevin and Ashley, as I would later learn through an informant.

Ashley was passed out in the armchair, a pile of fuzzy pink Juicy Couture. Kevin was at least awake, or at least he thought he was awake. He could see the woman that he had spoken on the phone with just five days ago.

"Excuse me. Mr. Sorin? Ms. Schmid? Are you two all right?" she asked again, although she already knew the answer. "Can you hear me okay?"

Kevin mumbled something, and Ashley nodded after a pause.

"When was the last time you took any substances?" Shawna asked again.

The words pulsed in Kevin's head. Should he tell this woman that they'd taken all the remaining pills they had in the car when they arrived in the parking lot? They had decided that if they were going to rehab they were going in stoned out of their minds. One last hurrah. He knew it wasn't the best idea, but no one ever said he was known for having the best ideas.

"Mr. Sorin? Ms. Schmid?" she said again, rising from her chair to check on them.

Kevin was conscious, and his eyes were open, but he was so high that all he could do was slur his words.

"I'm guessing you came in here rather high," Shawna said as she looked at Kevin's dilated pupils.

Kevin tried to nod and failed.

"Don't worry," Shawna resumed. "It's pretty typical. You seemed pretty desperate when we spoke on the phone. I am going to get an orderly to help me get you to your room. We can't start the procedure until we speak more; however, I will let you come down from this high in the room you will be in for the next several days. We can talk when you're feeling more up to it."

Kevin and Ashley woke up the next morning to find Shawna waiting, coffee and paperwork in hand.

"How are you feeling today?" Shawna asked, sounding as if she really cared.

"Like I got hit by a fucking truck," Ashley answered, rubbing her head and then massaging her temples.

"I don't doubt that at all," Shawna replied, ignoring the foul mouth. "I have all the paperwork about the treatment we will be providing you right here," she continued, as she handed them each their own folder. "As I stated on the phone, this is a bit more aggressive than your typical rehab facility, but from what you told me it seems that this is the type of treatment you require. What you will be undergoing is a rapid detox under sedation. All of the opiates will be removed from your system and your brain receptors while you are sleeping. Because of this, you will not feel any of the symptoms of withdrawal. You will be in this sedative state for three days. Any questions so far?"

"Are we drug-free after this?" Ashley asked.

"You will have skipped all the terrible withdrawal symptoms you hear so much about, but that is just the first start to your sobriety. You are going to have a long haul ahead of you. I highly recommend getting into a program when you return home. You may want to consider an inpatient program, as opposed to outpatient," Shawna suggested. "You made a big investment in your sobriety by coming here. But this is just the beginning."

Ashley rolled her eyes. Shawna had been in this job long enough to be able to tell the ones that were going to make it and the ones that weren't, and this one wasn't. Not with this attitude.

"We won't feel anything?" Kevin asked her.

"Not a thing," Shawna began. "We just need to get the paperwork filled out and then we can get started."

"Where do we sign?" Ashley asked.

She and Kevin had barely finished filling in all the blanks when a knock fell on the door.

"Oh, this is Chris," Shawna said, as a man wearing a similar identification tag clipped to his lapel entered. "He'll be your nurse. He'll get you both set up, and will be monitoring you throughout the procedure."

"Time to start prepping them," Chris told Shawna.

"Before that happens, do you have any more questions?" Shawna asked.

"No, thank you," Kevin replied. "I think we've got it."

"Chris can answer them, right?" Ashley said.

Chris gave Ashley a cheesy smile that made Kevin want to gag but evoked a chirpy giggle out of Ashley.

Chris was thirty-three with a potbelly and growing bald spot. Anticool, in Ashley's mind, and she couldn't help picturing herself in ten years or so going down this road, enough to make her question if listening to Kevin and giving up the oxy was such a good idea after all.

"I'm here for all your needs," Chris said to Ashley.

She wouldn't give this loser the time of day outside of this place.

"Seriously, dude?" Kevin asked Chris, before she could respond.

"Sorry, man, your needs too."

"Whatever," Kevin replied.

Chris began setting up two IV preps. He started babbling on about how he was going to put their IVs in and get them all ready for the doctor. That he was going to do all the work and he was going to be the one monitoring. Ashley was eating up all the bullshit, Kevin thought—that, or trying to piss him off for making her come here. Either way, he figured, they would both be unconscious soon.

Sure enough, they spent the next three days in a vegetative state, zonked out of their minds while the opiates detached from the receptors in their brains. They woke up on a sunny Thursday morning feeling fresh and renewed and were released the following morning to live a drug-free life.

"Aren't you glad we did this?" Kevin asked Ashley as he sped down I-90 East.

"As long as you don't think I'm ever going back."

"You're never going to need to go back. Now I just need to get out of the business. . . ."

Ashley practically jumped out of her skin. "What the fuck? No fucking way! How will we live?" she asked, infuriated. "Are you fucking nuts?"

Ashley, like just about all drug dealers and their significant others, had gotten very used to the lifestyle smuggling millions of dollars of drugs had enabled her to live. Luxury was not something she was willing to give up. Nor was the ability to buy anything she wanted pretty much anytime she wanted it.

"You know Chris gave me his number in case I needed him while I was transitioning to a clean life," Ashley said.

"Is that supposed to make me jealous?"

"I'm only talking here."

"Talking bullshit. I saw the way you looked at that guy. If he asked for your number, you'd make one up."

"Fuck you."

"You mean, as opposed to Chris the nurse. Why don't you move in with him, see if you like living in some ratty one-bedroom apartment?"

"Fuck you," Ashley said again. "And—"

Kevin's phone started ringing, and she stopped there. He flipped it open. At that moment even Ashley knew to stop running her mouth. Business.

Kevin answered with his typical greeting. "Yeah."

"K, it's V," said Mark Ververka.

CHAPTER THIRTY-SEVEN

Hey, Mike! Mike, wake up! We got something big this time!" Joe Miles yelled.

Mike and Miles had been working the wire room for a week, and nothing. The lines we'd secured warrants for had been silent while Kevin and Ashley underwent their pricey detox. My guys were getting the taste of what a true undercover drug case was about: waiting, lots of waiting for the targets to make their next move.

Mike wiped the bit of drool off his face and slowly stretched out. Sitting on the chairs was becoming achy even for his twenty-six-year-old back.

"Who we got on the line?" Mike asked, perking up.

"Kevin and a guy named V. I'm guessing it's Mark Ververka," Miles said, as the conversation scrolled up the right-hand side of the screen.

MARK: *The crew is asking for fish.*

KEVIN: *It may stay dry for a while.*

MARK: *Fuck that, dude. Don't be a pussy. I will come there and beat your detoxed ass if you think I'm giving up this gig and watch Cleveland go dry as a desert.*

ASHLEY: *(background—muffled) You tell him.*

MARK: *Dude, I'm serious. You gotta chill here. How can you let Cleveland turn into a desert? You have a responsibility here!*

KEVIN: *I'll figure something out.*

Click-clack.

The sound of the call ending.

"Should we tell Buck?" Mike asked Miles.

"Not yet. Let's see what the kid is going to do," Miles replied.

Miles and Mike sat quietly staring at the walls of computers, willing them to buzz. Both of them wanted desperately for the case to start heating up. It had been a slow go so far, and this wasn't what they thought it was going to be like. Sure, I'd warned and advised them on how things were likely to play. But some things have to be experienced firsthand, and a drug investigation, making a strong case, is one of them. Neither of them could say that putting all the paperwork in place and scouring through the thousands of pages of phone records hadn't been worth the time; it had. They had discovered several key players in the food chain.

I had taught them that while we were going after the big fish there were also several tiny fish in the sea we could catch along the way. Kevin's and Ashley's records had cast a large net. We were going to be able to grab a lot of little fish once the big fish were out of the way. It just took a lot of planning. We had to be ready to grab the little fish right after the big fish were snatched up. Cast one large net. Everyone gets startled when anyone gets hooked, be it above or below them on the food chain.

The central monitoring computer lit up with Kevin's number, the scroll on the other side of the screen commencing immediately.

MALE VOICE: Who the hell is this?

KEVIN: It's me.

MALE VOICE: Who the fuck is me?

KEVIN: Me, Harold, it's K.

HAROLD: Why didn't you just say so? What's up?

KEVIN: (clears his throat) Pick up next Sunday? Usual?

HAROLD: Whoa, that's such short notice and Sabrina ain't going to want to go over to the res. And what if I can't reach Noah?

KEVIN: Not this Sunday. Next Sunday. I think it's April fifth or seventh or something. Think you can make that happen?

HAROLD: That I can do.

KEVIN: Think you should write that down somewhere, so you don't forget?

HAROLD: You're a smart-ass, kid.

Click-clack.

And the line went dead.

Miles smiled wide, looking toward Hughes. "Hey, Mike, *now* it's time to tell the chief."

CHAPTER THIRTY-EIGHT

Franklin County, New York; March 2009

A lot of younger guys, and others new to the game, like to call me old-school, a dinosaur in how I go about running an investigation, and, you know, they're mostly right. They're all on Facebook and Twitter, while I can't always remember my e-mail address. But here's the thing: drug dealers don't use social media. They don't post pictures of themselves with their latest stash on their Facebook pages and don't use Twitter to communicate with their couriers. So you can be as savvy with social media as it goes, and you're still going to have to go out, do your surveillance, pick up the trail and follow it wherever it leads.

What's changed in the drug business that makes our job really difficult is the sophistication of big networks, like the one we were targeting in upstate New York, in their business practices. As far as the size and scope of the operation, this case kind of resembled another I'd put long years into around the same time as the Brancel case. It, too, covered much of the country, and it centered on an Ohio man named Richard Heckman, who was moving a thousand pounds of marijuana every two weeks. I worked that case for seven years. Ended up in Texas four times and California three times, with stops in Nicaragua, Costa Rica, Canada, and Colombia thrown in for good measure. This was a huge case too, and I ran it from the get-go.

That's my message to police departments across the country, no matter how small your agency: You can run any size case you want to run. A lot of the guys I work with say I'm a hard charger. I guess I am. I expect a lot from the people who work for me, but I don't ask anyone to do something I wouldn't do myself. That's why I've still got my nose in it; it's the only way I know.

The Heckman case revealed a massive, complex nationwide organization. His product came in from two sources: Robert "Robbie" Barnes in California and Frank Courtland Teek out of Texas. Richard Heckman might not have been as daring, but he had the whole operation down to a science, running like clockwork. He and his partner had built a network of thirteen or fourteen major players to move that thousand pounds of pot every two weeks. It would come in these Mylar-wrapped packets maybe two feet long, eighteen inches across, and four inches thick—hundreds of them packed into cardboard boxes loaded onto semis. That thousand pounds went for $1,600 per pound wholesale to their dealers. The street value of each ounce, meanwhile, was a cool thousand bucks. That meant they were moving $16 million street value of product every two weeks for however many months they operated during the year, which might have been only three or four. All the rest of the time was spent trying to figure out how to stash all those profits while enjoying them. Drug dealers, I guess, like to have lives too.

Heckman and his people ran their operation like a narcotics version of Walmart. Those individual packets trucked in from California or Texas came with bar codes that listed their precise weights. This was business to them and that's how they treated it when it came to keeping meticulous records, all by hand in ledgers. They even maintained a *restocking charge* for bags that came through damaged. They had it down to the point where they could off-load an entire shipment and have it on the street in two days. The affidavit that got us the wiretaps and search warrants on the organization was nineteen pages and listed a whole lot of names, dates, times, and locations. It makes the whole process look easy and doesn't account for the thousands of hours it takes to put a crack in an operation of this scale, or the kind that Alan Jacobs had established on the Akwesasne reservation, and that Noah King had taken over after Jacobs had been taken into custody on the Danny Simonds murder.

I'd like to tell you that busting Heckman's near-billion-dollar-annual drug operation, along with the national network behind it, was because of ingenious police work. Maybe it was. Depends on your definition, I guess. See, a lot of what a team, a task force, does is sit around and talk. Over breakfast, lunch, dinner, drinks—anything. We talk about what we've learned most recently and how that squares with what we already know. We basically think out loud. It's one of the reasons I never listen to the radio or talk on the phone through all the long drives I make when I'm normally alone. It's great thinking time to try to figure if there's anything I've missed and how exactly I'm going to nail this guy or that one. What's the angle? Where's their weak spot?

In the Heckman case, one of the guys we really wanted to nail was Frank Tawlberg. We knew Tawlberg was the main warehouser for a lot of Heckman's money and dope, working directly for an organization kingpin named McDivitt. We wanted McDivitt so he could give us Heckman, and Tawlberg was the direct link to McDivitt. But this guy was completely off the grid. He was dark. We could never pull a phone bill, a utility bill, a tax bill—nothing. As far as the world was concerned, he owned nothing and basically didn't exist. We had him narrowed down to a five- or ten-square-mile area in rural Trumbull County. But the roads were so flat and straight we couldn't risk a standard surveillance-style sweep operation because there's no place we could remain out of sight.

We looked for Tawlberg, the key to cracking the whole case wide open, for three years. Then one day I was out riding around on a beautiful fall day, covering the same five square miles I'd covered a thousand times before. I was running the case through my mind, trying to lock onto something I hadn't considered yet. So I drive down this rural road and it turns out to be trash day, and I looked over to my right at random and spot these four trash cans on the edge of somebody's yard that have TAWLBERG spray-painted in yellow on them.

Turned out I was finally able to nab a guy I'd been tracking and trailing for three years because kids had been stealing his trash cans, and he painted his name on them. So for something you can buy for ten bucks, I was able to finally find the man responsible for storing both the pot and the money that came in from selling it.

Tawlberg was a concrete worker and it turned out he'd built a secret passage under his garage leading to a thousand-gallon storage tank directly under a woodstove. That's where we found the drugs and the cash. Tawlberg also kept meticulous ledgers containing who was taking what and how much. But there were only initials, no names, so we needed him to do the math for us and send us up the food chain to McDivitt and then, ultimately, to Heckman himself. The goal then, as had been the case with Brancel, would be to get Heckman to roll on his suppliers so we could shut the whole network down nationwide. When you consider that Heckman was just one of the guys Barnes and Teek were distributing to, the sum total of their haul would stretch well into the billions.

The case got even stranger from there. Thanks to what we got from Tawlberg, we set up surveillance across the board, from Heckman himself to all his known associates, even to his mother. I was in a car, my Cadillac STS at the time, watching Heckman myself, and I had a DEA agent named Phil Garillo and my prosecutor with me. Phil was a vet of both Vietnam and the drug wars. A Special Forces type who was part of Operation Snowcap we ran against the coco labs in the Colombian jungles. He'd rappel out of helicopters to blow up labs and was no stranger to guns or actually using them.

It was a hundred degrees on a steaming July day and Phil wasn't even breaking a sweat, but my prosecutor was fidgeting like crazy in the backseat, when out of his house walked Richard Heckman himself. He came right up to the car, shaking his fist and threatening us.

"Why you guys driving down my fucking road?" he demanded.

By that time Phil had his .40 caliber aimed, ready to shoot through the door if it came to that. No way we could know if Heckman was carrying and a gunfight was in the offing. My prosecutor, meanwhile, had his fingers in his ears. Seven years we'd been after Heckman, seven years, and he had walked right out of the bushes and was now staring us in the face. We shrugged it off, telling him we were lost, and got out of there with no shots fired.

But it wasn't much later that Heckman went down anyway. Tawlberg gave me enough to go after his top two associates, Joe Thatcher and Robert McDivitt, but I still needed someone to roll on them so I could get them to roll on Heckman. The key cog in that machine turned out to be a guy who called himself Sundance, whom I paid a visit to lay everything out. At this point, I knew he had a bunch of cash stashed that he couldn't spend without getting nabbed. I proceeded to lay it out for him, a different variation on my Bad News Talk.

"I've got a hypothetical situation for you, Sundance. You've got a bunch of money put away you can't spend. But because you're going to be helping me make this case, I've got a proposition for you: Turn in your cash and I'll give you a finder's fee of sixty percent."

And damn if two days later he didn't show up at the station with a half million dollars in cash. I had the evidence officer inventory it, and within six months I cut him a check for $300,000 to keep all to himself while my department netted $200,000 on a deal where everybody came out a winner.

Well, not everybody. Sundance gave me Thatcher and McDivitt. As a local paper called the *Beacon* reported on November 19, 1996, "A drug ring investigation in Summitt, Portage, Trumbull and Mahoning counties has resulted in 13 defendants pleading guilty to marijuana distribution charges—and forfeitures of money, cars and other items with a total value of nearly $2 million. . . . The seized money and items include $1.3 million in cash confiscated at the home of the ringleader, Robert McDivitt."

A big chunk of that $2 million forfeiture went to my own department, funds crucial to bankrolling further drug efforts while supplying funding for additional personnel and training. By the way, the stash included a backhoe and a bulldozer.

But this complex case wasn't over yet. Heckman had a whole bunch of assets still floating out there, assets I wanted and was entitled to if I could get my hands on them. He would drive cash from Ohio to Miami and give the cash to a Miami attorney who'd then fly it himself to an attorney in Costa Rica. The job of the Costa Rican attorney was to buy and clear the land, and then build an oceanfront hotel to wash the money, managing the project from start to finish. The property would be in that lawyer's name along with another friend of Heckman's in Costa Rica he utilized because he didn't entirely trust the Costa Rican lawyer. Big surprise, right?

That trail took me all the way to Costa Rica, where I met with the actual attorney fronting the whole money-laundering operation through construction of the oceanfront hotel. He gave me the name of the Miami attorney who'd brought him the money, and two or three weeks later I found myself sitting in his conference room having a nice friendly chat.

"You don't want to be associated with this guy, you hear me?" I said, referring to Heckman.

He did but said nothing. Didn't even nod.

"Here's what we're going to do," I told him. "Your retainer represents proceeds of a crime. You're going to write me a check for the full amount of that retainer and I walk out of this office and forget we had this meeting. How's that sound?"

I knew it must have sounded good by the way he looked at me, still quiet. I'd just started to continue when his secretary walked in.

"Detective Buck has a call," she said.

Which was very strange because almost nobody knew where I was, and the few that did would've called me on my cell phone. So I took the call on an extension right there in the conference room.

"Detective Buck?"

I recognized the voice of Herb, the US attorney who handles seizures and forfeitures, immediately but didn't say his name out loud. "Yes, sir."

"You need to get out of that office," he said after introducing himself. "Don't take a check and call me back when you're in a safe place."

Now, as Herb said this, the lawyer walked back into the conference room with check literally in hand. But I excused myself anyway, went outside, and dialed Herb back.

"What gives?" I asked him. "How the fuck did you know I'm in Florida?"

"How do you think? The building is wired. We're looking at this guy for more than just this piddly shit."

"Piddly shit? The guy was getting ready to hand me a check for seventy thousand dollars. I'm going back in there and get it."

"You can't."

"Say that again?"

"As a favor to me, Detective. I'll make it up to you. I promise. But this is an ongoing case and we simply can't risk having it compromised."

"So what do you want me to do?"

"Get on a plane. Go back home."

I looked back up at the building, giving serious consideration to ignoring him, but I knew I couldn't, just like I knew something else. "No one will ever get this guy, Herb. I'm walking away from seventy thousand dollars that would come back with me to Cleveland for absolutely nothing."

"We'll get him."

"We'll see."

I hung up and went home, playing the good soldier. Ten years have passed since that day and no one has indicted that particular lawyer.

And that's not the only thing some officials don't get. The thing that makes me different is how I treat my informants. I treat them the way I'd like to be treated, with dignity and respect. And that's worked so well for me, I can't even begin to detail all I've gained from it. Most cops treat their informants like shit and then wonder why they never get much out of them. Not me. I take them to dinner, get to know them, what's up with their families, their lives—the whole drill. I let them see I care about them because I really do. Consequently, I'm able to make cases others can't. If you want to thrive in this world as long as I have, you've got to be good in the room; you've gotta mean what you say and have the integrity to back it up. I do the right thing. I mean what I say and the informants know it, just like they know if they fuck with me I'll put them in prison. But treat me fair and I'll go the extra mile for you.

The reality is you can't get something out of somebody if right from the start you're looking at them the way you would a sex offender. These guys are criminals, they're drug dealers, and once they're in that room with you, they know you've got all the power. Hey, I tell them, look, your back's against the wall but you can do something to help yourself. If you lie to me, you're going to get an extra five years. But if you work with me, I'll stand by you and try my damn best to get the lightest sentence possible.

They go along with it almost all the time, in large part because I've got a reputation and chances are they've heard of me. It's gotten to the point where I get calls from other jurisdictions sometimes far outside my own asking me to come in and mediate a case; that they've got a suspect in custody who'll agree to talk only to me. Almost all of the time, I'll make the drive and have the Bad News Talk with him on the other department's behalf. Sometimes it's even his lawyer who calls me. It's a big world, yet in this respect anyway, it's kind of small.

When I was sitting there in that wire room in March of 2009, though, the only part of the world I cared about started with the ice bridge over which drugs were flowing like water through the Akwesasne Indian reservation and ended up eight hundred miles away in Ohio, where I needed to figure out how to use Kevin Sorin to get me to the top of the food chain.

Before I could give that any further thought, though, my cell phone rang.

"Hey," my old pal Frenchie greeted from north of the border, "remember I said you'd be the first to know when we were ready to move on the Hells Angels?"

CHAPTER THIRTY-NINE

One month later, a task force led in part by my friend Frenchie managed a spectacular takedown of the Hells Angels motorcycle gang, focused primarily in Quebec. While this was without question the same group responsible for growing the weed that was coming into the country through the Akwesasne reservation, Canadian officials had actually been building their case against the HAs for over three years.

The gang's crimes dated much further back than that, even before the August 1995 death of Daniel Desrochers. The charges chronicled the entire heyday of the biker wars between the HAs and the Rock Machine. At long last the Angels were paying a much-deserved price. Turned out those infamous biker wars were just a battle and they'd actually lost the war.

In the meetings I'd had with Frenchie on the Canadian side of the border to keep the lines of communication open, he'd warned me it was coming, and he contacted me again shortly before the April 15 takedown to let me know it was imminent. Interestingly enough, we had to switch our meetings to a different location after the Akwesasne tribe barricaded the bridge that formed the border crossing at Cornwall with backhoes and bulldozers, chasing off the Canadian customs agents. Possession may not really be nine-tenths of the law, but in this case the land squarely and wholly belonged to the Indians, because no one was about to challenge them.

Frenchie didn't provide the exact date of the takedown, and I didn't ask; you never do in this business, because if something goes wrong, and a cop gets shot going through a door, you don't want anyone to feel in any way that you were somehow to blame. Much better to keep such intelligence on a need-to-know basis only, and I didn't need to know about the timetable for Frenchie's takedown any more than he needed to know the timetable for mine. And, I've got to tell you, the Canadian authorities that had formed a multi-jurisdictional task force similar to mine on our side of the border did an incredible job. They arrested 156 violent criminals without firing a shot and encountering barely any resistance.

This perfectly illustrates the point that successful drug investigations almost never end violently. Gunfights and all-out assaults are the product of either Hollywood or poor planning. Sure, Frenchie's team took down 156 suspects whose combined arsenals would've been enough to fight a small war, but almost all of them were taken down individually by strike teams capable of overwhelming whatever resistance they might have offered. When you crash through that door with warrant in hand, you want to catch the suspect by surprise before he can even contemplate going for a weapon.

It's not about the glory or glamour, it's about being a professional.

And that was exactly the case for the Operation SharQc task force Frenchie was a part of, consisting of more than a thousand officers. A small army constituted to fight a very real war on its northern front, so to speak, while my war was on the southern front. One hundred and seventy-seven individual raids were carried out by a staggering twelve hundred officers coordinated through the Royal Canadian Mounted Police and Frenchie's Ontario Provincial Police. The raids began in the predawn hours and continued through the morning of April 15.

"We believe we can dismantle the infrastructure, and disrupt their abilities to use our communities to carry out their criminal activities," Michael Martin, a Quebec provincial police inspector, told CBC News at the time.

Another organized-crime expert, journalist Michael Auger, told the same outlet, "For a long period they will be in court facing several charges. So the Hells Angels as such will be crippled for several years."

How did this huge takedown affect our task force's case on the other side of the border? The truth is it did initially, at least for a couple of weeks, but then it was business as usual again. How could that be? First off, because arresting suspects doesn't necessarily put the entire network out of business. As CTV news reported at the time, "The raids are designed to put the provincial Hells Angels out of the business—at least for the time being."

Emphasis on *for the time being*, because drug operations work with a "next man up" philosophy. Just as there was Noah King to step into the shoes of Alan Jacobs, there were plenty of underlings to step into the shoes of the arrested HAs to make sure their product continued to be shipped through the Akwesasne reservation. Beyond that, there was no reason for Noah, Kim, or the Frasers to suspect any connection and run for the hills, since the murder, drug, and gangsterism charges on which those 156 HAs were arrested dated back as much as twenty years. There was no reason for our task force's targets to suspect that a similar takedown was coming south of the border. They figured that they were protected by the peculiarities of the res itself, coupled with the layers enacted to keep them insulated. And they might have been right, if I didn't have Ashley and Kevin ready to lead me straight to their doorsteps.

Criminals often think they're invincible, coated in Teflon to the point where anything anybody in law enforcement throws at them will just slide right off. And there's actually some validity to that mindset. When criminals as powerful as the Hells Angels, or Alan Jacobs initially, get arrested, it doesn't mean they stand trial quickly or even remain in jail while awaiting trial. Some end up released on bail and resume their criminal activities while awaiting trial. Even in the case of Operation SharQc, The Canadian Press news agency reported around Thanksgiving of 2013 that "A Quebec judge has decided that fifty-one Hells Angels members and sympathizers who face a wide variety of charges including gangsterism and murder will be tried in two different groups. The accused were arrested in 2009 as part of the sweeping Operation SharQc."

While the bulk of the remaining suspects accepted plea deals, these hadn't and likely continued to at least coordinate the gang's efforts for that extended period after their arrest. You can do a lot of damage in three and a half years, and I probably witnessed some of it firsthand.

There's no way to accurately measure the collateral damage the drug trade does to society as a whole, economically as well as socially, in the number of ruined lives. And to me, busting a major drug ring, like the one still operating between upstate New York and Ohio with impunity, is about eliminating that collateral damage as much as it is about taking the weed and the network off the streets.

Back home in Ohio, one thing became clear once I got the word from Frenchie that Operation SharQc was moving on the Hells Angels: That it was time for our task force to move too.

5

TAKEDOWN

A hero is no braver than an ordinary man,
but he is brave five minutes longer.

—Ralph Waldo Emerson

CHAPTER FORTY

My team and I listened to and watched Kevin and Ashley for a hundred days. We had also followed them to the Frasers' five times when we decided that we would plan our takedown for Sunday, June 14. During that time we discovered that Kevin was a creature of habit, down to the minute. The only thing outside the norm was his brief stint in detox, but that didn't last long. He was back to his old habits, including the drugs, a couple of weeks later. Paranoia tends to drive drug dealers into complete randomness or a very strict schedule. The best of the best learned to follow a strict schedule that appeared to be completely random.

It took a while but we figured out the code words, the patterns, and the timing. That was the key to a successful investigation. I learned that from my undercover days. You needed to know your targets inside and out. You needed to know their every move, down to when they took a shit. If you didn't, you couldn't be prepared.

Kevin and Ashley took the drive up to New York twice a month. They left Sunday morning at five A.M. so they could be back by eleven P.M. They would pick up a rental car from Hertz on Saturday for the drive up to New York on Sunday because the office was closed that day.

Once Kevin returned home, he would work through the night to dump the dope. By morning it was gone. He didn't sell quarters or halves. He sold to the local dealers. He dealt in pounds, with only a few individuals that he knew and trusted. Less risk that way. I had to admit that I was impressed with this twenty-one-year-old; little more than a kid and he had made his way up the food chain, slipping a few times but always climbing. He had caught on fast and was following the rules. He wasn't typical for the business. Usually the good ones worked their way up and had mentors. Kevin had built his drug empire in middle-class suburbia on his own, a kind of twisted take on the Horatio Alger myth, the American dream turned nightmare. If he had decided to do something else, something legit, he most likely would have been very successful, even just as successful.

But he hadn't.

What always got me was how even the most skilled and experienced drug dealers, the cream of the crop, never figured out how to beat a wire; they hadn't yet and showed no signs of doing so. Every one of these guys used a burner phone and we were always able to get at least one of their numbers. From there, one group member would call another and then another. It was like a big spiderweb. They would all dump their phones at some point, but never at the same time. So, when a group member would call back into the spiderweb with a new number we could figure out who they were by the sound of their voice. We experienced that firsthand in the Franklin County wire room.

If I were the leader of a drug ring, I would have everyone dump their phones the same day and hand out new phones to everyone. Synchronizing their strategy and actions would be the only way to beat a wire. So simple it was scary. But they were too busy, and believed themselves too big, to be bothered by such mundane concerns, the kind of minutiae that dominated my working life and always had.

That's the thing about working undercover. It's dominated by detail, not excitement. Computer bytes instead of bullets. Glory hounds and thriller authors may want you to believe otherwise, but that doesn't change the fact that the way you bring down the biggest drug networks is to avoid the kind of violence, overreaction, and poor preparedness that will inevitably lead all the major players to run for the hills by severing ties with the underlings who otherwise could've delivered them to you. It's a painstaking process. Some would even call it dull. After all my years in the game, though, I can tell you it's the best recipe for success in putting the players away and getting their product off the streets.

Although huge, high-profile drug busts initiated by a single agent planted within a distribution network are great fodder for Hollywood, there's only so much a single undercover on the inside can accomplish.

And while it's been a prime component of my own modus operandi over the years, it has to be supplemented by an entire team of agents, often across a myriad of agencies, in a coordinated effort that makes heavy use of the mundane and even tedious.

With that philosophy in mind, I decided it was time for the takedown only when I was certain that the evidence against Kevin was strong enough that nothing would get thrown out in court. That is essential for leading a good drug investigation. While I have to think like a cop, I also need to think like a prosecuting attorney, a judge, and a jury. There can be no reasonable doubt once the investigation, especially the financial part, is completed. Otherwise, it all goes for naught and a law-enforcement operative like myself risks squandering thousands and thousands of hours of manpower.

I needed to coordinate with the St. Lawrence drug task force to confirm the date and time of the takedown. We decided it was best to make the grab at the Frasers', at the meet we'd learned about thanks to the wire. This would allow New York to snatch everyone up in one fell swoop and do the seizures at the Frasers' at the time of the arrest. Last thing we ever wanted to do was give time for the targets to hide assets, cash, and drugs. To stash them somewhere it might be hard for us to ever find, at least not without spending substantial additional resources unnecessarily. I always planned to do arrests and seizures simultaneously. So while the guys in New York were doing arrests and raiding the Frasers' and Noah King's homes, my team would be doing all the seizures in Beachwood, as close to simultaneously as was possible.

This was the biggest of all the jobs and challenges. While most of my guys didn't find it as exciting as watching the look on Kevin's face as the handcuffs were slapped on him, they did realize that such timing was the most critical element of our ultimate success and what our investigation would be judged by. This is how drug task forces accumulated the resources to continue the fight against the next big drug dealer. First we follow the money, and then we seize it, which helps to both take and keep the drugs off the streets. Seizing this money is what helped keep drugs off the streets.

Before all of this could start was where my real expertise kicked in: warrant writing. This is where a great investigation can fall apart. There's an art to warrant writing, just like there's an art to writing a book. I needed to write up arrest warrants for Kevin, Ashley, and the Frasers. I also had to write up search warrants for Kevin and Ashley's home, the Sorins' home, the Schmids' home, and Mark's home. All of this had to be well thought out. I had to consider everything when writing up additional search warrants to cover places, safe-deposit boxes, and cars that I had seen while following them. When it came to asset seizure especially, if it wasn't listed on the warrant, I couldn't take it, and that meant I needed to err on the side of excess caution. Leave no stone unturned, as they say, which turned out to be true literally in this case.

One of the biggest decisions in writing a warrant is deciding if it will be federal or state. As I mentioned before, in the state system the burden of proof is on the prosecution to prove that the assets seized were profits of crime, while in federal court it's up to the defense to prove that the assets were not proceeds of crime and that it was legitimate income. This is a huge distinction and one that obviously behooves law-enforcement agents to keep everything as much as possible on the federal side of things.

That said, I almost always start my cases with a state warrant. I do this because if you start with a federal warrant you're stuck with your decision, while if you begin with a state warrant you have the option to switch to a federal warrant during the duration of the case. This option gives me time to reflect on all the variables; it buys me time to make my case ironclad, in other words. I can review my search warrants, seizures, and indictments after everything is executed and decide which is the best fit for my case, federal or state, regardless of whether or not I began with a federal warrant.

This particular case posed additional challenges in that regard, since I needed to file warrants with both Cuyahoga and Geauga counties in Ohio. I had the option of either having municipal judges or county judges sign my warrants. I always take the time to get in front of the county judges. Not that there is anything wrong with a municipal judge. But, I've always found that a county judge is more learned in the law. And in all my years working drugs, I've never had a warrant suppressed, and I plan on keeping it that way. It's all in the details of the writing. It takes time and thought.

A defense attorney will do anything he or she can to try to suppress parts of the warrant for their client. And this kind of representation poses special challenges for the prosecution, because it's often taken on what amounts to a contingency basis comparable to personal-injury law. Top defense attorneys will often defend their drug clients in exchange for a share of the assets they are able to keep the government from seizing— I've seen and heard of such fees exceeding the 50 percent mark. My goal is to make it impossible for that kind of attorney, working as much in his own interest as his client's, to even try to make a motion to suppress evidence that will otherwise lead to a conviction and potential total forfeiture of assets. In that case, the lawyer could end up making nothing, which gives you an idea of the stakes involved in ensuring that everything I do leading up to the arrest and seizure is ironclad.

I knew here that I had solid warrants because I had run a solid case. I was sure not to include any nonpertinent information. And given the location in the country the case was occurring, we were able to call Border Patrol and get the drones up any time we needed them to further make and supplement our case. The process of requisitioning and utilizing drones didn't even require warrants, and any information we gathered in visible areas was fair game. Sometimes you get lucky with things like that. Once the warrants are signed, all that's left is to make your move, and as both Ohio and upstate New York began to warm for the summer, that's exactly what we were prepared to do.

Turned out we had a problem in that regard. A big one.

CHAPTER FORTY-ONE

W hat the fuck?" I asked Mike Hughes, needing to be absolutely certain we had all our ducks in a row. "You're sure they're about to make moves now?"

"Sure as shit, Chief. My buddy who works at the task force in Geauga County said that the two agents heading up the case on some Matt kid were going in to the prosecutor to get the warrants all set up," Mike replied from his chair in the wire room.

"Some Matt kid?"

"Far as we know."

"Hell, no! We've worked too damn hard setting up this case to let two ass clowns go in there and fuck it up. Do we even know who this Matt kid is?"

Mike shrugged and scanned the room for a reaction from the other officers gathered who'd been working the wire. "Anyone? Anyone got eyes or ears on this kid Matt? Is this even a name that has even come up in our investigation?"

Based on the empty glances and shaking heads, it didn't seem anyone in the room knew who Matt even was. This only caused me to get angrier and angrier. I was not going to let these guys screw this up over a nobody, over someone who was below a mope being pursued by these ass clowns who had no clue they were fucking with a case that actually involved hundreds of millions of dollars. I knew what I had to do.

"I'm heading back home. Take care of these bozos myself."

———

Geauga County, Ohio; June 2009

I left immediately, after calling ahead to set up an appointment. The long drive would give me time to unwind. I knew I had to be cool when I walked into the Geauga task force headquarters. There was always a chance that at heart they were drug guys and I could explain to them what was going on up here and they'd see the greater good. But I wasn't holding out hope in that regard. Essentially, I was going to ask them to stand down, which meant no bust, no glory, and all the potential commendations and promotions that might've otherwise followed. Law enforcement is a territorial world and cops will often defend their territory without listening to any explanation or rationale to the contrary.

I made sure to show up at the Geauga County task force with goodies in hand: a box of doughnuts and coffee from Dunkin' Donuts. It wasn't usually my style to kiss ass, but I was going in bearing gifts today. It might not have been bonding over food and beer, but it would have to do. I knew these cops thought they were going to be big shots for taking down some small-time drug dealer. I had taken down a few big guys in Geauga before and brought in millions for my city. They had as much of a chance of getting Kevin as they did of reeling in a giant marlin with an ordinary rod and lure. Maybe doughnuts would help ease the blow while I cut the line.

I knocked on the metal door of the drug task force. Like all DTFs, the building wasn't marked and was in a discreet location in the back of a shopping plaza in Chardon, Ohio. A cop from Chardon answered the door. He had to be a rookie, right out of the academy.

"I'm Jeff. I called ahead," I said to the kid.

"Nathan Zarando. Officer from Chardon. Just learning the ropes," he said.

"I'm looking for two guys about to bust a kid from Beachwood and a guy named Matt from Chardon. You know who I'm talking about?" I asked the kid.

"Yeah. This guy Matt was busted in a traffic stop—" Nathan started.

"Do you know who the officers are?" I interrupted before he could go on. New officers are always so easily confused! Drove me nuts. I needed to spell it out for him, like, one letter at a time.

"Oh, yeah. That would be Stevenson and Walters. They're in the back. I can show you, if you want."

"I got it," I said, pushing past Nathan and making my way toward the back, doughnuts and coffee in hand.

I was familiar with the Geauga task force. Hell, I couldn't think of a task force in northeast Ohio that I wasn't familiar with. I had been hooking up drug dealers longer than most law-enforcement officers even last on the job. I could only imagine that Stevenson and Walters were relatively new to the scene. Probably cops from somewhere in the county trying to make a name for themselves only to leave the task force behind for a promotion in their squad. If I got lucky, they'd be FBI or DEA and would easily see the whole picture, meaning they'd be glad to step aside. Nothing beats experience in that regard.

As I've alluded to several times before, all drug task force units are made up of several different types of law enforcement drawn from the likes of DEA, FBI, and local or state police. That doesn't hold true for just the high-risk areas like St. Lawrence County and the US-Canada border, but also drug task forces in local cities and counties.

As I stepped into the back room, it wasn't hard at all for me to pick out Stevenson and Walters. They sat in the corner with their backs toward me, huddled around a stack of papers. They looked like two schoolgirls sharing notes. That wasn't how I ran an operation or a task force. The more heads on a case the better. Hoarding and hiding information like small town gossips never benefited anyone other than the show horses and ass clowns doing it. Amateur hour, in other words.

Oh boy, I was thinking as I walked around to the other side of the table and placed the coffee and doughnuts in front of them.

They looked up, startled.

"What the—" the older of the two men began saying.

Before he could finish I had my hand outstretched, "Jeff Buck. You're Stevenson?"

"Walters."

"Nice to meet you."

Walters did not return the greeting or the gesture, so I moved my hand toward Stevenson. Stevenson, being younger and greener, reciprocated.

"What do you want?" Walters asked, clearly perturbed, as the three of us sat down at the table. His eyes looked too small for his face, a feature exaggerated that he still wore his hair high and tight, military style, as if he wanted everyone to know he'd been in the service, or at least looked like he did.

It was pretty clear to me at this point that both of them knew who I was, but Walters wasn't about to be deferential; he was already on the defensive. Yup, he knew who I was and he knew if I was there to see him it had to be because of his case.

"I hear we may have a mutual target and I came to discuss your case," I said plainly, leaving it there.

"And who's that?" Stevenson asked, playing dumb now and probably regretting he'd shaken my hand.

I hated that. It was one thing when a criminal did it to protect his own ass but it was beyond pathetic when an ass clown tried it. Oh, and the doughnuts and coffee just sat there. So much for my show of conciliation.

"Kevin Sorin. Drug dealer from Beachwood. Ring a bell?"

"Seems we do have a mutual mark," Walters conceded, his voice stern.

"I'm here to discuss what you have going on and what your next move is," I said, my voice measured and flat.

"We're about to get warrants signed off on to put trackers on the cars of Kevin Sorin and Mark Ververka."

"What do you have on them?" I asked.

"Plenty," Stevenson jumped in. "We picked up this Matt Cody two years ago and have been working on the case against Sorin and Ververka ever since."

"Can you show me your evidence?"

"No," Stevenson barked. "No way, Chief. It's our case."

"Okay, let me tell you about my case. Listen, man, my team and I have been tracking Kevin and his crew to upstate New York for months. We've created a historical case that goes back on him for years. Our case isn't going to just bring down Kevin Sorin, but also his suppliers and then their suppliers, not to mention his entire buyers on this end here. You getting the picture?"

Neither of them responded.

"Okay, this case is huge. Goes all the way up to the Hells Angels out of Montreal. No way do I want to deprive you of a major bust, if you've got a big case and you're sure you can bring down his whole enterprise. But I just want to make sure you have a rock-solid case. So, please, before you risk busting up my case for something that may not be a sure thing on your end, can I see your files to make sure you have all you need to indict?"

"We already told you no. We don't work that way," Walters snapped. "You're right, Chief, we know who you are. And just because we aren't the famous Jeff Buck doesn't mean we don't know what we're doing or how to do a case."

"Enjoy the doughnuts," I said as I rose and walked toward the door.

Nothing ventured, nothing gained, right? I'd tried things the easy way. Time to look for another.

CHAPTER FORTY-TWO

Patience is definitely a virtue when it comes to a well-laid-out historical drug case. The length of time that is put in to a case, though, isn't the final determinant of such patience. That was what these ass clowns didn't realize. Their two years didn't mean shit if they weren't patient enough to fill out all the right paperwork, go through all the right motions and research, work things right instead of waiting for something to just fall into their laps. Their vision was small-time because they didn't know any better. A drug case is 99 percent work and 1 percent ego. I left that DTF building thinking it was more like the reverse of that for these guys.

These guys don't want to hear how the biggest drug cases, the busts that really matter, are the product of hours and hours of hard work, with a multitude of different task forces and various other agents, that are little more than dotting the "i"s and crossing the "t"s. All the gunfights and car chases are mostly just fantasy dreamed up to sell movie tickets or grab television viewers. Sure, I've been in a few car chases and gunfights, but not too many. I work with criminal enterprises and they are just that, enterprises. Their goal is to stay in business, and make money. Killing people, the way Alan Jacobs inadvertently did when he sent Wildcat and company to teach Danny a lesson, only cramps their style and potentially lands them in jail. You think if Jacobs had it to do all over again, he would've dispatched Wildcat and the boys out to Danny's house that night? You think he would've taken that kind of risk knowing his entire enterprise might collapse beneath him as a result?

The criminal I usually chase likes to run under the radar. He is the person who lives next door to you in your comfy suburban neighborhood.

He drives an SUV and has a nice home. He doesn't get his hands dirty. He most likely doesn't even do drugs. A historical case is important because without it an indictment will never stick and you will never grab the mark's cash supply and his business will stay intact, for either the mark to run again when he gets out or his second-in-command to assume control over. Then what have you accomplished?

That was the point I tried to make to Stevenson and Walters, but it fell on deaf ears and I wish I hadn't bothered with the doughnuts. It befuddles me how some cops still don't get that the point of running an undercover operation is to get as many of the players on the food chain as possible. There will always be another ass to fill the seat, but as long as you're at it, you might as well take out as many asses as possible.

Stevenson and Walters weren't buying into that, and if I didn't act quick they were going to try to sneak up Kevin's driveway and put a tracker on his car. If Kevin got wind of that he would shut his operation down so fast that my trail would go cold, all would be for naught, and I wouldn't get to take out any asses, never mind those sitting in the biggest chairs. The time had come to call in a big favor.

"Geauga County Prosecutor's Office, Office of Chief Prosecutor David Joyce." The voice of the woman on the other end of the phone asked, "How may I help you?"

"Is Dave Joyce in, please?" I asked.

I'd worked with Dave on many cases. He was a good guy and a very fair prosecutor. He understood the importance of creating a complete case and would never indict someone unjustly. I knew that if I went to him he'd do the right thing, at least try to.

"May I ask who's calling?"

"Jeff Buck."

A brief pause followed before Dave came on the line.

"Jeff! How ya doing?"

Dave was a jovial guy and a true professional. His voice almost jumped through the phone every time I spoke to him.

"Good, real good. Except I have a small problem and it has to do with your task force. I feel awful that I have to come to you, but I went to your officers first and I got nowhere."

I told Dave about the problem and laid out my dilemma for him. He seemed to understand but also seemed to want to tread lightly, choosing his words carefully. He asked me to go back to Stevenson and Walters and ask to see their evidence again.

"Use my name. Tell them we spoke, maybe that will encourage them to open up to you," Dave suggested.

"Thanks, Dave. I appreciate it. This is a big case for our city," I told him.

"Sounds like it. I'd like to help in any way I can."

I hadn't driven very far from the DTF headquarters when I turned back around to have another chat with Stevenson and Walters. Nathan answered the door again.

"Hi Nathan, me again."

He eyed me first with suspicion and then with apprehension. "Ummm, they're still in the back. But, er, I don't think they want visitors," Nathan stammered.

"That's okay. I won't take much of their time," I said, and gave Nathan a pat on his back, as I slid past him just as I had the last time.

Stevenson and Walters hadn't moved from their spot in the back when I returned. I took the same seat I had before. The doughnut box was at the end of the table. I could see from the slightly raised lid that only three of the dozen doughnuts remained. My new friends had been busy. The corners of Stevenson's mouth were frosted with sugar, his eyes opened wider and looking like tiny marbles wedged in his head. Thinking back, I can't even remember much about what the younger Walters looked like. That's the kind of impression he made on me.

"Hello, guys. How happy are you to see me again? Before you say anything, I just got off the phone with Dave Joyce. He suggested I come back here and talk with you, again, so here I am."

I paused, waiting to see if there were any comments from the peanut gallery.

"I thought it would be in both our best interests if we could share information about our cases," I resumed when there wasn't. "What do you think? Would that be all right with you?"

I could tell that they weren't happy but they knew that if I had spoken with David Joyce they weren't going to have too much to say about it. They also knew that Joyce was the most reasonable prosecutor around and that he didn't take sides lightly. So even if we were friends, Dave wouldn't just go with my approach unless I had something worth listening to, so they better hear me out.

"Fine," Walters said gruffly, barely meeting my gaze.

"Great," I said, pulling up a chair between them. "I'm listening."

"Matt Cody was traffic-stopped around two years ago with an ounce of pot on him. We brought him to the station and got him to roll over on his dealer. Said the guy's name was Mark Ververka. After that we let the kid go with a warning and we began doing surveillance on Ververka," Walters explained.

Ververka was one of the dealers who bought from Kevin Sorin and also mostly lived in the house with him and Ashley Schmid.

"Do you have the evidence you gathered for me to take a look at?" I asked.

Walters pulled out a stack of photos from their two years of surveillance. The stack was awfully sparse and the notes accompanying it even more so. This was what I'd expect from two weeks, not two years. I began flipping through the photos. I couldn't find a photo of Kevin, not a single one. I could feel my blood begin to boil.

These guys are going to screw up my case for nothing!

Then I finally came upon a shot of Kevin, which pictured him golfing with Matt Cody and Mark Ververka.

"Is this your only eyewitness who can put Matt with Kevin together?" I asked.

"Well, we assume that one of those cars in some of those pictures was Kevin's," Stevenson jumped in.

"That wasn't what I asked," I said, straining to remain calm. Amateur hour indeed.

"We assume that Kevin was driving one of those cars," Walters repeated.

"Again, not my question," I said, more firmly.

The two men looked at each other. Neither of them wanted to answer.

"Okay, let me see if I can point you in the right direction here. None of the cars you have photos of belong to Kevin, Mark Ververka, or Kevin's girlfriend, Ashley. Does that help you to answer my question?"

"That's the only evidence we have of him with Matt," Walters conceded.

"Do you have any buys on these guys?"

Stevenson and Walters looked at each other. "No," they both said, one after the other.

"Then where's your criminal case? How did you think you could possibly get an indictment based on one photo?" I asked them.

"We were going to use a tracker to follow him," Stevenson said.

I fought the urge to shake my head. Hell, these guys didn't even know that Kevin didn't drive his own car to do work, and the tracker would have no evidentiary value.

"This kid Kevin is way too smart and paranoid for that," I told them, opting for the conciliatory approach. "He checks his car. He'd find your tracker day one."

The two men looked at each other. They didn't realize that another key to a good investigation was understanding the psychology of a drug dealer. They all tend to be pretty paranoid, whether they are on law enforcement's radar or not. They always live their lives on a nervous edge, obsessively cautious and aware, because someone is always after them, even if it's just the person who wants to knock them off their spot on the food chain.

"What do you think we're going to do, just piss away two years' worth of our work and all the forfeiture that goes along with that?" Walters asked me.

I wasn't quite sure what to say, because that was *exactly* what I expected, and there weren't going to be any forfeitures, because Walters hadn't really done any work. I could tell by what was in the case file. He was only writing his first warrant on the investigation now. We'd already written dozens.

"Well, yes, as a matter of fact," I said, trying to not sound too harsh but knowing I probably did anyway.

"That ain't happening. You want us to back down and off?" Walters challenged. "We want half of your forfeitures."

I had to fight not to lurch out of my seat. I couldn't believe the balls on this guy. Asking for anything at all was greedy and wrong, but half for doing and contributing zilch to the case? I mean, come on. But I knew I had to come up with something to appease these ass clowns.

"How about this?" I proposed. "What about when we go and pick up Matt Cody, you come with us? You can lead that operation and any and all forfeitures we obtain from the home or property of Matt Cody will be turned over to the Geauga drug task force. Free, clear, and in total. Does that work for you?"

Stevenson and Walters whispered among themselves. I sat uncomfortably as the two men went at it like fourteen-year-old girls: back and forth, back and forth, until they came to a decision.

"You got yourself a deal, Chief," Walters said, and stuck his hand out.

I shook it. "Thanks, gentlemen. I'll keep you posted as to the timing of when we're ready to do the takedowns. See both of you soon."

With that, I stood up and Stevenson and Walters followed.

"Would you like me to show you out?" Stevenson asked.

"No, thanks. I'm good," I replied as I headed for the door.

I made a beeline for my car, ready to put into motion the final steps that would take down one of the biggest drug operations in the country.

CHAPTER FORTY-THREE

I couldn't go directly to the manager of the Hertz car rental in Beachwood, because I had no idea how close he was to Kevin. Kevin did so much business there, I had to consider the possibility that they were acquaintances at the very least, and even that the manager was being paid to both keep quiet and warn Kevin if somebody like me came sniffing around. This could prove quite a quandary, given that I was going to be writing up the warrant, and the exact car needed to be detailed for the warrant to be valid.

Considering that there were probably a hundred cars on this particular Hertz lot at any given time, that was obviously a problem.

But there was a workaround. The increasing presence and popularity of navigation devices like OnStar were potential godsends to tailing suspects and targets without actually putting physical tails or trackers on them, either of which could be spotted. So I contacted Hertz's corporate office and got an older gentleman on the phone. I told him we were working a large-scale drug distribution network and that the couriers were using his vehicles. We could use his help, I said, in tracking them from Ohio to New York. All we would need would be for him to access the database to tell us which car they rented. He provided me with a list of the cars available on the lot for that weekend, and I wrote the warrant listing all of them. Once the warrant was signed by a judge, the Hertz specialty center that tracks its stolen cars was compelled to provide the information I needed. But I was working with a general manager who went that one better by actually emptying the Hertz lot of all cars that didn't have OnStar in advance of Kevin's Saturday pickup (because the Hertz in Beachwood is closed on Sundays). That eliminated any chance that Kevin would end up in a car without OnStar installed, meaning I'd have to use hard tails on him instead.

Once Kevin picked up the car Saturday morning, the general manager called and gave me the vehicle identification number. I then called OnStar directly at the number provided by Hertz and advised them of the court order. The car at that point was still parked in Beachwood, and I advised OnStar to call as soon as it started moving, because the surveillance team was waiting to do a soft tail, hanging back five or six miles, from the Ohio-Pennsylvania border on. This while I remained on an open line with OnStar for the whole trip so they could keep me apprised of Kevin's position in real time. Having that redundancy was crucial in this case, because Kevin was known to occasionally stop at the Syracuse Airport Hertz to switch rental cars. If he did that, we'd have to tail him the rest of the way in a more traditional fashion, because there'd be no way to get a warrant on the switched car in time.

That was more challenging in this case than it sounds because at the time much of this area of upstate New York, including Harold and Sabrina Fraser's farm and store, had no cell phone service. The only way we could communicate when up in that area was via old-fashioned radios with limited range. The fact that the Frasers relied solely on a landline, though, did have one important advantage. Kim Cook and Noah King would almost always use burner phones to call them. Normally, we'd have no way to get those numbers. But since we were up on the Frasers' number we got acquainted real fast with whatever number two of our other primary targets, Kim and Noah, were using. Interestingly enough, during another call that came in to the Frasers, we learned a two-kilo cocaine buy was about to go down and were able to alert the narcotics unit in Syracuse to make the bust.

Like me, they'd have to get a warrant in order to execute a search and that's not as easy as it may sound. Let's start with the true basics of writing and executing a warrant. There are two parts to a search warrant: the first is an affidavit detailing the facts of our case garnered through the course of the investigation sometimes years in the making to establish probable cause against our suspect; the second details the specific property address and descriptions and what exactly we're entitled to search from the house itself to those inhabiting it to vehicles. If there's a trailer or storage unit on the premises, we'd need a separate warrant for that if it wasn't mentioned in the original one, but could utilize the same affidavit.

So rule number one is to be keenly aware of what you're writing in your warrant, so you know what it is you're entitled to search. Assume your warrant allows you to search for documents that might include bank accounts, offshore accounts, investment accounts, real estate holdings, and especially those assets placed under what we call "nominees," or others the bad guys are putting properties in the name of to keep secret from law enforcement. You open up a drawer and find a kilo of cocaine, at which point everything has to stop until you can get a second warrant written that allows you to search for drugs. So rule number two is don't look at execution of the warrant as the end of things, as much as when things can really get rolling. If I find a key to a safe deposit box, for example, I don't have the right to search that safe deposit box. I have to go back to a judge, adding to the initial probable cause to enable me to get a warrant to expand my search. If I search that safe deposit box otherwise, anything I find is going to be suppressed as evidence as fruit of the poisonous tree and I can't touch whatever's inside for forfeiture.

Say I'm serving a regular search warrant on a place of business occupying Suite 201 in a strip mall. In the course of my search of those premises, I ascertain that the target also happens to be leasing Suite 202, something I wasn't originally aware of. At that point the warrant I have in hand doesn't entitle me to search Suite 202. I have to secure the scene and get a separate warrant to search that space as well. You never want to take a chance of having the product of your search suppressed because you rushed the process. The whole case can collapse under the weight of that.

Let's take another example. I learn a dealer is running dope out of some motel room. I set up an operation, go in undercover, make a buy, and arrest the target. But in the process I notice three zippered duffel bags in the corner. The bust doesn't allow me to search those bags or even open them. I have to go to a judge and articulate the facts of the arrest and undercover operation to create probable cause for a warrant that lists the bags specifically. If I open those bags without a warrant, it's pretty much a done deal the evidence inside them will be suppressed before we get to trial and I lose the chance to get the target on a much bigger score. The only thing we're allowed to otherwise search in such an operation is something that would pertain directly to the safety of the officers, like the closet or the bathroom, which falls under the auspices of "securing the scene."

And it doesn't stop there either. It's vital in cases involving especially high-profile targets that their attorneys never learn the contents of the probable cause affidavit that allowed us to obtain the search warrant in the first place. On the one hand, these warrants contain information we don't want the bad guys to know: the names of informants, investigative techniques and technology like the OnStar thing with Kevin. Court rules require that the warrant be returned within a specified time frame, but when I do so I make sure to obtain a judicial order to keep that warrant under seal. That way, it never becomes public record and its contents remain privy only to law enforcement. The bad guys have enough advantages already without us giving them more.

And so it goes.

I was exhausted that night but couldn't sleep. Tomorrow was the big day. Six months of work, countless man-hours, and a multi-jurisdictional, multistate, multinational case all came down to how tomorrow played out.

Beachwood, Ohio, and Franklin County, New York;
June 14, 2009

The day before, right on schedule, Kevin and Ashley had arrived at the Hertz car rental at the corner of Chagrin Boulevard and Brainard Road. The salesperson escorted them to a blue Ford Taurus. The two had no idea that this car would allow us to follow their every move, thanks to the warrant I'd written and OnStar. They had no idea that we were waiting for them.

The deal was scheduled to go down at the Frasers' around two P.M. Sunday. So we chose that as our zero hour to make our move. The Franklin County drug task force was in place to execute the arrest warrants on Ashley, Kevin, and the Frasers. Because the Frasers lived in St. Lawrence County, our task force would be working in tandem with that neighboring DTF that included Rick Sinnigan of the DEA; I might've had a poor first impression of Sinnigan, but when it comes to taking the bad guys down none of that stuff matters anymore. Mike Hughes was up on the wire keeping us informed, to avoid any potential surprises or pitfalls. That's the thing with a case like this; you just never know when something you're flat not expecting is going to pop up. You can get ambushed if you don't choose your steps carefully in this world. Just ask Danny Simonds.

I was in Cleveland with six men, and had narcotics units from Reminderville, Beachwood, and the Geauga drug task force ready to execute search warrants for Kevin and Ashley's home, Ashley's parents' home, Kevin's parents' home, and Matt Cody, the kid from Chardon, simultaneously. I didn't like that I was leaving another guy to go through the door on any one of these warrants. If someone is going to get shot, I want it to be me. I never want someone else taking a bullet on one of my warrants. But I had no choice in a four-house takedown. Wasn't like I could be in four places at one time. But I'd taught all my guys well. They knew what to do.

The timing had to be perfect. We wouldn't make our move until our counterparts in New York had made theirs. Then two o'clock came and went with no sign of Ashley and Kevin showing at the Frasers' place in upstate New York.

"What the hell is taking this kid so long? He's never late," Joe Miles said to me.

"Maybe he stopped for a little road head from that pretty little thing," one of the guys on my team said jokingly.

The guys all laughed, breaking the tension we were all feeling even though we were now behind schedule.

Then my phone started to ring. The name MIKE HUGHES flashed across my caller ID. He was calling from the Franklin County wire room.

"Yeah, what's going on with our boy?" I asked him.

"He just had a screaming match with the Frasers. He must not have the dope yet. He told Kevin it will be coming through soon. He told Kevin he could come by and wait. Kevin said he would call him later."

"Are you fucking kidding me?"

"Wish I was, Chief."

"Well, shit! Did it sound like he was leaving town?" I asked, my heart pounding.

"Hold on, he's making another call."

Hello?"

"Are you busy right now?" Kevin asked Kim.

"I'm eating breakfast with the kids," she replied.

"Can you meet me after?"

"There a problem, K?"

"I'm sick of these hillbillies. Their dumb asses can't do anything right. Shitty fish," he said, his usual code word for weed. "Can you meet me?"

"Yeah. But my lake is dry," Kim told him, utilizing more coded speech.

"I'm not looking to take any fish home from you today. Those idiots will come through at some point. This is about long-term concerns. Can you meet me at Target in twenty?"

CHAPTER FORTY-FOUR

Cleveland, Ohio; June 14, 2009

G ive me some good news," I said as soon as Hughes came back on the line.

"Our boy is going to meet Kim. There's some kind of holdup with the dope," Mike explained.

"Thanks for the update. I'll call Border Patrol and have them send drones up over Target. We'll hold steady in the meantime. Notify me if something new happens."

"Will do, Chief," Mike said.

I flipped my phone shut and placed it back into the case on my belt. I ran my fingers through the thin strands of my hair that were blowing in the warm summer breeze. My guys were not going to be happy about standing around; I wasn't either.

Patience, I reminded myself.

Even though waiting was part of the game, it was especially irksome today. I had twenty-four men standing in position waiting to do the takedowns, and now they all had to hold. That pissed me off no end! I had to make calls to each of the teams and give them the rundown.

I made all the calls and sat back to wait some more, willing the phone to ring with a call from Hughes in Franklin County.

Thanks to OnStar, we were able to follow Kevin's movements through upstate New York. He was taking every back road and side street along the way, even zipping through parking lots—"heat runs," as we call them. This is why using a tracker, or better yet OnStar, is much better than trying to follow a target manually, especially the really paranoid ones like Kevin. They're far, far more likely to spot a tail than sniff out a tracker.

And then there were the surveillance drones. They'd provided such an added bonus to the case. From the wire room, Mike Hughes was going to be able to watch, actually *watch*, whatever went down at Target, without the hassle, logistical challenges, and even danger associated with a stakeout.

Kevin and Ashley left Target around three P.M. after meeting Kim, where they had a spirited discussion in the parking lot, and then headed back to the Frasers' farm. The call came in from New York maybe twenty minutes later, and I listened to Hughes's report through ears that suddenly felt stuffed with cotton. This was a watershed moment, after all, six months of working coming to successful fruition right before my ears.

One team had arrested Ashley and Kevin without incident as they were leaving the Frasers' farm. Another task force team had arrested the Frasers at their home. Also without incident. And a third, led by the tribal police, was moving on Noah King, who'd no longer be protected by the fact that the Akwesasne reservation is sovereign land.

That meant it was my time to act. I made the calls to the other three Ohio-based teams at their locations and then moved on to address my team out of view from Ashley and Kevin's house.

"Huddle in, men," I called out, "it's time. Kevin and Ashley are officially in custody."

The team got ready to celebrate but I had to stop them. It wasn't the time; still too much work to do first. Executing the search warrants and the seizures may not seem as exciting as executing the arrest warrants, but it's equally important and requires much more skill. As I mentioned before, search warrants have to be executed in a specific manner, to ensure that nothing can be suppressed and so that seizures don't have to be returned to the perpetrators.

Well, not here.

"It's now our time to act," I continued. "When I give the word, I'll enter the house first. After we secure the premises we can begin the search. Everywhere in the house is fair game. If you have a question about what is permitted according to the search warrant, just ask." I took a deep breath. Played the scenario out in my mind one more time just to make sure I wasn't missing anything. "Okay, let's move on in!"

I started by knocking on the door. I waited for a minute. Another knock. When I was sure no one was home I called for the battering ram. I stepped aside for the officer to take his swing. After three swings and a giant slam, the door flew open. I entered first, the team behind me.

The house was clear.

I decided this would be a good time to head over to the other locations to check on the progress at all of them, starting with Kevin's parents.

"Hold down the fort, Joe," I told Miles.

When I arrived at Boris and Loudmilla Sorin's home, the search was well under way. Loudmilla and Boris were seated at the kitchen table, not far away from a secret panel behind a storage cabinet where we'd eventually find $300,000 in cash. She was crying. I realized that her English wasn't good enough for her to read the copy of the warrant that she had been given. I handed her the official copy and sat down to try to explain to her what was going on.

"Loudmilla, stop crying, please," I said or, maybe, ordered. Probably.

She sniffled and wiped her nose, but the tears continued to fall from her eyes.

"Do you know why we are here?" I asked.

"No. No idea," she said, her accent thick.

"Are you sure? Do you know what your son does?"

"My son? Which son?" she questioned.

"Your son Kevin," I said, humoring her.

"Konstantin? He sells computers," she told me. "Works with his friend Ivan."

Ah, good old Yulia, I thought, remembering the night I'd heard Kevin's name for the first time. I wasn't sure whether Loudmilla actually believed what she'd just told me or not, but I highly doubted that she did.

"Loudmilla," I resumed, "do you know what your husband does when he goes with Konstantin?"

"No, no, I don't," she said, and started crying again.

"Loudmilla," I said, using her first name again to emphasize the familiarity and provide the impression—illusion, more accurately—that I was on her side, "it's much easier to tell me the truth."

Loudmilla didn't want to talk. Could've been the language barrier or her general fear of cops. All I could do was explain to her the process of the search, her rights, what our search covered, and what we could seize. After my job was done there, I sped off to the home of Ashley's parents to do the same thing.

By the time I reached the Schmid home, my team there had already seized over $100,000, and that was just the cash they'd found in the home itself. I gave my guy in the driveway a big high-five before entering.

Ashley's mother and father were seated at the kitchen table, just as Kevin Sorin's parents had been, waiting for the team to start their search. I handed Ashley's father the warrant and made sure he understood everything that was going on. It wasn't easy, because Ashley's mother, Mary Louise, was busy screaming that she had earned all of this money on her own from working and we had no right to take it from her.

"Are you sure that Ashley hasn't dropped any of this money off to you?" I asked Mary Louise.

"What are you accusing me of?" Mary Louise screamed at me.

"Nothing, nothing at all. I'm just asking," I said, my utter calm the perfect counterpoint to her rage.

"I made all that money myself!" Mary Louise cried out, clinging to her story.

"You work at Target, isn't that right, Mary Louise?"

"So fucking what? I work overtime, double shifts!"

I wondered how many of those it would take to squirrel away a hundred grand. All I could do was laugh at the thought. I had explained the warrant; my job was done.

I needed to visit the cops from Geauga County at Matt Cody's house next, and then circle back to Kevin's. I pulled up to the Cody house and walked into the home. The Geauga task force was just about done with the search. The Cody family was seated in the living room. I met with the family first.

"Hello, Matt," I said, to get the kid's attention.

"Hey," he said, trembling and reluctant to meet my gaze.

I handed the warrant to the father. "Have you been explained your rights and what these guys are looking for?"

"Yes," he said, his voice meek. "We are so sorry our son did this, Officer. We are going to cooperate. Please tell us what we can do."

"Everything is going to be fine, Mr. Cody," I said.

I shook my head. I knew this whole part of the bust was going to be a joke. This kid Matt was some jokester who bought a bag of pot and went golfing with the wrong dude. That was the basis by which Walters and Stevenson almost sandbagged my entire case. I mean, they were this close! Now all I had to do was find them.

They were in the kitchen searching the cabinets. Their search must not be going well. Once you start searching the kitchen cabinets, it's pretty clear you haven't got yourself the big score you were expecting.

"How's it going?" I asked.

Walters puffed out his chest before answering, "We found a bag of pot in the kid's room."

"And a hundred dollars," Stevenson added.

"Big score," I said, trying not to laugh. "Seems you guys have it under control here."

It was eleven P.M. by the time I got back to Kevin's house. It was always easy to spot big ol' Miles; loudest guy in the room even after being on the job for over twelve hours straight with maybe a single bathroom break.

"How's it going?" I asked him.

"One million dollars in cash and assets. Not bad for a single sweep of a house," he told me.

"Pretty good," I agreed.

"I piled up all of Kevin's burners," Miles said, pointing to the cell phones on the kitchen table. "One of them should ring soon."

Kevin had kept to a strict schedule, so his customers knew that come eleven P.M. the goods would be in town and ready for pickup.

Miles was correct. Not more than a half hour later one of the phones began to vibrate across the table. I grabbed the phone. The message was cryptic and unsigned:

80lbs. Tomorrow. Time?

"Korinek, look at this," I said, showing the Beachwood detective the phone, since he was an expert on Kevin's texting patterns. "You thinking what I'm thinking?"

"Hell yeah! We're going to do a reverse. I'm in for the all-nighter to prep."

"I'll text him back," I said.

"Type 'K,'" Korinek advised. "Kevin always signs 'K' at the end of his messages."

So I pounded out a return text:

Got it. Noon. Where? K

"Let's see if this works," I said to Korinek, really hoping it would.

And sure enough, mere seconds later the phone buzzed again:

Summit Mall. South Side.

Korinek instructed me to text back:

C U there. K

Keeping with the pattern again.

I'd just been handed the opportunity to do a reverse deal: Go in with the dope and try to sell it to the target in exchange for cash, instead of walking the cash to buy the dope. That doesn't happen too often in my line of work. This type of deal is considered undercover work and requires a special certification from a prosecutor. This certification is something that I had acquired many years ago, back in my Dope Ghost days. It was once again going to come in handy.

Now, for the dope. I had to come up with eighty pounds of weed to show the perp tomorrow before we got ready to bust him and take out another link of the food chain. It so happened that I did have eighty pounds of weed sitting in my property room back at the station, but it was in no condition to pass the muster a dealer capable of moving that amount on the streets would surely give it. Far from anything this guy would be expecting Kevin to bring back from New York. Some of it had been sitting in the property room for over two years now, had dried out to the point where it wouldn't even pass visual inspection for someone who knew what he was looking at.

But there's an old trick in the undercover world for perking up your pot in this kind of reverse deal. It just took time and manpower. I called in Joe Miles and John Korinek and we headed to the station.

"Put on the coffee," I said to Miles, "it's going to be a long night. We've got some cooking to do."

"You got it, Chief," Miles said, trying to be chipper, but I could hear that he was tired. We all were. But I knew that we could push through, and headed back to the station to our evidence room.

It was the size of a bedroom and piled high with seizures that hadn't yet cleared court to officially allow us to reap the proceeds of their value. Our stock put the city of Cleveland's to shame because no one takes the time to worry about the seemingly small stuff. It all goes back to the show horse. The glory is always in arresting the bad guy. While that obviously needs to be done, law enforcement too often forgets that it's equally important to work at getting the dope, assets, and cash off the streets. Not only does it help to stop the targets and their associates in their tracks for a while, it also helps to feed the local police and drug task force drug funds, which assists in future investigations. So, while it seems humdrum, it actually makes a difference in the end.

A huge difference.

CHAPTER FORTY-FIVE

The night after the busts, I dragged the two large garbage bags out of storage in the evidence room down the hall to the guys. I opened it up and Miles took a peek.

"Oh man, worse than I thought. This guy is going to run as soon as he sees this merchy shit," Miles said, sipping the freshly brewed coffee.

"Won't look like stems and seeds when we get done with it," I said, a smile crossing my face.

Miles's face twisted up like it did when he got confused. "What, are you a magician?"

"Nope. A chef."

I went to the cabinet and pulled out a large pot and from the cabinet a box of green food coloring. I filled the pot with water, as my guys gathered around to watch what I was doing. I added green food coloring to the pot and stirred until the water was a nice shade of green.

Then I took a large handful of some still leafy, flaky buds of marijuana from our two-year-old haul and placed it into the pot to let it soak. Just enough to absorb the water in order to fluff it up and bring the color back into the dope by adding moisture.

After a short time I placed the pot on paper towels and put it in the microwave for two minutes. When it was done heating I had thick, fluffy, green buds, just like Kevin would have been bringing back from New York.

We worked all night cooking our dope to perfection. We didn't even have a chance to go home to sleep. I told my guys to run home and take a shower before we headed to Fairlawn to pull off the reverse deal. I was going to do the same, while multitasking and setting up the deal with Detective Al Beauchamp from the Fairlawn Police Department. Beauchamp was on board, and happy to do his part in getting rid of a local dealer. We discussed the logistics of the drop. Beauchamp was going to lend us four of his officers in two cars to be placed at the two nearest entrances of our planned meeting spot.

At this point, we still didn't know who was going to be showing up on the other end. This was somewhat typical. All I needed to do was text the guy and make up some excuse as to why Kevin was going to send some mope to make the drop, instead of coming himself.

*S*ending my buddy. Tan skin. Dark hair. Jimmy. K

The response: *Black Tahoe. Just me. GD Tie-dye shirt.*

A rich hippie kid who lived in Akron. Seemed a bit odd for Kevin. But that wasn't for me to judge; I'll leave that for somebody else.

I finished getting ready at nine A.M. I had some time to kill but I was afraid if I sat down I'd fall asleep after going nonstop for nearly three days now, so I headed to the station to meet Miles. From all my years undercover I had learned that if I just kept moving I could beat the exhaustion. My eyes were heavy as I drove to the station. After a couple of nights of no sleep, I knew that I had another long day ahead of me but it would all be okay once the adrenaline started pumping. The humdrum of the tires was broken by my ringing phone.

"Hello?"

"Chief Buck?" the voice on the other end asked.

"Yes, this is Chief Buck."

"Hi, my name is Ryan. I am the manager here at Hunting Bank in Solon. We spoke last Friday and . . ." His voice trailed off at that.

"Yes, I remember. How can I help you?"

"There is a Loudmilla Sorin here. She's insisting on taking the money out of the accounts you froze. And she's making a scene outside with my teller," Ryan told me.

"Would you mind putting Mrs. Sorin on the phone, please? I'll have a talk with her."

Ryan was more than happy to turn the dirty work over to me. And I was more than happy to remind Loudmilla why I had taken all of her money. This was commonplace during the time of forfeitures and seizures. The targets always ran to the bank hoping that they could make it there before I did. Praying that if they got there right at 9:00 A.M. they would beat me. But another key in this business is to always be a step ahead of them. That morning I had a uniformed officer waiting at the bank the moment it opened to ask the manager to freeze Loudmilla's account. I couldn't be there myself because the courts and banks open at the same time and I had to be in court to secure the warrant we needed to seize Loudmilla's bank balance as the product of ill-gotten gains.

There's no reason to rush a case. The more time you sit, the more evidence you have to gather. As long as no one's life is in danger, there's no reason to act fast, only to act smart.

I heard the phone picked up, and before I could say anything Loudmilla started yelling at me. Her Russian accent was so heavy that I wasn't sure if she was yelling at me in English or Russian. I let her yell for a few moments. I always found it a good tactic to let the perp vent. Get it off their chest. I would break in when they took a breath, when they felt it was time to let you speak.

"Loudmilla, I told you yesterday I was going to take all your money. Why didn't you believe me?" I asked.

"That is my money! Mine!" she yelled over and over.

I had to explain to her that even though it might be her money, and it might have been from her job, that didn't matter once it was commingled with proceeds of crime from her son's and husband's drug dealing. Commingled money could be seized just as if all of it, every penny, was Kevin's. It would be up to her to prove it wasn't Kevin's money, but until then it would sit locked up in court and if she failed to make her case, I'd formally seize it as the proceeds of a CCE.

I finished up the phone call just as I was pulling in to the Reminderville police station with warrant in hand. Once I served it, the bank would empty the account and cut me a cashier's check in the full amount to be deposited into an escrow account through the duration of the case. That call with Loudmilla had definitely helped to wake me up. I walked inside to find Miles sleeping facedown with his head on the table in the kitchenette. I clapped my hands loudly.

"Wake up, sleepyhead! Time to roll on out of here!"

Miles picked his head off the table, and a string of drool fell from his mouth. He wiped it away.

"Shake it off, pretty boy," I said to him. "Now grab the bag," I said, pointing to a hockey bag full of microwaved weed that now looked and smelled like fresh product.

Summit Mall was about forty minutes from my station. We took two unmarked cars for the deal: my Expedition and an unmarked police vehicle for Miles. This was going to be fun!

We met Detective Beauchamp at his station to prepare. He had a short list of who this guy could possibly be. He ran through the list with us. But no one on the list had a black SUV. This guy was either new at it, ran under the radar, or Akron was overlooking him. We were about to find out.

Our two cars headed to Summit Mall, accompanied by two marked cars and one unmarked one from Fairlawn PD courtesy of Detective Beauchamp, and took positions thirty minutes in advance. Since I was the only officer certified by the county prosecutor's office to do a reverse, I'd be the one doing the deal. I parked my Expedition in a middle spot, climbed out, and leaned against it. Twelve o'clock on the dot, a pimped-out Tahoe with speakers booming came whipping into the parking lot.

I had a feeling the deal would go down smoothly and without incident. The kid climbed out and left the door open behind him. I removed the hockey bag from the cargo area of my Expedition and tucked it through the Tahoe's back hatch. From prepping at the police station the officers knew it was time to move in without needing any prodding from me over the wire I was wearing. They rushed the target, and the kid didn't have time to make it back into the driver's seat. He ran around like a hamster on a wheel, easy pickin's.

Since I had vowed to give up running when Curtis flew out the window all those years ago, I let one of the uniformed officers chase the hippie kid around the car. After a lap or two the officer threw the skinny long-haired dude against the car. I had the other Fairlawn officer check the kid's address to make sure it was current while he was read his rights.

His name was Brad Kottler and he was just eighteen years old and actually fronting for his brother, who was Kevin's real contact. And he showed up with only $8,000 of the money and claimed he didn't have the rest. My mind started working on how I could get the rest of that cash from his brother, the real mark. I had maybe four minutes to figure out my next move before Brad Kottler's brother started figuring something had gone wrong. I made a snap decision and sped out with Miles to the kid's house in Akron, where I had no jurisdiction and no warrant yet.

It was a big house, ten thousand square feet or maybe even twelve. It was built in the sixties and sat square among other similar brick homes in a very affluent neighborhood ten minutes from the mall on Springside Lane. The yards were perfectly manicured, and expensive cars of BMW, Mercedes, and Lexus vintage dotted the driveways. As I pulled up on the driveway running down the right side of the house, I saw a car exiting fast with a woman behind the wheel and told Miles to take her down. Then I entered, and, through an open kitchen door leading to the backyard, I spotted a middle-aged man with handfuls of money rolled up in his shirt that he was stuffing one at a time in the bushes.

He came back inside the house and did a double take when he saw me standing there.

"We just arrested your son—Brad Kottler," I said, after introducing myself.

The guy looked genuinely scared. "You arrested him?"

"Sit down, sir."

I told him to have a seat at the kitchen table. The gourmet Victorian kitchen had brand-new stainless-steel appliances and marble countertops. This was not what I expected—rich parents supporting their hippie kids dealing drugs. And these kids weren't just dealing, they were dealing in bulk. What was going on here?

Next, I called the Akron police and positioned a uniformed officer in the backyard where the man had just hidden the money until we could obtain a search warrant. At that point, we'd be able to photograph and tag the money into evidence. So I asked Miles to bring my laptop and printer inside from the car. I always have them at the ready in case I need to write a warrant on the fly, which I did right at the table while Mom and Dad watched. I live by a single rule when I write warrants: If it's not true, don't include it. A lot of guys get in the habit of creatively writing their warrants. But you can't write anything, absolutely anything, in a warrant that's not 100 percent accurate, because everything is open to judicial review. I've heard about too many cases made by other guys crumbling under the weight of warrants containing falsified and inaccurate information. The best defense lawyers might even home in on a simple typo.

Once the warrant was ready and printed out, I sent another officer off to get it signed, with instructions to the judge to call me if he needed any gaps filled in. And while I was waiting for him to return, guess what?

It was time to have a Bad News Talk with the Kottlers.

Mr. and Mrs. Kottler, I'm Chief Buck," I started. "Your son Brad has been arrested for purchasing marijuana with intent to sell. That's a continuing-criminal-enterprise charge, and he's looking at a twenty-five-to-life sentence in federal prison, unless we can come to an understanding. So let's discuss your options, but understand the clock's ticking and I've got a very small window to help you out here."

They looked at me, nodding in obvious fear at what I'd just laid out. I jumped right back in and explained that I was here to gather the seizures. It was obvious that they'd been expecting me, I'm guessing because Brad must've had an opportunity to get off a quick text message before we caught him. Probably had the emergency signal ready to go at a press of the Send key. I hadn't even seen him do it.

The Kottlers and I continued our chat. I had to explain to them how it was going to go down. Either they were going to turn over all of their kids' cash from drug sales to me voluntarily or it was going to go very poorly for them. I laid it all out to them very calmly and clearly. Like most, they weren't very cooperative at first.

That changed in a hurry.

"Here's the way it is," I told them, the clock still ticking. "This isn't your lucky day. Because in addition to your sons getting jammed up, I happen to know that you own a small, but very lucrative grocery chain in northeast Ohio. Now, I'm not sure if you know how the law works, sir, but unless you cooperate with me, I'm going to freeze all the assets of your stores. The money in the cash registers, the real estate, the meat in your butcher shops, and the cereal on your shelves. The law allows me to do that because we have strong reason to believe that you are laundering drug proceeds from your son's illegal drug sales, since I just witnessed you hiding tens of thousands of dollars in the bushes as we were arriving. As proceeds of a crime, that means all your assets can be seized, and the fact that your funds are commingled with your son's makes them mine too in the eyes of the law.

"And, sir," I said to the dad, "you made yourself an accessory by trying to hide all that cash in the bushes outside the house. You may prevail in the long run, the very long run, because you'll have to go through a very long court battle to prove that none of the money, absolutely none, in your accounts can be classified as profits from your son's drug business. I hope I'm getting through to you here, because we can avoid the whole headache for you, make all this go away, if you turn the drug money over. What do you think?"

Mr. and Mrs. Kottler looked at each other. They hesitated briefly, and then the dad nodded.

"I don't want to lose my stores," he said, shaking a little. "I don't want my wife to go to jail."

"That's good thinking," I told him. "Because if I grab your assets, you'll never be able to do business around here again. You'll be finished."

"What can I do?"

"Let's wait for the warrant to come back and then you can show me the house."

Once I had the signed warrant in hand, I started my "tour" in the basement, where I found a whole bunch of shelves lined with mason jars containing weed in every strain from every country you can imagine. A smoke room with a bunch of chairs and a table, and I could tell from Dad that he was intimately familiar with the surroundings, like the family that smokes together stays together. Screw that, I thought.

"Is it any fucking wonder your kids got jammed up in the drug trade?" I accused him, really pissed, thinking as much like a father as a cop. "I'm seriously thinking about taking my offer off the table and seizing your assets, after all."

"No, please! What can I do to make this right?"

"You tell me."

He pulled a key from under one of the mason jars. "Here," he said, handing it to me.

"What's this?"

"Key to a safe-deposit box. There's money inside, lots of it."

I called the judge on the way to the bank with Mr. Kottler, and it only took a few minutes to get a telephonic warrant in place. The only way a judge does that without viewing the corroborating evidence is based on trust. Judges, especially in this area, know me from experience and reputation. The last thing they want is to be made to look bad down the road or have any order or warrant they've issued suppressed in court later for cause. And that's never happened with me. Through the hundreds of warrants I've written, not a single one has ever been suppressed in court. I like to make judges look good, not bad. And, as officers of the court upholding justice, they're normally more than happy to do their part to make sure suspects face the music.

Once we reached the bank, I provided the bank manager with a warrant entitling me to search the box. I had Mr. Kottler open the safe-deposit box, which was literally jam-packed with hundred-dollar bills amounting to over $200,000, making the total score closer to $300,000 when all that money pulled from the bushes was taken into account. I stuffed the money into a duffel bag and provided the bank manager a copy of the inventory. Ill-gotten proceeds from the drug trade of the Kottlers' two sons I'd now be able to put to much better use.

We had to gather up that money around the Kottlers' home where I'd stationed the Akron cops too, some of whom had ended up guarded by these sharp pricker bushes. When that was done, we were ready to leave, marking the end of another very long day by enriching the joint task force coffers by around $300,000. The Fairlawn Police Department received a check from the Reminderville Police equitable sharing account for $10,000 which was their share of the forfeitures.

So when was the last time I slept?

Maybe, just maybe I was getting too old for this shit. . . .

Nah!

I was leaving the Kottlers' home with one hell of a bonus in a case that was certain to yield a sizable amount more before all the books were closed. All because I'd answered a simple text message and followed it up the line. That's what it was all about and that's how you make a case.

CHAPTER FORTY-SIX

Everything had come full circle, perhaps described best by St. Lawrence County district attorney Nicole Duvé for a July 2, 2009, article in the *Daily Courier-Observer*:

"Little did we know," she told reporter Shelley Livernois, referring to the murder of Danny Simonds, "on May twelfth, two thousand and eight, we were walking onto the top of an iceberg. Clearly it started off as a situation, where we thought that it was—I guess you can't call any of them run of the mill—but thought it was more of a run of the mill drug rip."

The death of Danny Simonds, of course, turned out to be much, much more than that. The same article went on to detail the arrests of Harold and Sabrina Fraser and Noah King among eight others in upstate New York, along with Kevin Sorin, Ashley Schmid, and Mark Ververka back in my neck of the woods. The story went on to say that "over $2 million in assets were also seized, including $1.3 million in US currency, fourteen vehicles, two utility trailers, three ATVs, one snowmobile, and one boat." The proceeds of which would be put to good use for sure, namely bringing down other bad guys. And the hornets' nest we poked clearly was bigger than even we thought initially.

"This case is unfortunately the most recent example now of the extent and magnitude of the illicit marijuana and drug trade passing through the North Country," my new friend Derek Champagne, district attorney of Franklin County, told Livernois for her article. "Ohio is just one of the thirty-one states that have been identified . . . as having been directly linked to currency, drugs, or other criminal activity originating in Franklin and St. Lawrence counties."

The very definition of a continuing criminal enterprise we'd dealt a serious blow to. Not a mortal blow—I'm not naïve enough to believe that. But together with our sister investigation north of the border in which my friend Frenchie was involved, Operation SharQc, things would never quite be the same again on that infamous river that straddles both countries. And our case became a game changer for other reasons.

An Associated Press article on July 27, 2009, headlined "Anti-Drug Efforts Beefed Up at Border," went on to report about more agents being brought in on both sides to stem the flow. Ironic that the 5,500-mile zigzagging stretch is often referred to as the world's longest undefended border. That would at least begin to change now with the border being defended, better anyway, against a different kind of enemy in a different kind of war. For Derek Champagne's part, his Franklin County District Attorney's Office was awarded a $1.2 million grant to set up a surveillance system along the US-Canada border to further forestall the efforts of this CCE in ramping up again and to keep another of this magnitude from getting started.

Make no mistake about it, we'd won a battle in a much greater war that shows no signs of really abating.

As for me, my efforts led directly to my town of Reminderville seizing a whole bunch of money in assets. I was expecting more, to tell you the truth; it should've been more. But a forfeiture case like this is the very definition of taking money reaped through ill-gotten gains and putting it to good use. And my department is hardly alone in that.

According to an October 11, 2014, *Washington Post* story for which I was interviewed:

> About 5,400 departments and drug task forces have participated in the Equitable Sharing Program since 2008. Justice spokesman Peter Carr said the program is an effective weapon to fight crime but should not be considered "an alternative funding source for state and local law enforcement."
>
> "It removes the tools of crime from criminal organizations, deprives wrongdoers of the proceeds of their crimes, recovers property that may be used to compensate victims, and deters crime," he said in a statement. "Any funds received

through the equitable sharing program are meant to enhance and supplement, not supplant or replace an agency's appropriated budget and resources."

The point being that I use those proceeds from drug crime to put other drug dealers and organizations into our sights and then our jails. And the reason asset forfeiture remains so important is that with dwindling local and state funds, it's the only way to amass the resources you need to build the kind of long-term investigation to make a successful drug case. In the case of my department, the sole thing this money can be used for, besides some community policing, is to nail more bad guys. You take money from drug dealers to put other drug dealers in jail—that's the bottom line.

And the simple fact of the matter remains that in years following these 2009 arrests and subsequent convictions, those funds have been utilized to put more drug dealers, high and low on the food chain, away and taking more drugs off the streets. I don't normally use assets for equipment; I put them into the cases themselves so my guys can walk enough money to establish credibility with targets. It pays for things like the rental cars and hotel rooms my guys needed for all the months they were assigned to the wire room in upstate New York. Absent of having those forfeiture funds from past busts available, we wouldn't have had the resources to pull that part of the case off, and quite frankly, there never would've been a case to begin with.

No matter how things shake out, I'm a drug guy. I'm going to put the money I seize back into the game. And if I walk thirty grand to a target to make a buy, it's because I know the case I'm making will ultimately score me his house worth ten times that. Not a bad return on my investment, right?

According to Cleveland.com, the whole case I'd just closed all stemmed "from a local probe of alleged Russian organized crime in the Cleveland area. Officials here discovered last year that large, regular shipments of marijuana were coming to Ohio from Franklin and St. Lawrence counties along the Canadian border in New York."

In the months following our coordinated series of busts in both states, the price of weed in my Ohio backyard jumped appreciably. That's how you know you got the job done; taking more drugs off the streets means decreased supply which leads to increased costs. It's one of the best in-dicators when determining the success of a bust of this level. I'm not naïve enough to think those prices will stay high forever. Somebody else will inevitably move in to pick up the slack and the forfeited assets from the last case will help me build the next one.

The cycle continues, in other words, in self-perpetuating fashion.

Sometimes to move forward, it pays to look back toward the start, a start that seems innocuous in comparison to the level of distribution to which it led. Interestingly enough, most of the principals on both sides of the border, from the Hells Angels to the Frasers to Kevin and Ashley, never went to trial, accepting plea deals mostly on lesser charges. Kevin's out on parole now, as are a bunch of the Hells Angels north of the border, while fifty or so more HAs are still awaiting trials unlikely to begin before 2016. Included among them is Salvatore Cazzetta, who replaced Maurice Boucher as head of the Montreal chapter and now seems likely to join him in prison. For Frenchie and his task force, that made Operation SharQc maybe the most successful bust of an outlaw biker gang in North American history.

I hope that makes the parents of Daniel Desrochers, the boy killed by a bomb planted outside the Rock Machine biker gang headquarters by an Angel, sleep better. But somehow I don't think so.

Of the 156 Hells Angels arrested, thirty-one facing lesser charges were later freed. One of those initially released, Benjamin Hudon-Barbeau, later made headlines when he daringly escaped Saint-Jérôme detention center by holding on to the landing pod of a hijacked helicopter in March of 2013. Hudon-Barbeau had been arrested on weapons charges a few weeks earlier. He was also one of the runners the Angels trusted to pick up harvested weed from a collection of the grow houses they operated. The other HA assigned that task we met here, Frédéric Landry-Hétu, evaded Canadian police for four years on murder charges, until he was finally arrested north of Montreal in March of 2013. Another dozen or so Hells Angels, having been originally targeted as part of Operation SharQc, remain at large to this day. I'm not particularly worried and neither, I know, is my pal Frenchie who continues being a workhorse north of the border for the Ontario Provincial Police.

As for the Akwesasne Mohawk reservation, a US Justice Department report covered by CBC News on September 28, 2011, stated that ecstasy was being supplied by Canadian-based gangs and smuggled through the res on the order of "multi-thousand-tablet quantities." That's the same report in which Derek Champagne estimated drug smuggling by the Akwesasne Mohawks alone to be a billion-dollar-annual business. A billion dollars over a stretch of border measuring only six to eight miles. A *New York Post* article on November 8, 2009, just a few months after our busts went down, meanwhile, chronicled the involvement of the NYPD, who were sick of the flow of drugs coming from upstate New York into their city.

"I was astounded at how lenient the border is," Chief Joseph Resnick from the department's narcotics division told reporter Brad Hamilton of the *Post*.

"When the river freezes, there's so many snowmobiles out there we don't even bother," a US Customs and Border Protection guard told the *Post* for the same article. "If border patrol tried to police the traffic, there would be a war."

A smuggler from the Akwesasne reservation added, "We go at night and run all night. I get on my Jet Ski, put on a helmet and night-vision goggles and just go. The boats we have are way faster than theirs. They can't catch us."

"There are all these islands out here, and the snowmobiles just come shooting across," US Border Patrol agent Glenn Pickering told the Associated Press on February 15, 2011. "It's a constant battle."

And on June 20, 2013, the Royal Canadian Mounted Police arrested thirty-seven suspects in a Canadian smuggling ring they believed was directly associated with the Akwesasne. "Project O-TITAN was initiated in 2012," according to a report on the RCMP Web site, "and initially targeted individuals involved in the smuggling of contraband tobacco from the United States to the Cornwall area, and its distribution to various locations in Eastern Ontario. Through investigation, the police identified five separate groups operating together as required in the smuggling of contraband tobacco, and in the trafficking of marijuana."

The casual observer might read all this and believe that my take-down had failed to produce anything more than a negligible effect. And while we'd certainly won a major battle, I never believed we'd won the whole war. But the mere fact that so many other busts followed, thanks to the involvement of other agencies and departments, indicated that law enforcement was now paying very real attention to the problem. We had gotten the ball rolling and that's enough for me. Fighting this war is all about putting bad guys away, the more the better on both sides of the border, no matter who ultimately gets the credit.

It's also not just about the sentences, how long the people charged and arrested end up doing in prison. First off, people who belittle relatively minor sentences have never been behind bars. Two, three, or four years is a long time to be away from the world, especially for those who've never been put through the system before. Beyond that, the higher you climb up the food chain, the more likely it is we're talking about guys who've taken years to build their networks. Making a case that takes out the top dog means bringing down those networks. It's not just about taking down the individual, it's about taking down his entire criminal enterprise. So once they get out, what do they have to go back to?

Remember, putting them away means we've seized their assets—their money, their houses, their cars, pretty much everything—so upon release they have to start from absolute scratch, back to the bottom of the food chain. Pretty much nobody wants to do business with them, because everyone in the drug world knows they've been arrested. Anyone who does, meanwhile, isn't about to front them product on the arm. It's cash only now for these guys once they get out, only they don't have any because guys like me have taken it all through the federal forfeiture statutes. So, sure, they might get out after a relatively short stretch, but for all intents and purposes they're off the map.

What I've learned over the years is how to coordinate a major drug-enforcement effort built out from the local level. Local cops are the ones who know best the damage the illicit business does to their communities, so they've got the biggest stake in the action and the most to lose. They don't need a program to know the players. And other municipalities can do the same thing by finding their own Dope Ghost in the person of a good drug guy who wants to do the job. Find that person and let him do the job the way he wants to. Give him the funding he needs so he can walk money on deals to bring down major players. And have his efforts supplemented by those of the uniform guys. The uniforms are the ones best equipped to help with the informants, because they represent the first line. A uniform stops some seventeen-year-old kid carrying a half pound of weed, his first call should be to the department's Dope Ghost. Because traffic stops are a huge component of drug interdiction, along with manufacturing informants.

If you've got the right informant, you can do the world. You've got to put in the time not just to recruit them but to continually work them as they walk you up the food chain. A true Dope Ghost needs his CIs to know he's on the square to the point where when one of their "associates" gets jammed up, they call you. That's called street cred, and it comes from grooming and then treating an informant with respect to get the most out of them. I know it sounds easy coming from someone who's been at this for going on thirty years, but you've got to start somewhere.

I've learned plenty over the years, much of it from guys like this, who don't care how much harm they do to humanity and civilization at large. Sure, the Hells Angels are more dangerous and violent, but the Kevin Sorins, the Frasers, the Noah Kings, and the Alan Jacobses of the world aren't much better no matter how much their sprawling homes in tony neighborhoods may suggest otherwise. We truly have no idea what goes on beyond the drawn drapes. Neither did the neighbors of all those hydroponic grow houses run by the Hells Angels north of the border and the same almost certainly holds true for Kevin and Ashley's neighbors in my neck of the woods.

Speaking of Alan Jacobs and company, it was nearly three years after we brought down his network, in March of 2012, that he was sentenced to twenty years in prison for his role in the death of Danny Simonds. The thugs he sent to do the deed received similar sentences. Prevailing reports, like one in the *Watertown Daily Times* on March 10, 2012, labeled Danny's murder "a robbery gone wrong."

If only it were that simple. I know that now, just as I know that this case had given me a unique glimpse into the unholy alliances that breed greed and spread pain from one coast to another. I saw again how these people will turn on each other in an instant. Danny Simonds wasn't the first to perish to that proclivity, and he won't be the last.

But for those who survive, I'll be waiting.

EPILOGUE

Earlier in my career, I nailed a prolific drug dealer. I never gave up pursuit of him, even when he kept making bail or plea-bargaining down the charges. The first time I hit him I took five million in forfeiture and arrested a bunch of his guys. Then I did him again while he was out on bail, served him with a warrant one day before the statute of limitations was set to run out.

I'm sitting in the bedroom with him while my men are searching his house and I finally say to this guy, whose nickname is "Money Mike" on the street, "What motivates you?"

"What do you mean?"

"You're already rich. You don't need to still be moving two thousand pounds of weed per month. You've got enough money in the bank to last you several lifetimes. So why do you do it?"

"You really don't know?" Money Mike shot back at me, as if it were obvious.

"No, that's why I'm asking."

"It's not about the money anymore. It's all about seeing if a guy like me can get away with it and not get caught by a guy like you. It's all about the rush you get from that. Like a different kind of addiction, I guess."

In which case I guess my addiction is putting bad guys away and taking their drugs off the street. And, like everybody else, I've got a dream job. Mine is to work with the attorney general of Ohio to get his office to sponsor a drug task force connected to every municipality and law-enforcement body in the state. The problem right now is sometimes we're all chasing our tails, proceeding on our cases as if each is happening in a vacuum.

Well, what if this task force compiled a DNA profile on cocaine plants so we could trace the different sources of supply of coke across our state? The way it is now, some neighboring county could be working the same guy I want to do and I'd never know it. That's what almost happened in the case laid out in these pages when Stevenson and Walters from Geauga County almost ruined months of the big historical case I was building to go after a single small-time dealer. Cincinnati PD, for example, might be working an informant to get into a network I'm already into, or that I want to get into too.

Building a statewide drug task force from a law-enforcement standpoint would be a game changer. Right now, I could be working the same guy as a neighboring county or even two. Each of us might have only enough to get him a slap on the wrist and probation, while if we communicated and added up our hauls we'd be able to put him away for five to ten. I'm talking about building an information-sharing network in which we could all work together to identify and target the largest drug dealers across the state. And what I want to do in Ohio could become a model, a starting point for states across the entire country.

There's plenty of precedent for this. It took until around the year 2000 before we actually had a national database for sexual predators and serial killers so we could track their crimes across state lines. That's what I want to do with drugs *within* state lines. We're not there yet, not even close, but I have the sense we will be and I intend to work toward that goal.

Because it would help us put more bad guys pushing poison out onto our streets away, for longer stretches to boot.

And that's what being a Dope Ghost is all about.

AFTERMATH

Yulia Abramovich: Never charged.

Matt Cody: Never charged.

Derek Cooke: Sentenced to twelve years in prison.

Chad Edwards: Sentenced to ten years.

Harold Fraser: Sentenced to four years supervised release. His wife, Sabrina, wasn't charged.

Bryan "Wildcat" Herne: Sentenced to eleven years.

Benjamin Hudon-Barbeau: One of the 156 Hells Angels arrested in Operation SharQc. He escaped from prison in a hijacked helicopter in 2013 and was later recaptured.

Ivan Ivashov: Never charged.

Alan Jacobs: As part of the plea agreement, Jacobs agreed to a mandatory twenty-year term of imprisonment and the forfeiture of $666,466.82 in US currency. He also faces up to five years of supervised release following his release and up to a $250,000 fine.

Noah King: Sentenced to mandatory minimum of sixty months and four years supervised release.

Brad Kottler: Never charged.

Frédéric Landry-Hétu: Killed in a shoot-out with Canadian authorities in March 2013.

Brian LaTulipe: Sentenced to fourteen years imprisonment for the attempted robbery and death of Danny Simonds.

Ashley Schmid: Sentenced to four years supervised release. Her parents weren't charged.

Kevin Sorin: Sentenced to three years, ten months in prison and four years supervised release. His father was sentenced to four years supervised release. His mother wasn't charged.

Kaientanoron "Nolo" Swamp: Sentenced to twelve and a half years.

Mark Ververka: Sentenced to two years supervised release.